GRACE PERIOD

GRACE PERIOD

My Ordination to the Ordinary

MELINDA WORTH POPHAM

GRACE PERIOD
MY ORDINATION TO THE ORDINARY

This is a work of nonfiction. To protect the privacy and/or anonymity of certain individuals, their names have been changed or omitted. The author's name is other than her immediate relatives' names.

A portion of "My Getting-to-God Machine" was published under another title in the periodical *Berkeley at Yale* (Summer 2001 issue). Some of the essay "Malibu DPs" from *A Place Called Home: Twenty Writing Women Remember* (St. Martin's Press, 1996) appears in modified form here, as does some of an interview from *Listen to Their Voices: Twenty Interviews with Women Who Write* (W. W. Norton & Co, 1993).

The scripture quotations contained herein are from the New Revised Standard Version Bible, copyright © 1989 by the Division of Christian Education of the National Council of the Churches of Christ in the U.S.A. Used by permission.

iUniverse books may be ordered through booksellers or by contacting:

iUniverse
1663 Liberty Drive
Bloomington, IN 47403
www.iuniverse.com
1-800-Authors (1-800-288-4677)

ISBN: 978-1-4917-7601-8 (sc)
ISBN: 978-1-4917-7602-5 (hc)
ISBN: 978-1-4917-7600-1 (e)

Library of Congress Control Number: 2015916931

Print information available on the last page.
iUniverse rev. date: 11/23/2015

In memory of
Art Popham,
my brother and "Attagirl!" giver,
and
Quita,
my whither-thou-goest companion

You need only claim the events of your life to make yourself yours.
When you truly possess all you have been and
done … you are fierce with reality.

—Florida Scott Maxwell

God comes to you disguised as your life.

—Paula D'Arcy

CONTENTS

A Note to the Reader

When I first set out to write about my two years at Yale Divinity School, I was determined to reveal as little as possible about why I went. The readers of that early version were unanimous in telling me what I already knew: You can't write a memoir and pull your punch.

"More you, less Yale," was how one of them put it.

But it was the very one I wanted most of all to shield who freed me to tell about that anxious, fraught, turbulent time.

"Don't be self-censoring," she said. "Go for it, Mom!"

So I did, and that is how I've come to see that this book never was about my study of God at Yale Divinity School. It's always been about God's ongoing education of me.

—M. W. P.

PROLOGUE
LOOKING ON DARKNESS

My first class at Yale Divinity School met in a stifling basement room with two dozen of us crammed around a battered, old seminar table. We ran the gamut from a coat-and-tie, crew-cut evangelical to an ex-Catholic goth girl to me, an astonished Christian older than the teacher.

The enormous table left the professor—a burly, bearded, middle-aged African American—scant room to stand at the old-fashioned chalkboard, where, holding aloft a stub of chalk, he scoffed, "Yale University! And this is the best they can do?"

The class was Looking on Darkness. I knew from the title alone that, come hell or high water, I was going to take it, but I was already nervous about the way the word *ontological* kept cropping up in the professor's opening monologue when he casually referred to someone I had never heard of as "of course the foremost hermeneutic phenomenologist."

I almost bolted. I didn't mind being outgunned in theology—that, after all, was what I was there to study—but to find myself skunked in vocabulary on the first day was demoralizing. By the end of class, I had compiled a list of seventeen words. I came reeling out panic-stricken, depressed, and resentful. But it wasn't just because of the professor's big vocabulary. It was because of the paper he assigned at the end of class.

"This paper," the professor said, "will serve as a touchstone for your point of entry into this class. It is to be an account of a personal encounter with darkness. Two pages maximum. Due Monday. A personal experience of darkness."

I exchanged a stunned glance with a guy across the table from me; he looked about my son's age. He shook his head, jerked his thumb over his shoulder, and mouthed, "I'm outta here."

What have I gotten myself into? What am I doing here?

"You are here at the calling of the spirit of God," the dean had proclaimed from the pulpit in Marquand Chapel in his orientation welcome. "You belong here. Let me repeat that: you *belong* here."

His message now seemed about as credible as a fortune cookie's. But intimidated as I was, I refused to be scared off. I headed straight to the Yale Co-op (a Barnes & Noble *cum* Starbucks) for a double espresso and a Tenth Edition *Merriam Webster's Collegiate Dictionary*. Had I known at the time about the *Westminster Dictionary of Theological Terms*, I would have purchased it as well. I needed all the help I could get.

Really, though, it was the intimacy of the prayer with which the professor opened class that made me override my survival instinct to flee. His daunting erudition was disarmingly offset by the simple way he spoke from his heart to his God. Listening to the professor pray, I felt as if I were eavesdropping on someone talking to a God with whom he was on a first-name basis.

Students at Yale, undergrad and grad alike, have a week to sample courses before filing a final course of study. For some it becomes a shopping spree of dashing from class to class to seize a syllabus and size up the professor. The faculty hate the shopping period. Some professors devise winnowing techniques. But this professor's lofty tone that first day was not a ruse. Nor was the topic of that paper.

I should have seen it coming. I ought to have realized that a course titled Looking on Darkness might not be purely academic, that it might make painful memories reverberate. Still, I had not expected to be required to write a personal essay—much less an intensely *personal* personal essay. How often, after all, are we required to tell a perfect stranger right off the bat about an intimate encounter with darkness?

There was a time when the paper assigned at the end of class that first day would have upset me because I would have thought I had nothing to write about. Throughout my childhood and especially during adolescence, I thought my life utterly bland and lacking. I wanted answers to burning questions I didn't even know how to ask. I wanted to get beneath the lacquered beehives of '50s hairdos to know what went on inside people's heads. I knew in that inchoate way one knows uncertain things for certain that there was much more to life than anyone around me was letting on. I sensed there was a dark side, an underbelly, a something more, a *real* reality.

I wanted life to test me, to manhandle me. The rough of life was where I wanted to be, not the manicured fairways of my country-club upbringing. I longed for angst and in my callow shallowness plumbed what I thought were the depths. I yearned for some *sturm und drang*, envied those tested by tragedies, and cultivated emotion for its own sake.

The past five years, though, had provided me with a mother lode (oh ha!) of crises and sorrows. I'd had more than enough of what I used to call "real life" and plenty of material for my Looking on Darkness paper. But the one true subject for the paper was inescapable, even though divulging a mother's anguish over a daughter's suffering felt like a violation of privacy to gain admission to the course—a course I wanted to take precisely because I hoped it might shed theological light *on* that darkness. And so I titled my paper "*Chashekah*."

CHASHEKAH

What can I say in two pages? That darkness overcame my daughter so that her light no longer shone? That she dyed her blonde hair black as an outward sign of her inward state? That she did harm to herself and wanted to die? That the consulting psychiatrist she saw early on who scribbled a prescription for Zoloft and breezily assured me my daughter's depression was "eminently treatable" would not have recognized the erased girl with the leaden shuffle and lifeless eyes in the emergency room? That three days before her sixteenth birthday my daughter was hospitalized for fear that otherwise she would not live to see it?

"Fear not!" angels say to mortals.

But fear sent me tiptoeing into my daughter's room in the dead of night the way I had when she was an infant. *Is she breathing?* Now it was not crib death I feared but a quietly self-inflicted one.

Fear sent me to a lecture by the mother of a teen suicide. "Snoop! Pry!" she said. "Go through his backpack! Go through her purse! Read their journals! And if you get caught, don't make excuses and don't let their outrage intimidate you. What you are doing is trying to save your beloved son or daughter's life. My fifteen-year-old son hanged himself while I was downstairs watching *Antiques Roadshow*."

Perfect love casteth out all fear. But what I found in her purse and backpack and what I read in her poems and journal—words sometimes written with her own blood for ink—attested that my fear for her life was not irrational.

My God will enlighten my darkness. But fear was like a hood over my head with the drawstring pulled tight. It shut out the light, shut down my brain, and knotted my insides with terror. Of the four Hebrew words for "darkness" in the Old Testament, *chashekah* was the one that described mine. *Chashekah* bespeaks darkest darkness: terror and despair so extreme that the gloom seems godless.

Two-West, the adolescent unit at UCLA Hospital's Neuropsychiatric Institute, was a locked ward with dense mesh on all the windows. As part of the intake procedure, a staff person gave us a tour of the unit that concluded with her unlocking a door and stepping aside to let us look into a padded cell with a white canvas straitjacket lying in a strappy heap on the floor.

I swung my head sharply away, shocked by the ruthless, brutal fact of my daughter, my *child*, now being in a place where there was such a thing—a place I'd driven her to, in my car and in other ways as well … the same place where, in another wing, sixteen years minus three days before, the life she wanted to end had begun.

PART ONE

———

HOLY HELL

It is life-affirming to look at a dark history.
It lifts you to the pleasure of the truth.
—James Carroll

1

UNKNOWNS

I am that background figure, that
source figure, the mother. We are not,
strictly speaking, mortal. We cast
beloveds into the future.

—Sharon Olds

I don't know when it began. I can't pinpoint its onset the way I circled the day on my calendar when she got her first period. I can't say for sure when her despondency became entrenched, no longer burning off by midday like our coastal fog. But in hindsight, I came to think of the day after my mother's eightieth birthday as day one, because the photos from the party are the last of my fifteen-year-old daughter looking like herself.

The next day, towheaded Ella holed up in her bathroom with a friend and emerged a redhead. I assumed it was a dyed-to-match tribute to her elegant, red-haired Texas grandmother, but she bristled when I suggested as much.

"It doesn't have anything to do with Mema," Ella said. "I've always been a redhead on the inside."

"You *have?*" I said.

It was quite a revelation. I hadn't known my daughter was a blonde redhead. I didn't know I didn't know my daughter. As my grandfather used to say, "A whole lotta ignorance going on around here!" My daughter's story is not only not mine to tell; I didn't even *know* it. Although it was all of a piece—the whole slew of sorrows, fears, and hard blessings that left me convinced that pain is the Miracle-Gro of transformation—I can only tell my part in it, the mother's part.

My mother's birthday party was a "last" in another way as well: getting ready with Ella to host it was about the last companionable mother-daughter time the two of us would spend together for quite a while—the swan song of our kitchen camaraderie, incessant canasta games, daily race to solve the Jumble, origami napkin folding, and joint projects like the quilt we made from her baby clothes and the glorious garden we created from scratch.

Shortly after changing the color of her hair, Ella wanted to change the color of her room. The color she chose for the walls, woodwork, *and* ceiling was a visceral, crimson red like the glistening innards pulled from the cavity of a chicken. First with her hair, then with her room, she was exteriorizing her interior, trying to create a matchup. She was visibly manifesting her inner self the same way that Daniel, her seventeen-year-old brother, currently was with his dreads, dog collars, and metal-studded apparel.

I was just fine with it. Hair-color experiments, expressive clothing, secretiveness, and fury at parental vigilance and interference: these are all familiar stuff to parents of teenagers, par for the course, part and parcel of the battle adolescents must fight for separation/individuation from their parents. This battle, according to a recent study, makes parents of teenagers *the* single unhappiest group of people in America.

But it was fast becoming clear that Ella was not just undergoing a stage, a temporary outage of self, some developmental disruption of her ordinary state of being. Something more far-reaching than typical teenage antagonism and angst was going on with her.

Until that fall, her nature as well as her way of being in the world had been perfectly captured by the musical direction *con spirito*, "with spirit or animation." A dynamo of creativity, she filled sketch pads, tossed off easel paintings, designed newspaper ball gowns, collected sawn-off rounds in the Christmas tree lot to hand-paint as holiday decorations, won the Malibu library's bookmark contest, and concocted recipes for dishes such as Everything Stew. ("Gradually add everything in the world that would taste good.")

That live wire of a girl was fading before my very eyes into a dispirited shadow of herself, becoming like the barely legible letters of an erased word. Ella's descent into depression was so rapid and steep it was as if a sinkhole had opened up and swallowed her whole: *Where did she go? She was just here, and now she's gone!*

I sought out a therapist for her—a well-meaning but woefully inadequate novice, it turned out—and started madly reading up on adolescent depression. Reading at my desk instead of writing. Reading in bed at night. Reading in my meditation chair first thing in the morning, a shawl of sunlight around my shoulders. Reading but hiding the books, just as I'd hidden the divorce books I consulted, so she wouldn't know how worried sick and scared I was.

Oh, but she knew all right. There was no fooling Ella. Highly sensitive, with a capacity for unrestrained empathy, she picked up on my moods and states of being and made them her own. She epitomized what art critic John Ruskin called "the ennobling difference":

> The ennobling difference between one (human) and another—between one animal and another—lies precisely in this, that one feels more than another.

———

"Spinal menin*gitis?*" I said, as if it were some rare tropical disease my mother could not possibly have contracted.

It was ten days before Christmas. I had not seen her since her birthday celebration at my house in Los Angeles in September. I flew to Dallas. Having to wear a mask and gown to visit my mother in the ICU drove home the gravity of the situation, but she looked so beautiful lying there—conscious but confused, with her pampered skin, perfect teeth, and freshly coiffed red hair—that it was inconceivable she might *die.* The day before being rushed to the hospital by ambulance, she'd kept her standing hair appointment with Mr. Rick. An inveterate Southern belle and the first-ever Cotton Bowl queen, my mother had devoted her life to always looking her best. Doctors and nurses did double takes when they saw the age on her chart: eighty!

But she slipped into a coma and went rapidly downhill. My sister, Carole, and I leaned over her and sang Christmas carols into her ears. Our brother, Art, the baby of the family, came from Tacoma, and the three of us spent our mother's last night with her in the little room they transferred her to after we signed the DNR. They started a morphine drip. Art slept in the recliner chair. Carole and I shared a cot.

All night long I listened to the four of us breathing, being alive together: my mother, my brother, my sister, and me. It was transporting, like Buddhist monk Thich Nhat Hanh's meditation where you bring all your awareness to your breathing as you say in your mind, *Breathing in, I know I am breathing in. Breathing out, I know I am breathing out.* Later, at divinity school, when I learned that in Hebrew "breath" and "spirit" are the same word, *ruah*, I immediately thought of Mother's last night.

Her memorial service at Highland Park Presbyterian Church took place on December 23, the day she'd been due to arrive at my house in Los Angeles for Christmas. I returned home to find the personalized pencils I had ordered for her stocking. They were there, but she was gone.

My weekly sit with my Centering Prayer meditation group served as a de facto grief group, but mourning the loss of my mother, and in a way, of my daughter as well, I just couldn't seem to get my feet under me. The rug of my life had been pulled out from under me. On school days, after seeing Ella off, stooped with the weight of her backpack and depression, I would try to figure out what to do with myself other than lie down and stare out the window. I went to church on Sundays but slipped out the side door during the first verse of the closing hymn. At the grocery store, if I spotted someone I knew, I ducked up another aisle to escape an encounter. I couldn't write, so I rented office space to make it harder *not* to write, but all it did was compound my guilt: now I was paying rent *and* not writing.

Finally, at a friend's urging, I went to see a therapist she recommended, but I spent the whole session talking not about my mother's death but about my fears for my daughter's life.

"Next time," she said, pulling out her engagement book, "I'd like to focus on your dreams."

Had she said *nightmares*, I might have gone back. We say things like, "Traffic was a nightmare!" But watching my daughter spiral down, I was living one.

In April, a week before Ella's sixteenth birthday, I awoke with maternal ESP at 2:20 a.m., and as had become my habit now that I feared for her safety, tiptoed into her room to check on her. Her bed was empty, and with a visceral lurch, I knew she was not in the house. She was gone.

I thought of calling 911 to report her missing. I thought of going out to search for her on foot or in the car. I knew where she might have gone—a quiet little offshoot of a street about a half mile away—but I was afraid if I tracked her to her lair she might bolt.

Two months before, I'd chased her when she fled the house in a furious rage at me. Fight or flight: that time she had chosen the latter. What was I thinking? That I could stop a runner on the cross-country team from running away from me? What was I thinking, begging her to come back as I ran past a little kid who mocked me with falsetto cries of, "Ella, Ella, stop! Come back!" What was I thinking, chasing a teenager who wanted nothing more in all the world than to get the hell away from her anxious, hovering mother?

This time, faced with her empty bed in the dead of night, I mustered the self-discipline and the trust, both in God and in her, not to panic. I turned on the porch light, sat down in the living room, and, closing my eyes, settled into silent prayer. I could not help but peek at my watch every so often as the minutes added up to more than an hour, but I felt strangely calm and centered.

At last, I heard the door quietly pushed open. I kept my eyes shut, my hands folded in my lap, and my feet flat on the floor, and silently said, *Amen, amen, amen, amen …* I heard Ella come in, heard her breath catch and her feet stop when she saw me sitting there—*amen, amen, amen*—and then heard her tiptoe upstairs. I waited until I heard her bedroom door close; then I got up, turned off the porch light, went upstairs, and went to bed.

That night marked a milestone for me. I did not call up my friend Cory, who would have come to help me look for my daughter the way she had once helped me look for my missing Siberian husky. I did not call any of Ella's friends, who might or might not have known her whereabouts or been willing to tell me. I did not awaken my brother in Tacoma, Washington, or my sister in Parker, Kansas, to ask them to pray for her safe return. I turned on lights to beacon her home, sat down facing the door through which I prayed she would come, and anchored—no, lashed—myself to God to see me through the night. Confronted with my own insufficiency, God became what Psalm 46 says God is: "a very present help in times of trouble."

The plain truth is this: My daughter's suffering brought me to my knees, and it was while I was down there that I started to pray with an urgency that made prayer get real.

Two days later, Ella called from school at 10:20 a.m. She was sobbing.

"I can't do it," she said.

"Do what, sweetie?" I said.

"Get through my day. Can you come?"

"I'm on my way," I said.

I pulled up at her school, and watching her come toward the car, I saw that she could barely lift her feet. That leaden shuffle, a hallmark of severe clinical depression, convinced me to tell the psychiatrist she had been seeing for the past two months, a reputed expert on adolescent depression and suicide, that she needed to be hospitalized. In deference to his expertise, I had overridden my maternal instinct that my daughter needed the safe haven of a hospital.

But I didn't have to tell him the time had come. After squeezing her in for an emergency session that afternoon, he summoned me into his office when I returned to pick her up, and in Ella's presence, told me she needed to be hospitalized and that it needed to happen now … right *now*. I was not to take her home first. I was to drive her straight to UCLA's Neuropsychiatric Institute.

He flipped through his Rolodex, called NPI, and said he was sending an adolescent female for admission.

"Too late?" he said, glancing at his watch. "What do you mean, too late?" He listened a moment. "No, it *can't* wait till tomorrow, and a psych admission through the ER will take till midnight!"

He shook his head at me, tipped the receiver down from his mouth, and said, "They're saying new patients have to complete intake by 5:00."

I looked at my watch—four twenty—but despite what I saw, I nodded my head vigorously and stood up. We were not too late. *Too late* meant leaving Ella loose for one more day in a world filled with X-ACTO knives, razors, pills, and a tall building she may have scouted for roof access.

"Tell them we're coming," I said.

"The mother thinks they can get there in time," he said. "They're leaving right now."

He wrote down the address and scribbled a map on an index card. Traffic would be, as the KCRW traffic lady liked to say, "bummer to bummer." I stood up, shouldered my purse, and turned to Ella. "Come on, sweetie."

And so it began: a mad dash to get my daughter there in time. Her immediate hospitalization had suddenly become a high-tension, ticking-clock, life-or-death drama. She would be arriving like a refugee with just the clothes on her back and the contents of her purse, some of which would be confiscated as potentially risky. "Sharps," as they're generically called, include cigarettes, matches, lighters, and OTC pills.

Ella sat in the passenger seat twirling one long red hair at a time around her finger, yanking it out, and dropping it onto the floor mat. We did not speak. I did not think to pray. *Oh God, come to my assistance. Oh Lord, make haste to help me.* I drove the car, running traffic lights as they turned red and swearing under my breath at infuriating slowpokes. My emotional bandwidth narrowed to a slit. I did not dare let in what was happening: *I am driving my daughter to a psych ward. And I'm afraid we won't make it in time.*

I entered the UCLA campus through the Westwood gate, located the Neuropsychiatric Institute, and ditching the car in a loading zone, made for the door as if it were the finish line. I looked back. Ella was still getting out of the car. We were so close. But I couldn't tell her to hurry. How could she have hurried? She could barely walk.

We made it in the nick of time. We completed the preadmission review, and then an orderly escorted us up to the ward. We were buzzed in and shown to a small room, where the intake process continued.

A nurse leaned out of the nurses' station. "Food or mood?" she said. It sounded oddly jaunty.

"Mood," the staff person with us said.

That was how I learned that 2-West had two categories of adolescent patients: food disorders and mood disorders.

I was going to run home and pick up a few things just to see Ella through overnight, but they wanted her to start "settling in" and said they would provide her with toiletries and sleepwear. Hugging her good-bye and leaving her there was so hard I had to do it briskly in order to be able to do it at all.

Quita, my dog, greeted me at the door with her fleece man. I tossed it for her twice before I went to the kitchen, poured an off-duty amount of white wine, and leaning stiff-armed over the counter, let relief finally wash over me: *Ella was safe*. I sat down at the table and read through the Inpatient Adolescent Service packet I'd been given, including the section headed, "Preparing Your Family Member for Hospitalization," which detailed everything—every single thing—I had not had time to do.

Before bed, I went into her crimson room with a tote bag to round up what she'd asked me to bring. I found her sketch pad, Walkman, corduroy jeans, and the two sweaters; then, picking up her baby pillow, I pressed it to my face to inhale her salty sweet breath before dropping it too into the bag. On her bedside table was Sylvia Plath's *The Bell Jar*, a worn paperback of William Styron's *Darkness Visible: A Memoir of Madness*, and an overdue library copy of *The Diagnostic and Statistical Manual of Mental Disorders*. Too done in to soldier on, I fled her room, automatically closing the door behind me before realizing that tonight I didn't have to.

Two days later, I came home from making awkward, upbeat small talk during the 5:30–6:30 visiting hour to find an expensively overnighted FedEx carton on my doorstep. It was from my sister. I was puzzled. Carole's birthday presents to Ella and me had already arrived, both in one box because we have back-to-back birthdays. That day was my fifty-third; tomorrow would be Ella's sixteenth.

When I saw what was in the box, I knew just what had happened: My sister had thought of something she could *do*, under the guise of my birthday, to express her distress and sorrow over Ella's hospitalization. In a surge of profligate generosity, Carole had split up the pair of antique religious panels hanging in the foyer of her house and dashed off to the post office with the one I'd always half-kiddingly claimed ought to be mine since I'm the writer in the family: the one showing an angel holding a book.

My Popham grandmother had gotten the panels in New Orleans on an antiquing junket in the 1950s. The provenance, typewritten on age-yellowed paper taped to the back of one of the panels, attested that they were side panels from a Renaissance Italian altarpiece by the Dominican friar Fra Angelico: "Acquired by this shop from a famous American of Italian extraction who brought them from Italy about 1900." At the time my grandmother purchased them there was almost no demand for medieval art, but whatever my grandmother paid, my grandfather thought she'd been rooked and snidely referred to the panels as "Ethel's Fra Angelicos" in the way the purchase of Alaska had been dubbed "Seward's folly."

After my grandparents died, my sister wound up with both panels, and my hints to her about the "literary" one had fallen on deaf ears. Now, with Ella's hospitalization coinciding with my birthday, she'd hit on a sacrificial act of kindness, a *mitzvah*.

Funerals these days are called "celebrations of life," but Ella's sixteenth birthday was the saddest celebration of life I have ever attended. The four of us—a family in shambles crammed into a too-small room on an adolescent psych ward—went through the motions of birthday presents, funny cards that fell flat, and "Happy Birthday to You" sung with false gusto over my homemade cake decorated with "Happy Birthday Ella" and sixteen unlit candles ("sharps").

She spent twenty-six days in 2-West. The psychiatrist who wrote the discharge order told me early on that Ella would not be over her depression when she was released but that the worlds of feeling, thought, and action would be sufficiently distinct and unconfused for her so that thinking about or feeling like killing herself would not become an action taken. His evaluation of her safety was the major criterion for her release.

In meetings with Ella's team of doctors, social workers, and staff, I was told that no one thing "explains" depression. The weight of different factors is different for each individual: life circumstances, family history, biological factors, temperament. They said that her high intelligence and extreme sensitivity to others' thoughts and feelings—the ennobling difference—were a curse and a blessing, and the combination with adolescence exacerbated everything.

But everyone assigned to Ella's case considered her father's and my recent divorce—"the terrible, terrible divorce," as one doctor characterized it—a major contributing factor to her depression.

"The communication void your divorce created has left your daughter having to contend with each of you separately," he said. "It makes co-parenting simply impossible."

Well, Doc, just for the record, even when I was married, there was precious little "co-" anything.

2

UP IN SMOKE

It is easy to see the beginnings of things,
and harder to see the ends.
—Joan Didion

"Tell me!" he said. "Just *tell* me."

I shook my head slightly and sneaked a peek at my watch.

"Yeah, time's up. So tell me. *Tell* me."

The therapist jerked forward in his fake Eames chair with his arm cocked at shoulder height. I shrank back on the couch.

Smacking the side of my thigh, he shouted in my face, "Why do you want to marry the son of a bitch?"

I gasped and tried to pull my miniskirt over the burning place on my leg.

I was twenty-five years old and newly engaged. Alan and I had moved to Chicago two months before, but for now I was back in California and staying with friends in Santa Monica while seeing this therapist on a short-term, crash basis.

I was having a nervous breakdown. Or what I assumed was one. I don't know if "anxiety attack" was in the *Diagnostic and Statistical Manual of Mental Disorders* yet, but it was not in my lexicon. I did not know what was happening to me. My worst fear about therapy had not been what I might discover about myself but that I might discover I did not have enough of a "self"—a *there* there—to even delve into. So, in a way, I was fiercely proud of my shaky mental state. It meant there must be more to me than I had thought.

The idea was for the interim therapist to Krazy Glue me back together so I could return to my fiancé in Chicago. But wait. Why would any sane person *want* to return to a place that depressed her and to a man with whom she was madly in love but miserably unhappy? Why *did* I want to marry the son of a bitch?

In the middle of the night, I woke up on the hide-a-bed at my friends' apartment in Santa Monica with the answer stretched across my mind like a banner. It had percolated up from my subconscious like the answer to a Buddhist koan after deep meditation: because I am too scared not to.

I knew it was the truth. I was more afraid of hurting Alan's feelings than of honoring my own. I was willing to override my misgivings about marrying Alan in the belief that the sheer force of my love would change him into an appreciative and demonstrative spouse. Besides, even if I did know better than to marry him, I did not know how *not* to. After all, Alan's proposal had come in response to my ultimatum that I would not move to Chicago with him unless he made his intentions clear.

In the thirty years all told I spent with Alan, I stood up tall to him only twice: first in the hope of marrying him and then in the need to divorce him.

Our marriage ended one sunny, breezy afternoon in Malibu some two and a half years before the date stamped on the divorce decree.

I was writing in my office at the far end of the garage, and Alan was on the tennis court shooting baskets with the kids. When the sound of the ball and their horsing around suddenly stopped, I figured Alan was taking a cigarette break. I wondered if he would ask Daniel and Ella where we had gone that morning. "Running errands" was what I had said.

When the door slammed back and Alan stormed into my office, I knew why. I had seen it coming since the day our son was born: this very moment, this exact scene.

"How dare you show Daniel schools!" he shouted, looming over me and banging down his fist on my papers.

I leaped up so fast my rolling chair shot away. "I didn't!" I said. "We were out getting school uniforms, and I drove by a couple of schools just to see where they are."

"Don't play the innocent with me!" he said, jabbing his finger in my face. "Daniel is going to Deerfield, and you'd better goddamn well get used to it."

Alan liked to recount the story of how after Daniel's birth at 4:34 a.m., as he stood waiting for the maternity-wing elevator before heading back home to Malibu to get some sleep, he found himself weighing—seriously wrestling with—what seemed like a burning question that had just come to him: *Should my son have golf lessons or not?* Though meant as an amusing anecdote of new fatherhood, it had made me uneasy that Alan's first reaction was to start mapping out our newborn son's future. It worried me because it was what Alan's overbearing father had done to *him* and it had not served Alan well.

His adoption as an infant into an East Coast family of wealth and prestige personified the adage that in any given situation the best thing and the worst thing about it are identical. But it doesn't begin to convey what it was like for Alan, an introspective, eczema-suffering child, the youngest of four, in a family with a domineering father and a patrician mother whose children came a distant second to her larger-than-life husband.

Now, on that late August afternoon in Malibu, he brought dramatically to the fore the issue that had been simmering on the back burner since Daniel's birth thirteen years before. Now, here it was, right in my face, not an amusingly trivial decision—To golf or not to golf, that is the question!—but a unilateral decree that our son was to be sent three thousand miles from home to the school Alan's father had shipped him off to: the venerable, top-notch prep school in the boonies of eastern Massachusetts, where Alan made no bones about having spent the bleakest, most miserable years of his life. That it was an open-and-shut case of "like father, like son" became crystal clear when Alan admitted to me that, though his alma mater was now coed, he did not plan to send our daughter there.

But I was not about to be prematurely deprived of my brainy, droll, tall, tender son, nor would I let Ella be robbed of her god of an older brother. I stepped back from Alan, glowering down at me like a gargoyle, and folded my arms across my chest.

"Over my dead body," I said.

———

When Daniel was born, Alan's sister Charlotte sent a silver baby cup and the family heirloom christening gown. Alan and I had no church affiliation—or any thought of having one—but I felt obliged to put the gown to use and suggested we have an impromptu little ceremony at home in Malibu. So on a Sunday afternoon in March—during what was, unbeknownst to me, the penitential season of Lent, when the church suspends the sacrament of baptism and even the word *alleluia* is banished—I got our six-week-old baby all dressed up in the freshly starched and ironed christening gown. After taking archival photos, I set him in his infant seat on the redwood table on the terrace, dabbed his noggin with champagne from the silver baby cup, and ceremonially spoke his full name. I associated christenings with champagne because of a photo I'd once seen of First Lady Jackie Kennedy dubbing a nuclear sub with a magnum.

I poured some of the christening champagne for the two of us, and raising our glasses in a toast to our firstborn, Alan said, "To Daniel!" and I said, "*L'Chaim!*" because it was the only blessing I could think of. We then took turns telling Daniel a little bit about the two men he had been named in honor of: Alan's father, a Fortune 500 dynamo and public servant, and my maternal grandfather, a southpaw pitcher in the Texas League and much loved butcher at the Piggly Wiggly market in Cleburne, Texas.

That evening, smack in the middle of *60 Minutes,* Alan said, "I want you to find an Episcopal church so that damn christening thing can be done right."

The next day I called my sister in Kansas City. "You're not going to believe this," I said. "Alan wants me to go find a *church*, an Episcopal one."

"Well, guess what?" Carole said. "Our associate rector just moved to Los Angeles and is at one."

And so it was that our son, wearing the christening dress a second time, got officially baptized on Easter morning at an Episcopal church in Pacific Palisades, California, the town right next door to Malibu. I considered being at St. Matthew's a one-time thing until I heard about its highly regarded pre-K–8 school and found out that nonparishioners' kids didn't have a prayer (as it were) of getting in. So I became a churchgoer with an ulterior motive. Alan backed my efforts to gain admission slots but attended church with us only on Christmas Eve and Easter morning. God, being God, "to whom all hearts are open, all desires known, and from whom no secrets are hid," knew what I was up to, but once I started going to church, he took it from there.

I say "church," but there *was* no church. It had burned to the ground six months before Daniel's baptism in one of those seasonal wildfires that Southern California is famous for. Having been *un*churched for so long, it suited me fine being a member of a clergy-led but nonphysical church. It was a churchless church that came into being solely through its various ministries and outreach activities, and our Sunday gatherings for worship in the school gym, or weather permitting, on a grassy slope on the church grounds. Two years later, when Ella was born, there still was no church, and she too was baptized alfresco in the heirloom christening gown.

———

Growing up, my sister and I had attended Sunday school regularly, but my parents skipped church about as often as not. In the 1950s, belonging to a church was the norm, but attendance was optional. My childhood church in Kansas City was named, I kid you not, Country Club Christian Church. Since just about everyone who went there also belonged to a country club, I didn't think twice about it, but *The New Yorker* magazine had a field day with it in one of their little column-fillers—something about the holy-in-ones praying for short putts and a good lie.

My father would toss on his bathrobe over his pajamas—the wool plaid robe in winter, the seersucker in summer—and drive Carole and me there. Mother liked to get her beauty sleep on weekends, and Daddy, an avid outdoorsman with a trophy room of hides and heads at home and a wing of Kansas City's Natural History Museum named in his honor, revered nature but never could buy into God. Or maybe he would have agreed with Frank Lloyd Wright about believing in God but spelling it N-a-t-u-r-e.

When I was twelve, I was baptized at Country Club Christian in the sacramental dunk tank located behind a wooden panel raised for viewing by the congregation. I remember wearing my turquoise Jantzen bathing suit under a white robe and how the pastor's robe had weights sewn in the hem to prevent it from billowing up around his underwear. I also remember how scary it was when he put a folded handkerchief over my nose and mouth, and bending me backward into the water, proclaimed me to have died and to now be Christ's own forever.

But in our family, God was strictly quarantined to church. His name was never spoken, not even to be taken in vain. God just never came up. I was taught to say "please" and "thank you" to everyone, it seemed, but God.

Then my baby brother, Artie, suddenly got very sick and was found to have type 1 diabetes. He was five years old. My mother fled in denial to the Christian Science Church and tried to take my sister and me with her, but we flat refused to get in the car. Since she was always running late to church, she soon gave up. It's a toss-up whom I was madder at: Mary Baker Eddy for proclaiming an incurable disease "mental error" or my ostrich of a mother for closeting herself upstairs in her sitting room reading *Science and Health* while my father jabbed Artie with insulin every morning in the breakfast room.

In sympathetic accord with my rosy-cheeked baby brother, whom I simply adored, I forswore dessert and all sweets, even sugar on my Cheerios. I anxiously watchdogged Artie and came unglued every time I caught him crouched on the kitchen counter with his pudgy little hand in the box of C&H brown sugar. I was terrified he would die.

On Saturdays I rode my bike to the science library at the University of Missouri's Kansas City campus to secretly bone up on the disease my family was treating like a dark, shameful secret that was never to be spoken of. Believing the cause of Artie's diabetes was genetic, I wrote out a vow not to have children and hid it in a little china slipper on my whatnot shelf. I was eleven.

Twenty years later, married, living in Chicago, and longing for a baby, it was not my girlhood vow that restrained me but doubts about my marriage. Then Alan and I moved from Chicago to Malibu, and in our geographic euphoria at being liberated from his family's corporate headquarters, blamed Chicago for our unhappiness and started a family right away.

Having children was not only the salvation of our marriage but the meeting place of our greatest happiness. I took to motherhood like a duck to water, and fatherhood took Alan's heart by storm. His capacity to love shot up overnight like a surprise lily.

But fatherhood, like everything Alan did, was strictly on his time and on his terms. He had a way of imbuing his activities with a highly official aura and capital-letter status meant to command respect and brook no interruption. If he was reading the paper, he was Reading the Paper. If he was on the phone, he was On the Phone. When he stretched out on a chaise on the terrace and snoozed, he was Taking a Nap. When he sat down on Sunday morning with an emery board, he was Filing his Fingernails. I bought into the Do Not Disturb image he presented and, cowed by it, let him off the hook when it came to household chores and the more *un*fun tasks of child raising.

A video I shot at the beach when the kids were four and six captures Alan's once-removed, there-but-not-there aloofness perfectly. While the kids romp and cavort, shoveling sand, patting sand castles, chasing sea gulls, dashing in and out of the shallow, foamy brine, Alan is stretched out, propped on an elbow, smoking a Lucky. He stubs it out in the sand, lies back, closes his eyes, and dozes. Daniel and Ella keep running up to show him things, and he opens one eye to squint at whatever it is this time, nods, and then closes his eye, and the children, satisfied enough, scamper off.

It is a family outing—there we are, the four of us—but the dad is a man apart, unto himself. Looking at that video now, I find it so poignant I have to remind myself that Alan was not being excluded; he recused himself from *us*.

Our marriage was not a partnership but an alliance of fiefdoms, of his-and-her domains. We didn't function as a couple, a twosome, but as separate entities. We played singles, not mixed doubles. I did not even buy joint gifts and sign the cards, "Love, Mom and Dad." In every sense, we each gave our own gifts to our children.

Our alliance worked well enough until the August afternoon he burst into my domain and attempted a takeover of our son. This was about far more than where our son would go to high school. What was at stake, for me, was the integrity, the fastness, of our family. What I wanted was four more years of Daniel as an embedded member of our family … four more years of Daniel at the dinner table, Daniel in his room, and Daniel in our daily lives, lollygagging over his homework, maddening us with the hard bargains he drove in Monopoly, skylarking at the beach with his sister, and shooting up to six six before our very eyes.

Alan's power over me had always resided in his clenched intensity when angry. He never hit me. He didn't have to. He intimidated me by slamming things down, stomping around, shoulders sawing, growling, *goddammit*-ing. I walked on eggshells to avoid his displeasure. I safeguarded his sleep from disturbance, ran the house to suit his schedule, and made sure to never ever run out of Lucky Strikes, Oreos, and Medalgia d'Oro espresso.

But it was the furrowed intensity of Alan's craggy face that had instantly, viscerally attracted me to him. I was on spring break with my family in Scottsdale, Arizona, when I met him through friends. It wasn't even a blind date; he was just a guy giving me a ride to our newlywed, mutual friends' for dinner. I knew nothing about him except that he was a grad student in philosophy at King's College, Cambridge University, who was spending spring break at his family's winter home in Phoenix. What grabbed my heart was not his dark-blond hair, piercing blue eyes, deep suntan, and six-one height, but the blemished complexity and fierce intelligence of his face. I was attracted to Alan because he was *not* a blandly handsome, nice-looking man.

Here was someone who looked conversant with the tumultuous depths I had craved growing up in the stifling niceness of midcentury

Kansas City society. At age twenty, I was a seeker of just the sort of truth I saw in Alan's face: hard, angry, expensive truth. I thought of it as *authenticity*, and at twenty-two, Alan's face already had it writ large. Everything that made his physical appearance so compelling was borne out by the aloof reserve of his temperament. *Laid-back, carefree,* and *easygoing* were antonyms of him. *This is the one.*

Intense, instantaneous attraction—"love" at first sight—is often, I think, based on an inchoate sense of recognition. In some embryonic way, I sensed that we were equal and opposite reactions to the same stimulus: He did anger; I did fear. His fear took the form of anger; my anger, the form of fearfulness. (At *Jaws*, when the shark burst out of the water and came within an inch of snatching the guy from the boat, Alan leaped up out of his seat, jabbed his finger at the screen, and yelled, *"No!"* with such fury it sent a ripple of nervous laughter through the theater.) I recognized in him someone who could act out my suppressed side. And I think Alan saw in my overt anxiety and fearfulness an embodiment of his own long-suppressed vulnerability and fears. Our balanced imbalances made us two sides of one coin: the perfect couple.

But on that August afternoon when Alan burst into my office, my set-apart writing place, my holy of holies where he rarely set foot, as he craned over me and got in my face, intimidating me in my inner sanctum, I suddenly saw him as if through the wrong end of a telescope. I viewed him as if from a safe distance, and speaking from there, in a preternaturally calm voice, I said, "Alan, you are not in control of yourself right now."

What he heard in my voice and saw in my composure was fearlessness. He did not know it was completely involuntary. A part of my mind had momentarily separated from the rest, and it was that disconnected part that spoke and changed, once and for all, the dynamic of our relationship. I later learned that what I experienced was the defense mechanism of dissociation.

In that moment of fearlessness—of being so overcome with fear that I overcame my fear—something fundamental shifted so radically it ended our marriage. Even had I stayed, it would have been over, because in that moment I had seen Alan on a life-size, human scale, and I did not like what I saw. For decades I had lost self-respect because of how I let him intimidate me. Now I had lost my respect for the man I had put on a pedestal, revered as an angry god, and tried so hard for so long both to please and to placate.

He glared into my face, coming so close that, in my detached state, I noticed the stray eyebrow hairs slanting this way and that in the vertical grooves between his brows, and how his lips, compressed with anger to a thin hard line, paralleled the welt of the scar across the groove of his chin. Then he swung around, threw open the door, banging it so hard against the doorstop that it ricocheted off his shoulder, and strode out.

He stopped speaking to me from the moment he banged out of my office. He ceased communicating with me because of the shift that had happened. From then on, he ignored my presence as if I had become what was known in the Stalin era as a *former person*. From then on, he referred to me to Daniel and Ella as "your mother" instead of "Mom."

Always before, after cold-shouldering each other for a while after a disagreement, there would come an easing up, a backing off, a gradual resumption. We'd let enough time go by, and then, as sure as spring follows winter, the ice would gradually thaw. This time our silence reached the state of permafrost. This time my heart hardened so obstinately against him it seemed to have lost the very capacity to melt. In church, kneeling for the prayer of confession, I always welled up over the line about "deliverance from hardness of heart." But it never softened my heart past the "Amen."

I became habituated to our silence, but it never seemed normal. Hoping to ease some of the awkwardness and strain, I suggested we at least observe the bare-bones civility of saying "Good morning" and "Good night" to each other. The next morning as we got out of bed— we still slept in the same bed but miles apart—I said, "Good morning, Alan."

"Yeah, sure," he snarled.

I suggested we see a marriage counselor. He refused. I let a few more months go by and then approached him about seeing a family therapist. He refused that as well.

"What do you think will make things improve between us?" I asked, standing beside the chaise where he was sunning with eye protectors over his eyes. More than a minute went by as I stood gazing down at the white plastic orbs that made his eyes look creepy.

"Time," he finally said.

———

On a hot Tuesday afternoon during Southern California's annual autumn fire season, an arsonist in Thousand Oaks succumbed to the temptation of tinder-dry chaparral, and an hour later, over on the ocean side of the Santa Monica Mountains in Malibu, I saw the sky take on the eerie copper luster that meant a wind-propelled Santa Ana fire was heading our way.

By then, Alan and I had not been on speaking terms for over a year, and Daniel had been in boarding school six weeks. His school was located just an hour up the coast from Malibu and was modeled on East Coast prep schools like the one Alan had attended. I considered it a painful compromise, but Alan didn't and had made arrangements to fly back East with Daniel for an interview at his alma mater. I had begged him to reconsider uprooting our son just six weeks into his freshman year. Now, with Malibu in flames, the Pacific Coast Highway closed, and our house threatened, Alan had to cancel the trip for the time being.

After Daniel left for boarding school, stranding his sister with parents locked in icy silence and headed for divorce, Ella did not know what hit her. At an age when belonging is everything, she was being snubbed by girls she had been friends with since preschool. Now, with their Victoria's Secret bras, menstrual chitchat, and heartless preteen hauteur, they wanted nothing to do with a late-bloomer. On top of that, a broken wrist had sidelined her from sports at school and her horse world in Malibu.

No wonder she's depressed! I told myself. *Her brother's gone, her dad and I aren't speaking, she's having a horrible year at school, and she can't ride till her wrist heals.*

It grieves me to speculate on the extent to which my having let her depression when she was twelve go untreated contributed to the terrible severity of the one that began three years later. Alan told her to stop feeling sad and "buck up."

I kept track of the Malibu wildfire on the nonstop TV coverage. Gauging its distance from our house made me think about the way danger is often measured in terms of distance. I was thinking about how, with a house, the closer the fire, the greater the threat; but between husband and wife, the wider the gap, the greater the danger. Around midnight, before going to bed, I went outside to check the sky and sniff the air. No stars were visible, but it was windborne smoke, not fire glow, that was blotting them out. The table on the terrace had a light dusting of ash.

To stay or to go? It is the hardest decision of all. Which is better? To face an inferno with a water bucket and a garden hose or get the hell out of there? To abandon a threatened house or try to save it? To pull the plug on a lifeless marriage or stay on in the false hope it might somehow be revived? In divorce, 75 percent of the time it is the wife who wants out. In wildfires too, it's the women who leave, taking the children with them, and it's the men who, even against bad odds and their better judgment, stay to try to save the house.

Once you have decided you cannot save your house or your marriage by staying, there comes the decision of when to go. Do you hang on until the eleventh hour, hoping for a shift in the wind or a change of heart, or do you get out immediately? Most people, I think, stay as long as they possibly can—and probably longer than they ought to. I did. And when they finally do bail out, and even if there should not have been any question about it in the first place, they still feel terrible about leaving. I did.

After the fire, Alan never rescheduled the trip back East with Daniel for an interview at his alma mater. I left well enough alone and did not bring it up.

But, for me, Daniel's departure from home at fourteen, even for an in-state boarding school, signaled the end of us as an intact family. Had our children remained at home until their timely departures for college, I would have stayed married to Alan until death, not divorce, parted us. The breakup of our family came not when I left the marriage but when our son left for boarding school. It was, to borrow a psychological term, a "nodal event" that destabilized the family equilibrium and left us, each in our own ways, traumatized by Daniel's absence, shell-shocked by his vacant room, his empty place at the table, his unoccupied seat in the car.

Nothing drove it home harder than when he said to me, "Do you realize, Mom? From now on, I'll be a visitor at home."

Even so, even *with* Daniel away at school, had I known what lay just ahead for Alan, my heart's blockade of him would have lifted. I would have made my peace with him and stayed. In a cruelly ironic way, he would have been right about what would end our impasse: time, the little he had left of it.

———

Three months after the Malibu wildfire, on January 17, 1994, Martin Luther King's birthday, a magnitude 6.7 earthquake struck Los Angeles at 4:31 a.m. Alan and I nearly collided as we rushed from our respective bedrooms—I now slept in the guest room—but not even an earthquake in which seventy-two people died and nine thousand were injured jarred us out of our silence.

Our house withstood the quake, but it left me badly shaken that such a calamitous event had failed to jolt us out of our impasse, and I started seeing on my own the family therapist Alan had refused to see. After a half-dozen sessions I knew that for me divorce was a lesser evil than remaining in a marriage beyond resuscitation. Alan might be prepared to settle for a marriage of convenience, but I wasn't. I had a Taoist sense of "right action" about my decision to leave. But anyone in agreement with the Authors Guild poll that concluded the smartest thing a writer can do is find a lifelong partner with an independent income big enough for two would have told me I was out of my mind to leave my marriage and walk away at age fifty from all I had. What more could I possibly have wanted?

I wanted to become recognizable to myself. I wanted to hear the sound of my own laughter again and for my kids to hear it too. I wanted to start living in accordance with who I was and not the person I had contorted myself to be. I wanted to reconnect with the optimistic, all-embracing spirit of my twelve-year-old self who had believed she could be a writer *and* an artist. I wanted to explore those inner promptings and spiritual inklings I was having. The concept of the true self in the writings of Trappist monks Thomas Merton and Thomas Keating resonated so deeply with me in part because of how not-myself I always felt with Alan, how slight a resemblance I bore to what I thought of as "myself" with him. I wanted my children to understand that, profoundly sorry though I was for the pain my decision to divorce would bring them, I was even sorrier for the example of marriage we had set before them.

Despite the sense of "right action" I had about my decision to leave, I was in such a state of anxious dread over telling Alan that, before facing him, I wrote out what I was going to say on index cards and pulled off the Pacific Coast Highway at Zuma Beach to practice in the car.

But I didn't need my index cards after all. It was as if the prayer I had not thought to pray beforehand for what to say had been answered. In one short sentence, I said the one true thing: "I can't stand the pain any longer, Alan."

I did not say "divorce," but he knew that was what I meant, and in an agitated state, he immediately called the family therapist I had been seeing alone and told her he wanted her to broker a reconciliation.

The therapist laid it out in plain terms in a joint session: "Alan, Melinda has told you she plans to leave you. Melinda, Alan has told me he wants you to stay. Are you willing to hold off and give Alan six weeks to prove he wants your marriage to last?"

I said yes. I had to. It was only fair. But it felt wrong.

The therapist turned to Alan down at the far end of the couch. "Okay, Alan," she said. "You've got your six weeks. The ball is in your court. It's up to you."

That night I sobbed with unguarded ferocity in the outpost of the guest room, too distraught to muffle my despair for the sake of Ella in the next room. I felt trapped, doomed. Having agonized for so long over whether to stay or leave, no sooner had I come to the decision to leave the marriage than I was being hauled back in to give Alan a chance to demonstrate his desire to save it. Just when I had finally managed to get one foot out the door, I had been grabbed by the other ankle and dragged back in. I had a profound sense of self-betrayal. I had let this man's wishes overrule my own deep inner sense about leaving. I was suffocating the truth as I knew it.

I hauled out the cache of divorce books I kept hidden under the bed to find the one with the Biblical bookmark stuck in it. I sometimes winced at the religious stuff my sister sent me, but I latched for dear life onto the bookmark she'd tucked into my fiftieth birthday card the month before:

> Do not be anxious about anything,
> but in everything,
> by prayer and petition, with thanksgiving,
> present your requests to God …
> Finally, beloved, whatever is true,
> whatever is honorable, whatever is just,
> whatever is pure, whatever is lovely, whatever is admirable—
> if anything is excellent or praiseworthy—
> think about such things …
> And the God of peace will be with you.
> —Philippians 4:6–9

I had read it so many times I knew it by heart. It had become a touchstone to steel my resolve not to let divorce bring out the worst in me but to make it a shining hour for the angels of my better nature. "Do not be anxious about anything." I wanted to know how to use prayer as an antidote to anxiety, as spiritual Valium, but the idea of presenting my requests to God, of flat-out asking God for what I wanted, was stunningly radical to me: *Please help me not to be too scared to leave. Please keep me from speaking ill of Alan to Daniel and Ella. Please help me not be greedy for stuff when I leave.*

The reconciliation attempt proved not only an exercise in futility but also a kind of mutual humiliation. Having never been a demonstrative man—we never held hands, never walked with our arms around each other's waists, never spontaneously kissed—Alan could not suddenly become one. Under the gun to be expressive toward me, to show me that he loved me, honored me, cherished me, *somethinged* me, he just could not do it. Nothing changed. I kept waiting for some sign, some gesture. It would not have taken much. After all, in thirty years he had told me he loved me a grand total of three times, and one of those didn't count because I extracted it from him when we were drunk.

Flying off on our honeymoon, in an outburst of newlywed elation, I had reached across the first-class armrest for his hand. He yanked it away from me, and with a backhand wave, said in a weary, tutorial tone, "Melinda. Just because we're married doesn't mean I'm going to pay attention to you."

Blinking back tears, I picked up my book and pretended to read while my insides sank with a leaden premonition of the humiliation and loneliness in store for me in this marriage I had longed for and sought, despite knowing better, with such ardent determination.

I took Alan's last name, but it did not redefine me. I continued to write under my own name. I had been writing since I was seven, when my father brought home a Remington Noiseless typewriter from his law office and installed it down in the basement. I fell in love with that machine—it was not noiseless, it was gloriously audible—and with writing as a subterranean activity. But I thought of myself as far more than a writer. I was a *typist*.

After marrying Alan, I no longer had to teach to support myself while writing my first novel, but I did not identify with my in-laws' wealth and was embarrassed enough at having married a businessman that I let friendships with fellow writers lapse.

Intimacy in a relationship comes from the risk you take by letting yourself be vulnerable to each other. Early on, Alan and I became adept at avoiding that. Rarely did I glimpse the abyss of vulnerability beneath his reserved manner. Once, when we had been dating for two years, he waited in the car while I dashed into the market. It took longer than expected, and afraid he'd be mad, I got back in the car babbling apologies and explanations.

He cut me off in a tone so naked it laid his core wide open for me to see. "I felt abandoned," he said.

But I kept jabbering about long lines and slow clerks, and he saw that, though I was the one always claiming to want more emotional candor in our relationship, I couldn't handle it. I could not bear to know how he really felt deep down—his excruciating vulnerability, his primitive fear of disconnection. Besides, feeling *abandoned*?

One of my earliest memories is of being in the bathtub when I was big enough that I could be left alone in it but was still small enough that I had to be helped in and out of it. My mother would run a shallow tub, swirl the water with manicured fingertips to test it, and then put me in and return to her dressing room to resume her nearly perpetual personal grooming. The water went from too hot to lukewarm to stone cold while I waited for her to come back. I did not call out to her. I had already concluded it was futile to ask for what I wanted or needed. Instead, I made up a little song and sang it to the soap dish while I hoped my mother would remember me. I pretended the recessed peach tile niche of the soap dish was a little house, and peering into it, I softly sang,

> Nobody home.
> Nobody home.
> Nobody,
> nobody,
> nobody home.

So when Alan, in a unique moment of raw truth, confessed that my delayed return to the car had made him feel abandoned, I could not acknowledge it. Abandonment? That's *my* issue. Mine! You can't have it.

When the six weeks' reconciliation attempt was up, the family therapist asked me what direction I was inclined to take. I glanced at Alan hunkered down at the far end of the long couch.

"I'm going to proceed with the divorce," I said. "He's given me no reason to stay."

That afternoon we called the children into the living room. Daniel was home from school for the summer. Because we rarely gathered there other than Christmas morning, our being there had a cruelly Christmassy feeling, all the more so since we all were sitting where we always sat opening our presents.

Alan said, "Your mother has something to say."

I had read four books about how to tell the kids you're getting divorced, but nothing I had read, reread, and underlined in those four books, and nothing I could have scripted on index cards and rehearsed, would have made it any easier to deliver that life-altering, heart-shattering sentence: "As you both know, Dad and I have been having problems for a while now. And I'm so sorry to have to tell you this, but Dad and I are going to get divorced."

It was so painful I don't remember what else was said, but as I recall, it was over fast. We scattered to our individual home bases: Alan to the study, the kids to their rooms, and me to my office. Daniel was fifteen and Ella thirteen.

"SM Canyon furnished apartment; short-term ok," the ad in the paper said. A converted two-story beach house, it had hardwood floors, glass doorknobs, and the right number of bedrooms. Even the name of the street boded well: Entrada.

The gated isolation of my oceanfront former life at the far end of Malibu now seemed peculiar. The urban orchestra was music to my surf-deafened ears, and the quickstep pace of city life gave me the solace that others seek by going to the beach. In that most uprooted, stressful, and crazed of times, life seemed unexpectedly grounded and sane. Ella's school was now three miles away instead of twenty-three, and for the first time in her life she could see friends at the drop of a hat and make last-minute plans. Watching her blossom socially now that we were living in town made me kid myself that my pending divorce had conferred an unforeseen benefit on her. Both of us relished the elbow room in the way we lived there. We made it up as we went along, winged it. Instead of waiting for the Dinner Hour, if we were famished at 5:00, we'd just go ahead and damn well *eat*.

I went for long walks with Quita and discovered old, wooden, vine-festooned staircases connecting the upper and lower parts of Santa Monica Canyon. I rediscovered peanut butter on celery sticks, and when

I banged out a short story from scratch at the big Mexican desk in my bedroom, I noticed that the tone of my writing was as changed—and unpredictable—as my circumstances were. I had a sense of having been catapulted onto a rising arc of exhilarating, burgeoning newness.

But I was like the woman in the news-looped footage of the Indonesian tsunami: frolicking at the shoreline with her back to the ocean, she does not see it coming.

3

MY GETTING-TO-GOD MACHINE

Be still and know that I am God.
—Psalm 46:10

Three months after separating from Alan and moving to Entrada, I signed up for a Centering Prayer workshop. I was so nervous and excited you'd think I'd agreed to go on a blind date with God. What if it didn't work out? What if it *did*?

The last two years I was married, every time I saw publicity for a Centering Prayer event somewhere in Los Angeles, I'd found myself drawn to whatever this contemplative prayer of "unknowing" might be. What stopped me from going was picturing the way Alan would have screwed up his face and said, "You want to go to a *what*?" And I knew I would have flapped my hand in that self-deprecating way I had and said, "Oh, nothing. Never mind."

But this time when I saw the publicity for a Centering Prayer workshop, there was nothing—or no one—to stop me. What's more, as luck would have it, the workshop was being held at my own church. The publicized event was from nine to three on Saturday, but the chaplain from Sewanee who was conducting it had offered to give the host church's parishioners a preview on Friday morning. I was one of a scant eight or nine who showed up for his early-bird special. He had us go around the circle and introduce ourselves and say why we had come.

When my turn came, I said I had come because regular prayer

made me feel awkward and hokey and I liked what the flyer said about Centering Prayer changing your way of seeing reality. What I didn't say was this: I'm here because after two and a half years of not being on speaking terms with my husband, I'm ready for a silence that's receptive instead of stony. I'm here because I feel guilty and worried sick about my teenage son and daughter having to cope with my pending divorce from their dad. I'm here because I have to find something besides wine that I can count on to lift my spirits.

After we had gone around the circle, the chaplain said, "Whatever you said about why you came, I'm here to tell you you're here today because God brought you here."

The Sewanee chaplain told us about the prayer's origins in an ancient monastic manuscript called *The Cloud of Unknowing* and its updating in the 1980s by Trappist monks in Spencer, Massachusetts. He quoted Christian mystics like St. John of the Cross, who'd coined the phrase "the dark night of the soul," and read us poetry by T. S. Eliot, John Donne, Billy Collins, Mary Oliver, and Gerard Manley Hopkins. Even before I gave the prayer a try, the rich context and tradition in which he embedded it made it feel alluring and right up my alley.

After running through the guidelines of the prayer, he led us into a twenty-minute period of practice. I shut my eyes, planted my feet, cupped my hands in my lap, and sat up straighter than usual, and at some point, for a moment or so, the "I" of me went away. I became momentarily *un*selfed or, I don't know, *de*selfed. I no longer was aware of sitting in a circle of people on a chair in the choir room. I no longer heard the fountain in the courtyard. I had not nodded off. I had a moment of blissful cessation. Only momentarily, yes, but long enough for me to sample the rest St. Augustine is talking about when he says, "Our hearts are restless until they rest in thee." The prayer had such an immediate take with me it was as if God had had his ear pressed to the door of my heart all along, and when I opened it just a crack, he came tumbling in. It was the first form of prayer I had ever engaged in—not counting the panicky kind—that didn't make me feel stiff and inauthentic.

First of all, it was silent prayer. That alone lent it considerable clout with me. This prayer didn't put words in my mouth or force me to come up with something to say to God on my own. Its silence felt like the densely compacted distillate, the irreducible essence, of the Biblical injunction "Be still and know that I am God."

Be still and know that I am God.
Be still and know that I am.
Be still and know.
Be still.
Be.

Centering Prayer was the BC/AD of my spiritual life. It was my portal to God. It activated God for me, throwing the switch that gave God the go-ahead signal and jump-starting my awareness of being *on* a spiritual journey. Centering Prayer not only deepened my relationship with God, it gave me to know I actually *had* a relationship with God.

No doubt the prayer's quick take with me was accelerated—and its hold on me strengthened—because of what was going on in my life at the time: a snail's-pace divorce; money worries; Alan's unrelenting hostility; and the threat of Daniel's expulsion for teenage shenanigans having put me in the paradoxical position of now hoping he would be permitted to *remain* at boarding school. Things with Ella, who'd just turned fourteen, still seemed copacetic, but all those other concerns left me sorely in need of the respite the Sewanee chaplain quoted Jesus as offering: "Come to me, all you who are weary and carrying heavy burdens and I will give you rest."

After that introductory workshop, Centering Prayer anchored my day and became the spine of my spiritual life, the crucial toothpick holding the messy triple-decker sandwich of me together. Twenty minutes, twice a day, first thing in the morning and just before fixing dinner with Ella, I put down my load and rested. Twenty minutes, twice a day, I sat down in my Entrada bedroom, closed my eyes, and bent the knee of my heart so that God, if he so desired, could bend my ear for a while. Day by day, month after month, I sat down, set the timer, and with varying success, quieted that noisy trio in my head: me, myself, and I. As Jesuit Anthony de Mello says, "Silence is not the absence of noise, it is the absence of self." Buddhists, bless their hearts, put it more succinctly: "No self, no problem!"

The flotilla of random, passing thoughts in my head was much easier to ignore than the unruly tremors, weird tics, and deluge of tears I experienced those first months. The most disconcerting side effect was one particular twitch that raised and lowered the left side of my upper lip. During group sits at the follow-up sessions I attended, I hoped to God no one peeked and saw me deep in prayer with my lip curled like that of a snarling dog.

The prayer's initial results were transformative. I later learned that this euphoric phenomenon is referred to in monastic circles as "the springtime of the novice." My springtime didn't last. But it didn't have to: I was hooked. My capacity for noticing and experiencing signs and glimmers of God's presence dramatically expanded. I saw what poet Elizabeth Barrett Browning meant when she wrote, "Earth is crammed with heaven."

Through my practice of contemplative prayer, I came to picture the divine presence as a pilot light deep within me. The South Side apartment where I'd lived as an undergrad at the University of Chicago came with a cruddy old gas stove. Having grown up around electric stoves—"Everything's up to date in Kansas City!"—I had been enthralled to discover a staunch little pilot light way at the back of the oven's nastily encrusted insides. To this day, whenever I come across a reference to the "divine spark" or "inner light," I picture that little lick of flame, that stubby blue nubbin, that tiny eternal flame steadfastly burning away in that ancient oven's innermost recesses. I was always elated by the way the pilot light would come to life when I turned the knob to Broil, leaping up, elongating to ignite the oval ring of broiler jets into a crown of bright flames. Because of it, I came to envision just such a tiny flame—a sacred speck, a mote, a fiery freckle of God's DNA—buried deep at the core of my being, the source of everything of height, heat, heart, courage, and beauty I am capable of.

By the time I attended the Centering Prayer workshop, I had been a faithful churchgoer but what is sometimes termed a "functional atheist" for sixteen years. By that I mean, based on how I went about in the world—harboring grudges, making uncharitable snap judgments, waking to a new day not with rejoicing but with free-floating anxiety and semi-sadness—you would not have guessed that I believed in God. There was apartheid for me between *life* in all its confusing, messy profusion and *church* in all its Sunday-ness. Though I never got through a worship service dry-eyed (in clergy lingo, I was a "weeper"), just what I was crying about was a complete mystery to me. All I knew was that being in church triggered tears the way a breast-feeding baby triggers the "let-down" reflex in the mother, allowing her milk to flow.

Sometimes the Eucharist really did seem like holy food and drink, not just a memorial gesture. But the moment of encounter would fade and, hit-or-miss Christian that I was, I thought that was all there was to it. I did not yet know how to carry the momentum of such a moment into a way of being in the world. I hadn't a clue how to bring God into whatever was going on at home. Until Centering Prayer, I was worlds closer to my women friends than I had ever been to God. It had always been my women friends, not God, I turned to when I needed to unburden my heart. They, not God, were "my strength and my refuge, a very present help in times of trouble."

The idea of integrating the happenstance of daily life with a regimen of spiritual practice was unimaginable to me. Which is to say: I did not yet *have* a spiritual life. I hadn't the foggiest idea how to get acquainted with God, be a conduit for Christ, or wing it with the Holy Spirit. ("Wing it" sounds flip, but it best conveys the intuitive, off-the-cuff nature that my interactions with the Spirit have had.)

Contemplative prayer was where the rubber met the road for me. It created a channel between my daily life and the divine indwelling and equipped me with the spiritual means to detect God's presence and action in myself and the world around me. The surface of my everyday life became richer, sweeter, as if raised from two-dimensional flatness to bas-relief. I began to experience the healing process that Trappist monk Thomas Keating calls "the divine therapy," the integrated realm of psychological change and spiritual transformation. My center of meaning—of who I hold myself to be, of who I am—began to undergo a radical shift. I started to grasp that I am not here *in propria persona*—a legal term meaning "in your own person"—but as a creature of God. Ordinary things now seemed opaquely sacred and my daily life a cocreation of the divine source and me.

One night about a month into my practice of the prayer, I saw an angel in the magnolia tree outside my bedroom on Entrada: a slender, grayish seraph every bit as real as the glossy, dark green foliage surrounding it. I called to my father and stepmother, who were visiting me, to come quickly. Ella was over at a friend's. I wanted them to hurry because I thought the angel might be a short-lived phenomenon like a rainbow.

"Look!" I said, pointing to the open window.

They looked and saw it: an angel in the tree. Even my super-rational, hyperanalytical father with his souped-up, finely honed legal mind had to admit he was seeing an angel in the tree. Phoebe and I stood close together, arm-hugging in awestruck reverence.

"I wish Ella was here," I said.

My father went into overdrive to figure it out. A man who could not stand being stumped, he pursued a logical explanation for it with dogged resolve until finally, pulling the open window a little inward, he made the angel disappear.

We had been seeing the ethereal reflection of a statue of an angel high in the tree—How? When? Who? Why?—projected onto a window open at just the right angle for visibility to us inside.

Though disappointed at the outcome, I did not feel silly to have believed the angel was real, and my father, to his credit, did not gloat at being right. Besides, to see my agnostic, skeptical father given pause for a while? That alone was a miracle.

I was on a month-to-month lease on Entrada. Four months after we moved in, my landlord informed me he needed my apartment for his elderly father. The idea of having to find *temporary* temporary housing for Ella and me and perhaps even needing for her to live in Malibu with Alan for the interim sent me into a tailspin—and cranked up my sense of urgency to arrive at a marital settlement so that I could make an offer on a house I'd found.

On the morning I'd told myself I would do it, as soon as the timer went off at the end of my meditation sit, I stood up and, as if propelled by the momentum of the prayer itself, sat down at my desk, and crossing my hands on the phone's cradled receiver, bowed my head and whispered, "May the words of my mouth and the meditations of my heart be always acceptable in your sight, oh Lord my God."

Then I picked up the receiver and dialed my former home number. It was 7:30 and, knowing Alan's ironclad schedule, I knew he would be back from his beach walk and awaiting the daily call from his broker in New York.

"Hi, Jim," he said pleasantly. "How's it going?"

"Good morning, Alan," I said. "It's Melinda."

He took a beat to readjust and then said, "Yeah, yeah. What?"

I delivered an ultimatum with a deadline about revealing—in court if need be—a certain asset he had left undisclosed in the financial discovery phase of our divorce proceedings. And it was just like what had happened in my office that August afternoon, when my calm detachment and nothing-to-lose tone said it all. There was total silence on his end. He didn't swear at me. He didn't sneer at me. He didn't slam down the receiver. He was palpably silent. For once, I was the one who hung up first.

All at once, with an eleventh-hour flurry of faxes, speakerphone conferences, and a motorcycle courier, our signatures were on the settlement. Three hours later, my real estate agent presented my offer, and the following day, after accepting the sellers' counteroffer, I had bought a house—the one with the address that was Daniel's birth date. Both my engagement to Alan and my divorce from him had required ultimatums from me.

Between Martin Luther King Day, when I left Malibu, and Memorial Day, when I was handed the key to my house in Los Angeles, I lived on Entrada with Ella, at two friends' places, and at two pet-friendly motels in Malibu so that I could drive her to school from Alan's. Everything for my post-Entrada, *temporary* temporary life was contained in one duffel bag, one tote bag, and grocery bags from five different markets: The Hughes Market bag was my desk. The Gelson's bag had my real estate documents. The Von's bag had my divorce-related documents. The short story I was working on was in the Westward Ho bag, and the Vicente Foods bag was my laundry hamper.

There is a Quaker saying, "Way will happen." Centering Prayer was mine. The prayer gave me a method, a means, a *way*, of entering into the incomprehensible mystery of a loving God. By the time I moved into my house, I had been practicing the prayer twice a day for three months. Fifteen months later, as Ella slid into the abyss, Centering Prayer would be my salvation.

4

THE RED PHONE

How can you let me die
in the midst of
this cloudy, secular electrical caution?
—Anonymous

One morning, way at the back of my desk drawer, I found a small blank notebook. It was shiny black with an exuberant red cloth binding. Inside, it was inscribed, "Happy Mother's Day, Mom! I love you, Ella."

It gave me such a jolt of joy to come across it that I decided every morning, before meditating, I would do a Five Things list, jotting down off the top of my head five things to be glad about even now. This was my first list:

1. Finding this notebook from Ella
2. Quita's goofy, toothy attempt to smile back at me
3. the cypress trees lining the driveway like sentinels
4. the hope that ECT will bring Ella back
5. the "FOUND!!!" poster for a missing cat

I put ECT—electroconvulsive therapy—on the list because I had to be glad there was something left to try, even something so drastic, terrifying, and last-ditch. The very thought of it being done to my child made my hands tremble, my heart cave in, and the soles of my feet ache the way they do when a nightmare wakes me up.

It had been one full year since the onset of Ella's depression. Now, over Labor Day weekend at the start of her junior year, she had been hospitalized for the third time in five months. As always, her safety was the primary concern.

At 7:20 a.m. on the first day of school, I parked in the loading zone at NPI's side entrance, went up to the ward, signed Ella out, wearing her school uniform from last year, and drove her across town. Commuting from NPI was her idea: Ella was bound and determined to graduate on time with her class. After school, I picked her up and returned her to the ward.

But the routine ended three days later when her NPI doctor said, "We've come to the end of the road with antidepressant drug options."

Effexor had made her violently ill. After a promising start, Wellbutrin had caused hives. Paxil, Lexapro, Prozac, and Zoloft had each been tried. Her depression had proved resistant to them all. There was one last one that had been around since the 1950s, but its prominent side effects and potentially fatal interactions with common foods and OTC medications made it so risky that even shock therapy was considered preferable.

A feeding tube is to anorexia what electroconvulsive therapy is to mood disorder: a last-ditch treatment considered so extreme the very mention of it causes a frisson. But whereas a feeding tube always works—willy-nilly, life-sustaining nutrition is delivered to the unto-death anorexic—ECT does *not* always work.

Ella's doctor arranged for Alan and me to be shown a video of the ECT procedure and to meet with someone from the ECT Department before we came to a decision.

Alan and I watched it sitting awkwardly close together on a two-cushion couch in the same little conference room as Ella's sixteenth birthday "party." He left immediately afterward, brusquely refusing to meet with ECT staff, and as far as I could tell, washing his hands of any further involvement in the decision.

The ECT video allayed but by no means quashed my deep-seated fear of shock therapy, stemming mainly from Jack Nicholson's benchmark portrayal in *One Flew over the Cuckoo's Nest*. Research was how I tried to subdue my fear, and books were what I turned to. (The Internet was not the resource it is now.) Acquiring knowledge has always been my chief coping strategy for dealing with fear. When I was contemplating divorce, I consulted books. When Ella was spiraling down, I read up on adolescent depression. Now it was ECT I needed to become informed about.

In my research, one brand-new book stood out from all the rest, a book that presented electrical therapy as a valuable emergency medical procedure used by both the cardiologist and the psychiatrist. Similar in principle and practice, defibrillation is to the heart what ECT is to the mind.

But what ultimately gave me the courage to sign the ECT consent form was a serendipitous human factor. The jacket flap on this new book said that the author had just been named director of UCLA's Neuropsychiatric Hospital.

Simply *knowing* that the man I saw through the venetian blinds in the ground-floor office I passed coming and going from my twice-daily visits to NPI to take Ella out for fresh air was none other than the author of the most reassuring, up-to-date, and informative book I'd consulted gave me the courage to consent to ECT for my daughter.

After the ECT video and Alan's abrupt departure, an ECT staff person showed me the treatment room itself and the adjacent recovery room; then she took me down to the NPI lobby to show me the area reserved for family members of ECT patients. I made note of the fact that it was not twenty steps from the NPI director's office.

She pointed out a red phone mounted on the wall. The sign above it stated that it was reserved for the exclusive use of ECT staff and patients' families. She told me that on the days Ella would be receiving a treatment I should be in the lobby by the phone at 7:30 a.m. I would receive two calls on the red phone. First they would call down to tell me they were taking her in for the treatment; then they would call me when she was in recovery. Only one patient at a time was treated. Once you knew yours was the one in the treatment room, you would wait, knowing the next call would be for you.

The ECT consent form required Ella's signature and one parental signature. I had always been the one who signed consent forms for the kids' school field trips, summer camps, rental horses, and dental procedures—any activity deemed risky enough to require parental consent. Over the years I had scribbled my name on dozens of forms, but until leaning over that clipboard in 2-West, I had never given my consent with a shaky hand and a leaden ache in my chest.

At seven thirty on the morning of Ella's first treatment, nine of us were in the waiting area by the side entrance of NPI: this solemn cluster of disparate people whose loved ones' intractable suffering brought us to sit in a designated area under the aegis of a wall-mounted red telephone. We did not speak to one another. No one read a book, a newspaper, or a magazine. We sat with averted eyes, waiting for the red phone to tell us about our loved one going in and coming out.

At seven thirty-five a car pulled into the handicapped space at the side entrance, and a white-haired couple unloaded a wheelchair and brought in their middle-aged daughter. She appeared catatonic. The practiced manner of the father calling on the red phone to announce his daughter's arrival made it clear this was an outpatient routine they had down pat. An orderly came and greeted the woman in the wheelchair by name and with a warm smile. She did not respond. The mother leaned over her daughter and gently kissed her cheek. When the mother straightened up, the look of weary hope on her face might have been the expression of a miracle-seeking medieval pilgrim at a holy shrine.

I was the only one waiting alone, and I felt very solitary. I closed my eyes and tried to enter into Centering Prayer, but thoughts ricocheted through my mind like bullets in a shoot-out.

After they called to say Ella was next, I did not know how long it would be before they would call again to tell me she was in recovery, so I did not think anything of it when two white-coated doctors—a man and a woman—came striding toward the side entrance. I had seen lots of white-coated doctors coming and going.

But these two stopped in front of me, and the woman doctor said, "Are you Ella's mother?"

And for one second I thought how nice it was of them to have come down to report to me personally about how my daughter's first treatment had gone. But then I saw their somber faces, and a massive sense of knowing I was about to receive bad news hit the pit of my stomach and sent my heart careening … news so bad it couldn't be phoned down but had to be delivered face-to-face by a team of doctors.

"Yes, I'm her mother."

The woman doctor sat down, perching sideways on the chair next to me. The name on her white coat was Russian. She looked severe, stringent, like a pre-Glasnost Soviet. The man stood in front of me with his hands in the pockets of his white coat. My body shivered. My legs shook in a terrified palsy.

"There was a problem," she said.

They had not been able to stop the seizure. She said how long the seizure had lasted and what the maximum was supposed to be. My mind balked at the gap, the gaping discrepancy, between the two numbers. I couldn't think. I could barely breathe. Something in my middle—my solar plexus or diaphragm—was so tightly squeezed with terror I could only take in shallow little sips of air.

Perhaps, she explained, my daughter had been dehydrated. That would cause the seizure to be prolonged.

I asked to see Ella. I would have to wait, she said. She was going to be seen by a neurologist, and they would need to run some tests on her.

"What kind of tests?" I asked.

"An EEG and an MRI."

I complied because I was petrified. I did not come unglued in front of them—*Why didn't you make sure beforehand that she* was *sufficiently hydrated?*—because I needed them to take care of my daughter. I did not want to present a problem. I was determined not to be an obstruction, not to make a scene, not to cause their attention to be in any way diverted. I would be docile so they could focus on my daughter and not have to tend to me.

I did not think to race around the corner to the NPI director's office, just as I had not thought to pray as I was driving my daughter to NPI: I behaved as if it was all up to me, that I had to be self-sufficient and up to whatever needed doing. "My grace is sufficient for you, for my power is made perfect in weakness."

Late that afternoon I was allowed to see Ella. She was back in the ward. She was in a wheelchair, but she was not like the catatonic outpatient in the wheelchair that morning. She was pallid and tearful and uncommunicative other than to say she had the worst headache of her life. I don't know if the sense of reproach I felt was self-reproach or came tacitly from Ella's distressing state, but mixed in with the fear and sadness swamping me on sight of my daughter was my sense of needing her forgiveness: How could you have let this happen to her?

A doctor went over the neurologist's report with me. Her reflexes were good, the dilation of her pupils, etc. Next time, he said, they would have intravenous Ativan ready to stop the seizure if need be.

Next time?

That I would have even considered signing a consent form for a second treatment says how utterly desperate I was for my daughter to be liberated from the grip of her now yearlong depression. But I left it to Ella's doctor to persuade her to sign it. I couldn't handle it.

I got to the ECT waiting area at 7:15 a.m. This time, instead of sitting with the others, I went and sat off by myself over by the closed convenience shop. At eight thirty they called on the red phone to tell me they were taking Ella in. I hung up, returned to my chair, doubled over, and covering my face with my hands, collapsed into prayer, whispering into my hands, "Please, God, oh please, please, please, please." I wasn't praying for ECT to work, just for it not to do her harm.

Then, as I prayed my plea, God gave me to know that Ella was safe. Contrived and awkward though it sounds, *gave me to know* is the closest I can come to expressing how I knew what I did. God's reassurance was not to *tell* me that she was all right—no voice spoke—nor did God show me. What I was given was a sure and certain knowledge that my daughter was all right. I understood that the medical personnel hovering over her were emissaries of God, angelic presences. My daughter was surrounded by ministering angels in white coats. God instilled in me the words with which angels begin their messages to mortals—"Fear not!"—and gave me to know that I need not fear because my daughter was attended by angels.

Suddenly there was a sharp tap-tap-tapping on my shoulder blade and a man's voice in my ear. "Ma'am? *Ma'am!*"

I jerked upright, jangled and disoriented at being brought back so abruptly from the safe haven of God. My eyes flew open and my head snapped back, recoiling from a man's face just inches from mine, a man bent over with one hand splayed on his knee and the other on my shoulder. I once caught a bathrobe's kimono sleeve on a doorknob as I ran to answer a crucial phone call, and the abrupt reversal of momentum yanked me back so hard I almost somersaulted. That was what it felt like as I blinked into the brown-eyed, brown-skinned, worry-furrowed face of the uniformed security guard in front of me.

"You okay there, ma'am?"

I rubbed my face, smearing my tears. I did not know how to answer him. I bobbed my head.

"You take care now, ma'am," he said, patting my shoulder; then he moved off on his appointed rounds, his weapons-laden body rocking slightly from side to side.

A gift of divine reassurance had been interrupted by a UCLA security guard. But maybe that security guard was part of what God was providing me with—not only the knowledge that my daughter was safe, but also a solicitous stranger, a guardian of security, who felt prompted to check on the woman in the Neuropsychiatric Hospital lobby sitting off all by herself collapsed over her lap with her hands covering her streaming face.

The second treatment did not have any glitches. But Ella received no benefit from it either.

After the third treatment, she came out of the recovery room and—poof!—Ella was back. Ella was herself. Ella was restored. ECT had *worked.* She was famished. She was laughing. She was giddy. It had been so long since I'd seen her smile I had forgotten how pretty her teeth are. As we left the hospital, walking to lunch in Westwood, we looped arms and laughed and joked and—my God, my God, thanks be to God!—my daughter was *fine.*

After lunch, I took her back to the ward. When I returned at five thirty to see her, she was gone. *Gone.* Leaden of gait. Wooden of affect. Sunk back into a depression that seemed, if possible, even worse.

No one had informed me, no one had *warned* me, of this potential outcome of an ECT treatment: the bounce effect.

In the course of Ella's long illness, there were other times I despaired, but my lowest point, my below-sea-level, Death Valley nadir, was witnessing her total relapse after she had been herself again for a cruelly joyous interlude of three hours.

In Compline, the seventh and final canonical hour of daily worship, there is a prayer asking God not only to "give rest to the weary, bless the dying, soothe the suffering, and pity the afflicted" but also to "shield the joyous." It is a stunning recognition of how fleeting and precious a thing joy is, how worthy of protection, of being safeguarded, it is. This devastating phenomenon called "the bounce effect" had given rise to joy—not the hope of joy but joy itself—and then destroyed it utterly. *Shield the joyous.*

After further treatments also proved futile, ECT was abandoned, and Ella was discharged, still suffering from major depression but not deemed suicidal. Three weeks later, when she was readmitted again, all I could think was, *Now what?*

One Friday evening, hoping it might provide some respite, I took her out on a pass to attend a candlelit contemplative worship service based on chants of the monastic community of Taizé in Burgundy. It had been quite a while since Ella and I had been in our church together, but she headed straight to the pew where we'd always sat when she and I were the regular churchgoers in the family.

Whether it was that Ella, growing up, had liked being in church or liked having me all to herself, it was uncanny the way she never made a peep. Not once did I have to hustle out the side door with a wailing baby or an irrepressible toddler. She had always been, quite simply, happy as a clam being in church with me.

Now, on this autumn night, as soon as we sat down in our usual place, she did exactly what she had done as a child: She keeled over sideways on the pew cushion, drawing in her legs and curling up with her head in my lap. It was as if a sort of Pavlovian response to her surroundings had kicked in, and so, though no longer a toddler, she lay with all five nine of her long-limbed, adolescent self drawn up into a ball like a doodlebug.

Her long hair, now dyed black, was covering her face, hiding its loved familiarity, and for a moment I thought, *Who is this stranger in my lap? Where is my sweet blonde Ella?* Smoothing back her hair from her face to find her, I remembered her telling me she had always been a redhead on the inside. Now, with her hair a ruthless black, I concluded it must be, once again, to match the color of her interior world, to manifest an outward and visible sign of the darkness within her: "If the light that is in thee be darkness …"

Holding this Morticia-haired teenager in my lap, I could not help but overlay the towheaded toddler who had lain there with a panel of her beloved, bedraggled crib bumper pressed to her cheek and two yummy fingers in her mouth, including the one she thought was called the Windex finger because it went *pssht, pssht* on the sprayer. I missed that joyful, quixotic child. And I missed the daughter who had once so adored me that when I shut her out of my bedroom while I worked on the life-size doll I was making her for Christmas, she curled up on the floor right outside, her fingers waving forlornly to me through the crack under the door.

I rested my hands on her uppermost shoulder and the blade of her hipbone, and after a while, working up my courage, fearing I might scare her off, I began giving her a gentle scalp massage, formerly one of her favorite things. At certain points in the service the small congregation stood or knelt, but I remained seated, not about to deny my daughter my lap or myself the euphoria of having her there.

Sitting in our usual spot but with a different daughter in my lap, I chanted, "My spirit is longing for you, oh God, my spirit is longing for you," but my heart substituted "Ella" for "God."

As we filed out in silence from the sanctuary, my friend Sarah slipped up beside Ella, put her arm around her, and leaning in close, whispered, "Hi, Ella. I love your mom."

"So do I," Ella whispered back.

The "now what" was an antidepressant dating back to the 1950s, the one considered so outdated, risky, and potentially fatally interactive that her NPI doctor had recommended ECT instead. But now they were saying that, despite its "downside," it was still considered a valuable treatment for atypical, major depressive disorder. The downside was that common foods and meds—such as fava beans, cured meats, aged cheese, and Sudafed—could cause hypertensive crisis and death. As with any antidepressant, it would be several weeks before they would know whether this one would prove of benefit.

But gradually, oh so slowly, like winter solstice's longest night fading to feeble but strengthening light, Ella's mood began to brighten until, finally, five weeks after the trial began, her depression had receded enough so that, on the day after Thanksgiving, she was discharged. By now, we had the routine down pat—the metal cart piled with her belongings; the discharge instructions gone over with us; the good-byes and thank-yous to the staff; the hugs with her food and mood buddies whose portraits she had drawn and whose hair she had French-braided; the buzz of the door being unlocked—but this time it felt like a *final* discharge. There were signs that this time it would stick. Not only was she on a medication that was letting her hold her own, but for the first time since turning sixteen eight months before, she wanted to get her driver's license. So normal! So typically adolescent!

How was I to know that Ella behind the wheel would prove disastrous?

5

PERFECT SYMMETRY

It is always the children who distance themselves,
their fingers welded to great suitcases
in which their mothers have saved both dreams and horror.
—Heberto Padilla

After her final discharge in November, Ella went at her adolescence with such a vengeance it was hard to bear in mind that it was "just a phase." Every single thing about me infuriated her. My very existence sufficed as provocation. Tensions between us finally reached a breaking point during a fight in the kitchen one morning in early July. Her fury at me was of a whole new order of magnitude. It became so intense I got scared. There is something terribly demoralizing about being afraid of your own child. It ended in her storming out on foot with just her purse.

I called her doctor.

"You'll have to make other arrangements for her housing," he said. "Her volatility toward you has reached the point where she can't be under your roof."

I did the only thing I could: I called Alan.

"Please don't hang up," I said. "I need to talk to you. It's important."

I told him what had happened in the kitchen and what her doctor had said. He listened in such total silence that if I hadn't heard him inhaling and blowing out smoke from his cigarette, I wouldn't have known he was there.

"If we had any family in the vicinity—grandparents, cousins, aunts, uncles—I would ask them to let Ella stay with them," I said.

I paused.

Alan said nothing.

"But we don't."

Nothing.

"Alan," I said, "I need for you to provide a home for Ella."

"Okay then," he said and hung up.

One week later, on a Tuesday afternoon, a new priest at my church called. As I was leaving church on Sunday, I'd mentioned that I wanted to talk to her about something. The spur-of-the-moment thought I'd had was so minor I was going to just let it go, but all at once I'd felt strangely compelled to tell her I wanted to talk to her.

"How nice of you to call," I said.

"I know what you want to talk about," she said.

"You *do?*"

"Your ex-husband's terminal cancer," she said.

The shock of it—the staggering, blindsiding *wham* of it—knocked me back into my childhood stutter. I could not get a clear word out, only stuttered fragments.

"Oh! You didn't *know?*" she said. "I'm so sorry. You said there was something you wanted to talk to me about, and, well, I just assumed that's what you meant."

Alan had told no one but Daniel and Ella about his diagnosis, and he'd imposed a blanket gag order on them. The total secrecy he demanded of them was the very thing that, in Greek myth, drove the keeper of an unbearable secret to dig a hole, whisper it deep into the earth, and then cover it up with dirt.

Inevitably, each of them did confide in a trusted friend, but then they felt just awful about it. That was how the priest had learned of it in a baroquely circuitous manner through a comment by a neighbor of hers whose daughter was the friend Ella had confided in. Coincidence, it's been said, is God's way of remaining anonymous.

Now I understood that what was *really* behind our fight in the kitchen was the news her father had delivered to Daniel and her while

I'd been in Kansas City. Her fury at me was in direct proportion to her very real fear of losing her father.

"What kind?" is usually the first thing you say after hearing someone has cancer. But I could not ask my children for details, and the priest knew only that it was terminal. Though I desperately wanted to know, I also knew that ultimately it was only a piece of information, nothing more, and that my having it wasn't going to change anything. Whatever kind it was, it was not survivable.

Alan—my husband of twenty-five years, the father of my children— had a terminal form of cancer, and I was supposed to play dumb about it. I spent a day composing a letter to him, but at the end of the day, out of respect for his privacy, I could not bring myself to mail it.

But Ella had not left home to go be with her dying father. She'd left to get away from me, the Anathema Mother. My fear of losing her, my anxious vigilance, drove her away. Her doctor had told me to "dissipate" my fears, but I could not make myself stand down. The easily fatal reactivity of the atavistic, last-ditch antidepressant she was taking kept me in a permanent state of high alert. I brought upon myself the very thing I did not want to have happen.

Ella's abrupt and total absence left a *nada* so vast it was a struggle to get out of bed, fix myself a bite to eat, or glance at the newspaper other than to look for a movie that might let me forget for a little while that she was gone. I signed up for a UCLA Extension course called The Art Scene in LA just to get myself out of the house, and then I felt oppressed by the time and energy it took to get out. I could barely bother to watch *Jeopardy* while I ate what passed for dinner. I still went to church and to my weekly Centering Prayer group, but I was like a blind woman running her fingers over the pages of a non-Braille Bible.

My life felt emptied of its purpose. Like a drained swimming pool, it just collected whatever fell into it—leaves, rainwater, the dog's old tennis ball—since its true and meaningful content was gone. I had lost the things that once gave meaning to my life. My marriage was gone, and my ex-husband was dying. My son was gone. My writing had become a slog of procrastination and guilt. And now my daughter. My greatest and most primitive fear had come to pass: abandonment.

There is a pregnancy emergency called "placental *abruptio*." It is a dire situation caused by the placenta tearing away from the uterine wall and the afterbirth threatening to become the "prebirth." Ella's *abruptio* exit from home and from my life left me feeling that something direly out of sequence had just happened: First my son, and now my daughter, had left home prematurely. Separations from those who once were within and utterly *of* us need to happen in timely fashion, not precipitously.

Jesus said, "Come to me all you who are heavy-burdened and I will give you rest." I wanted to take him up on his offer of respite, but I did not know how to go about it. Then one day, I was taking Quita for a long walk—something I had often failed to do since Ella left—and farther down the block, I saw a short, squat woman with a thick black braid down her back, a big black purse on her shoulder, and a white, kitchen-size trash bag balanced crossways on her head. The bag was full but in a squared-off manner that suggested stacks of neatly folded clothing. She was carrying it effortlessly on her head the way women the world over have carried burdens since time immemorial. The trash bag's two red ties floated jauntily like streamers.

And that's when it came to me that what I was witnessing was a woman who had transformed her burden into a hat. When I reached the foot of the street, she was standing at the bus stop, and her hat was now at her feet.

I took in what I had learned from her: First she had lightened her burden by the way she bore it. Then she had done just what Jesus wanted me to do with my burden: put it down at his feet.

On Christmas morning, six months into our estrangement, Ella showed up unexpectedly, ringing the doorbell before tentatively cracking open the front door and slipping inside sideways as if to minimize her arrival. Quita ran to greet her. Daniel waved hello from the couch amid gifts and crumpled wads of wrapping paper.

"Ella! Oh, Ella, it's you!" I said, leaping up from my chair. "Merry Christmas!"

She came in just far enough to prop a painting against the wall, and then she waved to Daniel. "Merry Christmas," she said, turning to go. "Watch out; it's still wet. I just finished it."

"Wait!" I said. "Come in!"

"I can't. I left the engine running."

"Well, go turn it off," I said, laughing, "and come open your presents."

She looked and saw wrapped gifts arrayed on one end of the couch: a heap of love with her name on it. What she did not say was almost audible: *What if I hadn't come?*

She went out and turned off the engine, then came back in, and perching formally on the edge of the couch, she said to Daniel, "I didn't bring your present. I hadn't planned on coming in. I'll give it to you later at Dad's."

It was not that I'd secretly believed I would see Ella on Christmas. It was that I just could not *not* have gifts ready for her. Had she not come, I would have put them away with the Christmas decorations. But apparently she woke up on Christmas morning and found she could not *not* give me a present either and set about creating a mixed-media collage on a plywood panel.

Sitting on the couch with her brother, she opened her gifts and expressed thanks for them. It was the first time she had been under my roof since storming out on July 1. For one holy hour, I was not Ella's archenemy. It was if she had called a Christmas truce, like soldiers in World War I emerging from opposing trenches to smoke cigarettes and sing "Silent Night/*Stille Nacht*" together in no-man's land:

> All is calm. All is bright.
> Heavenly hosts sing hallelujah.
> With the dawn of redeeming grace …

After she had gone, it occurred to me that my Christmas gifts for Ella were like God's love for me: freely offered and just waiting for me to show up and claim it as mine.

On Ash Wednesday, seven months to the day since Ella had stormed out, I told my Centering Prayer group I was giving up anxiety for Lent. The priest sitting next to me in the circle nodded and said, "Good! It's your biggest sin, Melinda."

Whoa! My head snapped back.

"It doesn't mean you're quote-unquote *bad*." She laughed, patting my arm. "Sin is whatever separates us from God. For some, it's an addiction. For you, it's anxiety."

In the New Testament, the Greek word *hamartia* is translated as "sin," but it is an archery term that means "to miss the target." Being anxious about Ella was the way I missed the mark by the widest margin: scaring myself with dire what-ifs. Worst-case scenario was my default setting. No wonder I latched onto that Philippians quote: "Worry about nothing, pray about everything."

But I not only gave up anxiety for Lent, I also devised a makeover regimen. Since Ella had been gone, I had gotten heavier in every way, weighed down in body, heart, and spirit. To keep myself on track and hold myself accountable, I wrote out a Rule of Life on an index card, a framework to shape, schedule, and order my daily way of life. The rubric of Saint Benedict's *Rule,* written 1,500 years ago for the monks at the monastery of Monte Cassino, was "Nothing harsh, nothing burdensome." The rubric for my rule was, "For God's sake, lighten up, Melinda!"

Devising my Lenten agenda, I followed the Book of Common Prayer's suggested practices for the observance of a holy Lent "by self-examination and repentance; by prayer, fasting, and self-denial; and by reading and meditating on God's holy Word." These practices for the forty days of Lent are intended as a way of imitating Jesus's time of trial for forty days in the desert.

I ramped up to four or five hours a day of meditation, prayer, and study in my prayer chair. The hours flew by. The stacks of books beside my chair grew ever taller and wobblier, and my Centering Prayer sits sometimes went so deep that when the timer went off I had to remember what the sound I was hearing meant. I started keeping a journal again. I had stopped when Ella was disappearing into depression, and it was all I could do just to keep my chin above water. "Save me, o God, for the waters have come up to my neck."

I gave up wine and carbs, weighed and measured everything I ate, drank gallons of water, and worked out at the gym six days a week. Doing cardio on the treadmill, I read manuscripts from the fiction course I was teaching that winter in UCLA Extension's Writers Program.

It took four months, not forty days, but I lost twenty-five pounds of fat and sadness. Psychologist B. F. Skinner gets at a compelling reason behind the practice of self-denial: "The denial of the self is the beginning of any change."

At the Easter Vigil that marked the end of Lent, I allowed myself the festive exception of a glass of champagne—or was it two?—as we proclaimed, "Alleluia! The Lord is risen! The Lord is risen indeed!"

There was at that time a priest at my church with whom I shared a penchant for the mystical traditions of Christianity as well as the Buddhist psychology of attentiveness. When it was Deborah's turn to preach, she would stand in the pulpit and sing her sermon *a capella* in a voice so beautiful it made me weep: a hymn from the breastplate of St. Patrick or one by metaphysical poet George Herbert. Deborah saw how disproportionate and out of whack my life was becoming. Enraptured and consumed with God, I had disengaged from my community as well as from my friends. I was living almost exclusively on a vertical axis without the stabilizing crossbar.

One day deep into Lent, Deborah led me aside and, taking my hands in hers, said, "I want you to know I'm keeping an eye on you. It can get pretty hairy way out there where you're going."

I was developing a "nose" for God the way oenophiles educate theirs for wine. But it would be more accurate to say I perceived God's scent in the once-removed manner of a nondrinking wine-lover "tasting" a wine through its bouquet alone. It was an *as if* aroma. It was reassuring to learn that the ancient church fathers spoke of the initial perception of God's presence as "perfume" and attributed it to the spiritual sense of smell. Centering Prayer guru Thomas Keating describes the spiritual senses as an analogy of the material ones: not a sensible reality, but a spiritual experience. The spiritual sense of smell, he says, manifests as an "inner attraction" for prayer, solitude, and silence. During my intense Lenten "lighten up!" regimen, my sense of this inner attraction was at its keenest:

We experience the inner attraction of God *as if* his presence was a delicious odor arising from within and attracting us to him ... Since God is present within us, he may reach up and pull us down anytime, or let a wisp of the delicious perfume of his presence escape from his secret place within us ... We cannot control this perfume; we can only receive it or place ourselves in its path. It communicates itself on its own terms, when and as God wills.

But the odd thing was, I had never been a scent-oriented person. Fragrance was my mother's domain, an intrinsic element of her being. Her perfume, potpourri, lotions, potions, and high-end cosmetics blended into a smell that was hers alone. At my sixth birthday party a little girl whispered to me, "Your mommy even *smells* pretty!" After Mother's burial in Athens, Texas, when the funeral limo returned us to her house in Dallas, I went straight to where I knew I would find her: her walk-in closet. I gathered a big swath of her elegant empty clothes on their sacheted satin hangers into a hug, and burying my face in cashmere, linen, and silk, inhaled my mother's lingering presence.

God's scent was far less explicit. Like a mariner who detects the fragrance of land from far at sea, I was hard put to say just what the sweetness was that I had caught wind of. But God somehow insinuated his presence in me through it, and it became his way of leading me. Maddeningly fleeting and elusive, it came and went, but every time I detected it I knew I was on the right path—on the trail of something I felt very much drawn to follow. It stimulated in me the behavioral response a pheromone is meant to: powerful attraction. I was finding out that seeking God develops the capacity to detect God.

Once I had detected his aroma, I found allusions to the mystical sense of smell cropping up all over the place. All at once these lines from a French carol leapt out at me:

What is this fragrance softly stealing?
Shepherds! It sets my heart a-stir!

Never was sweetness so appealing!
Never were flowers of spring so fair!

Edna St. Vincent Millay's reference to a spiritual fragrance in her poem "Renascence" spoke directly to my own experience:

I know not how such things can be;
I only know there came to me
A fragrance such as never clings
To aught save happy living things; ...
... and with the smell—
I know not how such things can be!—
I breathed my soul back into me.

St. Augustine, distracted by passion—"Lord, make me chaste, but not quite yet!"— acknowledges his tardy response to God's appeals:

You breathed your fragrance upon me,
and I drew in my breath
and now I pant for you:
I tasted you and now I hunger and thirst for you;
You touched me, and I have burned for your peace.

My Lenten sojourn was the most spiritually saturated, God-besotted period of my life. Nothing before or since has been so spiritually formative or transformative for me. Jesus became Jesus during his forty days in the wilderness. My spiritual identity accrued and grew by leaps and bounds during those forty days of Lent. My spirit was open to the transcendent as never before. It opened wide, letting in more and more of God the way the pupil of the eye opens wide in darkness to let in more light. That consecrated time of total submersion in the sacred was when I figured it out: The more open I was to God, the more space I created for God to transform me.

In March, I surfaced from my Lenten regimen long enough to attend a prom-planning meeting at Ella's school. I did not know if she even planned to go to the prom. I knew nothing about my daughter. I went to the meeting in the hope that I might catch a glimpse of her in a classroom, corridor, or the Seniors Only hangout room. By then, she had been living with her father and estranged from me for nine months. I had not seen her since Christmas morning when she'd stopped by to drop off the painting, but then, stunned to find gifts awaiting her, had come in and joined Daniel and me for a little while.

At the mother-daughter tea at the Biltmore and the mother-daughter luncheon at school, it killed me to see mothers and daughters laughing, posing for pictures with their arms around each other's waists, hugging hello and good-bye, and calling "Love you!" to each other. I fled to the ladies' room, locked myself in a stall, and overhearing mothers and daughters laughing and chatting at the sink, rocked back and forth, self-soothing, autistic with missing her.

When I showed up at her school for the prom meeting, the hallways were plastered with posters for the citywide high school art show that her school hosted annually. The opening reception was the next day. I had already decided to go in the hope that Ella might have a piece in the show when I saw a poster for the exhibit showcasing the competition's featured artist: Ella. Had I skipped that meeting, I would have missed my daughter's first show.

When I arrived the next day for the opening, I went upstairs to the mezzanine, and through the crowds of people, saw several of Ella's friends gathered around the punch bowl. I waved hello. Seeing me, they automatically glanced around to find her, and they were all looking in the same direction: toward a room at the far end of the mezzanine. I made my way through the crowd ranged along the exhibit and went into the room. It was dimly lit with spotlights trained on the artworks. I spotted Ella talking to a teacher. She saw me and, caught by surprise, for an instant her face became animated with an uncensored expression of joy, and her arm shot up to wave hello. She tried to rescind her unguarded expression by turning her back to me, but her photography teacher asked to meet me, and in introducing us, Ella said, "This is my *mom*," with a lilt in her voice that gladdened my heart.

This room, it turned out, was the Disney Pocket Gallery, and all eight of the pieces in it—"New Work"—were Ella's. From scrounged construction site debris—scrap-pile plywood and jagged chunks of drywall—she had created lyrical bas-reliefs of stenciled calligraphic landscapes and seascapes of midnight blues, turquoises, and rusty, earthy oxides. They were so unlike any of her previous work I would not have known they were hers if her signature weren't on them: a cloth name tag from her childhood glued to the lower right-hand corner.

Instead of boasting "That's my daughter!" I eavesdropped on artists and art teachers who leaned in close, intrigued and puzzled: Encaustic? Beeswax? Resin? Gesso? They simply confirmed what I had known since Ella was a toddler with a fat crayon in her hand: a born artist.

I caught her eye to say good-bye, and we traded little waves, but when I raised my hand to my mouth to blow her a kiss, she turned away.

Two days later, meditating in the chapel with my Centering Prayer group, I began to feel very agitated. My heart began to race. My legs began a palsied jiggling. My hands shook. Tears streamed down my face, and my torso jerked with silent sobs. I had no idea what was happening. I was overcome by a dizzying sense of impending revelation, of *déjà vu.*

In my mind's eye, I saw the gallery; then, overlaying it like a double exposure, I saw Ella sitting in the *same room,* the Disney Pocket Gallery, with the dean and all of her teachers and me. The space where her art was currently being showcased had served as a conference room for the academic summit meeting held in September of Ella's junior year. The purpose of the meeting had been to discuss how the school could help Ella meet her academic requirements "under the present circumstances," meaning hospitalized and undergoing ECT.

Just enough chairs had been brought in to seat the nine of us in a tight circle as if around an imaginary conference table. The dean of students, two other administrators, and all Ella's teachers were there. I sat next to Ella. There was a kind of defiant bravado about her chosen outfit: a sleeveless, bright green Mexican shift that was a far cry from the drab school uniform.

The sorrow and sympathy for this brave, brilliant, gifted girl was palpable in the room. Glances veered uneasily off the IV needle taped to the back of her hand. Ella held up the hand with the needle left in place for the next ECT treatment, and waggling it back and forth, cracked a joke about "Edison's medicine." It did just what she intended: it put everyone more at ease.

Ella then spoke eloquently and with great self-assurance about her determination to graduate on time with her class, summoning herself to instill confidence in her teachers and the administration that she could cope with honors and AP classes along with her regular classes while hospitalized and receiving ECT treatments. By granting her leeway on deadlines but not cutting back on her workload, the school, for its part, pulled off the impressive feat of accommodating her situation without condescending to her.

On the drive back to NPI, depleted by her bravura performance, Ella slumped back into mute, unresponsive silence.

Then, as my sense of *déjà vu* dissipated and I became aware of my immediate surroundings again—of the chapel and of the others in the prayer circle—it came to me that in the same space in which Ella's illness had been on display now it was her creativity on exhibit. There was this balance, this exquisite equipoise, this perfect symmetry between the purposes the exact same space had served: before and after; weight and counterweight; darkness and light; nadir and apogee. It had a harmony requiring both sides to achieve the result.

That my epiphany had come during silent prayer made perfect sense. My receptors for grace had been honed by all the turbulence, grief, and sorrow of the last five years. It was grace that let me recognize the perfect symmetry of the two events that had taken place in that one space, that let me *see* the other side of the equation:

> Those who sow with tears
> Will reap with shouts of joy.
> Those who go out weeping, carrying the seed,
> Will come again with joy, shouldering their sheaves.

———

Pink's Hot Dogs is a Hollywood landmark founded in 1939. It's famous for its chili dogs; long, slow-moving lines; and celebrity sightings. I'd heard of it but had never been there until meeting Ella there after school one day in early May. It was our first planned get-together in almost a year, and it came at *her* invitation. Driving there, I was so nervous and excited I had to keep telling myself, *Calm down. It's Ella, for Pete's sake!* But that's why I was so nervous and excited: I was going to be seeing *Ella*.

We hugged hello without a moment's hesitation and chatted away easy as pie in the line, which was indeed long and slow, concurring with a laugh that the only hot dogs we'd ever had were the Dodger dogs at our annual family outing to a game at Dodger Stadium. When we got to the window, we exchanged a look and ordered hamburgers. We agreed to share an order of fries. I got iced tea, and Ella, lemonade. *That's right*, I thought. *That's what she always gets.* She reached into her purse for her wallet.

"No, no," I said, touching her arm. "My treat!"

We sat out back on the patio. I asked her who was going where for college. She asked about Quita and Pop and P.K. and Auntie Carole and Uncle Art. I wanted to ask how Alan was doing. She knew I knew, but since I wasn't supposed to, I didn't ask. We pooled our news about Daniel, and then she said that Alan was taking them to Spain and England right after graduation.

"Dad's letting me stay on in London for a month afterward," she said. "I'm meeting up with Jane, and we're renting an apartment, I mean a *flat*, in Chelsea."

I felt sucker punched. It was the first I'd heard of it. My insides clenched. I swallowed hard. The Rodney King voice in my head kicked in, pleading, *Can't we all just get along here?*

"What fun!" I said. "I'm going to England this summer too."

"You *are*? When?" Ha! Now the shoe was on the other foot, and I saw her mouth get the prim look that meant her feelings were hurt.

"July and part of August," I said.

"Where are you going?"

I put down my burger. "First, to Betsy's place in West Sussex, then to Oxford for a summer course, and then to Norwich."

"What's the Oxford course?"

"It's called The Medieval Church in England: Monasteries, Churches, and Cathedrals."

"How perfect!" she laughed. "Why Norwich?"

"Well, for one thing, the university where Daniel's going to spend his semester abroad this fall is there. But mainly because it's where this amazing fourteenth-century mystic lived—St. Julian of Norwich. I'll get to visit her actual *cell*."

"Cool."

When I'd ordered my burger, the guy at the window had said, "Whadaya want on it, the works?"

"Nothing," I'd said. "Just plain."

But that hour with Ella on the patio at Pink's was such a deluxe event I came away feeling as if that's just what I'd had: the works!

Pink's did not mark the end of our rift—our "disrupted attachment," in clinical parlance—but it did mark the beginning of the end.

———

The speaker at Ella's high school graduation was author Joan Didion. I don't remember one single thing she said. I was there not as a writer but as a mother. All I cared about, all I saw, was Ella in her white dress on the stage. She had done what she had set out to do: graduate *on* time *with* her class *and* on the dean's list.

She looked out from the stage at the four people to whom she had given her allotment of tickets for the privileged seating section, the four central figures of her life sitting there all in a row, side by side: her difficult, demanding father; her adored older brother; her anxious, overprotective mother; her overdevoted doctor.

After the graduation ceremony, there was a tea. I longed for Ella to have a picture of the moment during the father-daughter dance when she leaned back against Alan's arm, threw back her head, and laughed at something he had said; but I found myself unable to raise my camera and point it at them. I let them be. This was her last dance with her dad. He looked the same as ever—suntanned, intense, striking—and apparently was still well enough to travel. But there would be no father-of-the-bride dance for them.

6

THE INCITING INCIDENT

To fall in love with God is the greatest of all romances;
To seek God, the greatest adventure;
To find God, the greatest human achievement.

—St. Augustine

Two weeks after Ella's graduation, I was on duty at the welcome table on the patio during coffee hour after the ten-fifteen service. A guy from the choir stopped to say hi, and as we chatted, he kept slapping a brochure he was holding in one hand against the palm of his other hand. I didn't think anything of it. It's hard to walk out of church without some leaflet, bulletin, or pamphlet.

Then I noticed the brochure was from Yale Divinity School.

"Russell!" I said. "Where did you get that?"

"From them," he said, nodding toward two congenial-looking, middle-aged men standing by the table with the coffee urn and the Krispy Kreme doughnuts. The one in the seersucker suit had on a necktie; the one in the linen suit wore a priest's collar.

"Those guys are *from* Yale Divinity School?" I said.

"Well, yeah," he said. "They gave a talk at Adult Ed this morning."

Without a millisecond's hesitation, I abandoned my post at the welcome table and made a beeline for the two visitors. I introduced myself. They introduced themselves. Steve, the priest, was the director of something or other; Bill was a dean, but I didn't catch what of.

I told them I was *devastated* to have missed their talk. What had they said and did they happen to have any more of those brochures? They pointed to a little stack by the coffee urn.

"Which degree," the dean asked, "might you be interested in?"

"No, no, it's not for me; it's for my son," I said, and I proceeded to explain how I had long thought that Daniel, presently in college and an atheist or at most an agnostic, would relish a graduate program in theology. It had to do with how Daniel's intellectual approach and imaginative interactions with his *Star Wars* action figures had always struck me as not just cosmic or mythic but downright biblical.

Then, waving my hands in front of my face, simultaneously amazing and alarming myself, I said, "No, wait! The hell with my son! *I* want to go to Yale Divinity School!"

All three of us laughed in surprise.

But I knew that what I had blurted was the absolute truth. This notion I had foisted off onto my son was nothing less than my own secretly incubated desire, a desire so secret it must have been known to God alone. I had never stopped to wonder why it was that any time I read or heard a reference to Yale Divinity School, I would sense my attention quicken the way a dog pricks its ears and suspends its panting in order to listen harder to something of interest. The magnitude of my disappointment at having missed the YDS envoys' talk left me with the feeling I hadn't just missed an opportunity, I'd missed the whole damn boat.

"So!" I said. "What are my options?"

The dean rattled off the various degrees offered, concluding with the possibility of applying as a nondegree student.

"Come visit us this fall," he said. "Come and see."

I got goose bumps. The dean had offhandedly used the exact same words to extend a personal invitation to me that Jesus utters to his first disciples, Simon and his brother, James. They ask Jesus, "Where do you abide?" And Jesus replies, "Come and see."

I came home from church with brochure in hand and visions of theological sages dancing in my head and tried to wrap my mind around the notion of going to Yale Divinity School. In screenplay lingo, my suddenly noticing the brochure in Russell's hand—and my amplified reaction to it—was the inciting incident: the thing that had to happen for there to be a story to tell. The fact I'd planned to play hooky that Sunday until suddenly remembering my assignment at the welcome table made my coffee-hour encounter with the last-minute visitors from YDS seem all the more divinely engineered.

I had known Ella's departure for college in the fall would be a watershed event for me: the point at which I would officially become an empty nester and need to get on with the next phase of my life. Technically, *un*officially, I had been an empty nester for a year, but I never thought of it that way, since Ella's absence from home was due to estrangement, not college. Now I felt as if I had just been handed the itinerary for the ensuing stage of my journey. The YDS brochure was like a Pony Express rider's fresh mount for the next leg of the ride: *giddyup!*

Before encountering the YDS envoys on the patio, I'd had other plans in mind for after Ella left for college. I'd decided it was high time to get going on my Kansas City novel. I'd been thinking about traveling to the Holy Land or joining a Celtic pilgrimage to the tiny isle of Iona in the Inner Hebrides. I'd even been toying with the idea of signing up for Match.com or eHarmony.

Now those plans were shoved to the back burner, and all of a sudden, there I was, wanting to dash off to Yale Divinity School to study theology without having ever attended so much as the Bible study class at my own church. Something irresistible grabbed hold of me and said: You must do this. This is what you must do. I felt as if I had run smack dab into my *himmah*, a Sufi concept concerning spiritual aspiration as it relates to your intended purpose. The coordinates of my position not only in life—divorced, unattached, empty nester in my midfifties—but also in my *spiritual* life put me at a juncture that made this the perfect time to go to Yale Divinity School.

At various times in my life I had dabbled in God like a Sunday painter with pastels, but even after my spiritual awakening by means of Centering Prayer, I had not proceeded to wade into Aquinas, Anselm, and other such hard-core theologians. After God snagged me, I skewed to the contemplatives and the mystics: Thomas Merton, St. Julian of

Norwich, Thomas Keating, St. John of the Cross, and the like. I valued the institutionalized spirituality of the liturgy in church worship, but my own spiritual life was more self-guided, like a nature trail through wilderness. Now at last I felt ready to *study* God. That is what *theology* means: the study of God; loving God with your mind.

Of course, I could stay put and pursue the study of God locally, but taking theology classes at a Southern California seminary would lack the element of lavishness of uprooting myself from home to study at Yale Divinity School in New Haven, Connecticut. I wanted to go whole hog. Like doing the Hokey Pokey, I wanted to put my whole self in. A divinity school is a seminary but one that offers a university setting for the scholarly assessment of the religious features of human existence. Yale's is one of only eight such schools in the United States. If I really did want to give theology the old college try, then where better than an Ivy League divinity school?

I only hoped my graying gray matter could handle the intellectual rigor of such an institution. I would soon have a chance to find out. The summer course at Oxford would provide me with a golden opportunity for an academic dry run for YDS.

When the dean rattled off the various degrees offered, I'd known immediately which one grabbed me: the MA combining the study of religion and the arts for secular purposes. It thrilled me because it meant that I could apply to go there as a layperson who fully intended to remain just that: an *amateur* Christian.

One thing I knew for sure was that my sudden desire to go trooping off to Yale Divinity School had nothing to do with a vocation, a "calling," to the ministry. If I applied and actually got in, I most definitely would not be going in pursuit of late-call ordination. *Ordination?* Are you kidding? I was still an I-can't-believe-I'm-a-believer.

Nor, for that matter, was I out to deepen my religious beliefs. Religion might provide the framework for my studies, but even God is interested in more than mere religion. I envisioned Yale Divinity School as a Juilliard for the soul as well as the ideal place to honor the "mind" part of the commandment to love the Lord your God "with all your heart, with all your soul, and with all your mind."

But what could I say when people asked me why I was going? Because I didn't want to chicken out on my *himmah*, my spiritual purpose? Because God—or what I summarized in a lump-sum way as God—had radically happened to me? Because now that I was taking God seriously I couldn't just tra-la-la along in my life? Because grace had handed me a personal invitation on a silver platter, saying, "Come and see"?

———

At the tail end of summer, two weeks before leaving for college back East, Ella burst into my house, calling, "Mom! Mom? Where are you?"

"Ella? What is it? I'm here. I'm coming!" I dropped the hose. I'd been watering plants out on the deck. Something must have happened. Something serious. It must be about Alan.

She was leaning over, patting Quita, when I came rushing in. Then she straightened up, and I saw her face.

"Mom!" she said. "I've met someone. I'm in love!"

"Ella! Oh, sweetie!" I clapped my hand to my heart. "Wow! Tell me!"

But she didn't have to. She didn't have to say a word. Taking in my radiant redheaded daughter, I could see it was true: Ella was in love. Head-over-heels, madly in love! I had not seen her look this happy since the fleeting elation of the bounce effect. But this was not an upbeat, transient emotion caused by a brief convulsion in her brain. This was a profound, intuitive, head-to-toe recognition sparking a *yes* in every fiber of her being: "Shield the joyous."

Far more than having witnessed a medication's mood-brightening effectiveness, seeing Ella in love gave me, at long last, soaring confidence in the solidity of her recovery. Love is simply too exhilarating and daunting a venture for someone with severe clinical depression.

Later that day, pondering it in my heart, I remembered the time when Ella was eight and Daniel ten, and I'd had some very good news of my own to share: My agent had called to say that a novel of mine that had been rejected by umpteen publishers had just been accepted by a prestigious small press. When I picked them up at school that afternoon, instead of telling them my news in the car, I led them to a bench under a magnificent old sycamore tree on the campus and knelt down in front of them so I could see both of their faces at once.

"I have good news," I said. "My book is going to be published!"

Daniel shot up off the bench like a rocket, shouting, "It's wonderful! It's wonderful, wonderful, *wonderful!*"

And Ella? Ella burst into tears, doubled over her lap, covered her face, and said, "Oh, Mom! Your sadness has ended."

The day that Ella came to tell me her good news I was both a rocket of happiness shooting into the stratosphere *and* a mother doubled over with joyful relief.

Oh, Ella, your sadness has ended. It's wonderful, wonderful, *wonderful!*

7

COME AND SEE

Hello, Mom,

So you're going back East to do some interviews, then? Good, I'm glad to see that you're really going ahead with applying to divinity school. I was thinking about it the other day, and I decided that I think that you have quite a good chance of getting in. I'm obviously no stranger to the whole college application process, and in thinking about your credentials, as well as the life experience that you have had that the average undergrad applying hasn't, well, I think that you should maybe be getting your hopes up.

The only concrete tip that I have for you is that you sleep, shower, and wear neat and tidy clothing before you head into the interview, all things I managed not to do for most of the interviews I had. I would get all nervous about the interview, not be able to sleep, and then would get up with no time to shower in the mornings. I probably could have put in a slightly better appearance.

What are the requirements for divinity school? I suppose that an undergrad degree and some really good grades are par, but do they ask for some sort of demonstration of your interest in matters of the church/spirit? Maybe if you healed a leper or turned some water into wine or founded a new religion or something … it couldn't hurt.

Love,
Daniel

———

I had such a "thing" for Yale Divinity School I hadn't even planned to check out Harvard Divinity School. Finally, though, at the urging of friends, I scheduled an interview at Harvard as well, and it turned out to be a damn good thing that I had it as practice for Yale.

The Harvard Divinity admissions interviewer asked me why I thought I wanted to come there, a perfectly reasonable question I should have anticipated and had a sound byte prepared for. But I hadn't and didn't. After listening with a slight but discernible wince to my rambling, overly intense response (I fear I may actually have used the word *numinous*), she suggested that, should I be interviewing elsewhere, I might want to summarize it simply as "personal edification."

I would gladly have adopted "personal edification" as my standard explanation from then on if it weren't for the trivializing "just" that people always appended to it: "Oh, so it's just for your own edification?" "Oh, then it's just for your personal enrichment?" No! Yahweh does not lead us into the wilderness *just* for PE.

At both Harvard and Yale, the intellectual exhilaration of the classes I sat in on whetted my appetite for the courses offered at a divinity school. But Harvard Divinity was predominantly a community of scholars; Yale Divinity was a community of scholars and believers—or as the YDS motto puts it, "Faith and Intellect." My visit to YDS assured me that its mission-statement commitment to foster both the knowledge *and* the love of God meant I could have my cake and eat it too. And unlike my interview at Harvard, the one at Yale went so swimmingly I emerged from it feeling on top of the world.

I also liked it that the original Yale College *was* a divinity school. When Puritan clergymen founded it in 1701, the course of study was largely intended to educate young men for the Christian ministry. And these Laws of Yale College from 1787 make it clear they were dead serious about it:

> I. If any Scholar shall be guilty of blasphemy, cursing, robbery, fornication, forgery or any such atrocious crime, he shall be immediately expelled.

> II. If any Scholar shall deny the Holy Scriptures, or any part thereof, to be of Divine Authority, or shall assert any error or heresy, subverting the foundation of the Christian Religion, and shall continue obstinate therein, after the first and second admonition, he shall be expelled.

> III. If any Scholar shall be guilty of a profane oath or vow, of profaning the Name, Word, or Ordinances of God, of contemptuous refractory carriage towards his Superiors; of fighting, striking, quarrelling, challenging, turbulent words or behavior, drunkenness, lasciviousness, *wearing women's apparel* [italics mine], fraud, injustice, idleness, lying, defamation, or any such like crime, he shall be punished by fine, admonition, rustication, or even expulsion, as the nature and circumstances of the crime may require.

A flipbook would dramatize how nonmainstream the study of theology had become by 1932, when with the completion of the Sterling Divinity Quadrangle, Yale's Divinity School had shifted from the epicenter of the campus to a location so far on the fringe of Yale's real estate fiefdom that today's campus map indicates YDS with an arrow pointing off the page. But far-flung though it is, the Sterling Divinity Quadrangle is a gem. Modeled on Thomas Jefferson's classically inspired University of Virginia, its colonnaded pavilions of handmade brick surround a virtual town green of lawn crowned by Marquand Chapel, its soaring steeple a New Haven landmark.

What sealed the deal for me was what I experienced at an evening service at Berkeley, the Episcopal seminary officially affiliated with YDS—a divinity school within a divinity school. Whether it was the acoustic intimacy of a chapel in the former living room of an elegant century-old mansion or the antiphonal arrangement of chairs facing *faces*, not an altar, the hymns sung in the service in that homey sacred space had a richness and depth that made me brim with longing to be part of this community, a yearning so intense it was like homesickness for a place that already felt like home.

I drove from Visitors' Day at YDS in Connecticut to Parents' Weekend at Ella's college in New York. I had never been there before. Our rift during her senior year had precluded my having any involvement in her college selection process, though the college counselor at her school had been kind enough to quietly keep me in the loop. Alan had masterminded both Daniel's and Ella's applications and campus visits—especially to Yale, his alma mater—with the sole exception of my having taken Daniel to visit the college he'd gotten into that was *his* first choice.

When Ella left for college, Alan had brought her to LAX from Malibu for her 6:45 a.m. flight to JFK. I'd been waiting at the gate, farewell present in hand, to see her off. The time grew short: Where was she? I waited in the state of intense expectation conveyed by the Inuit word *iktsuarpok*, meaning "to go outside often to see if someone is coming." Had she overslept? Had Alan overslept? Had they had an accident? Had she decided not to *go* to college? Had she eloped to Vegas with the boyfriend I hadn't even yet met, the one she'd fallen in love with just two weeks ago?

The flight was called. No Ella! The plane loaded. Standby passengers got on. Still no Ella! The Jetway door closed. The plane left. My daughter had missed her plane to college.

I went back home in hopes of finding a voice mail of explanation. My home phone was, at the time, my only phone. An hour later, she called from a pay phone. A curbside line of college kids with excess baggage to check was why she'd missed her flight.

Her new flight was leaving before I could get back to the airport. Not getting to see my daughter off for college about killed me. I remembered my "school butter" ritual from preschool through grade school with each of my children at bedtime on the eve of a new school year: mixing up a batch of my top-secret concoction in a gaudy, bejeweled chalice brought forth only for that occasion, dabbing it on their backs and ceremonially rubbing in their requests for the coming year—good grades, courage, kindness, new friends, being well liked … Now my daughter had left for college and I hadn't even gotten to hug her good-bye.

Throughout Parents' Weekend we ignored the scheduled activities and just played it by ear. It felt both totally familiar and utterly exotic to be with Ella for hours on end, in a new place with her, being on *her* turf, having her show me *her* world—her room, her studio space, her favorite places—walking around campus and town together, sitting across the table from her in coffee shops, restaurants, and the campus cafeteria, getting to look at her, talk to her, listen to her. I felt like a nature lover sitting very still in the woods, trying not to scare off a skittish creature by making any sudden moves or noises, hoping it will stay put, or better yet, hoping it will choose to come nearer.

I refrained from asking her everything I wanted to know about Guy, the man she'd fallen in love with, and how her dad was doing. It wasn't worth the risk of her finding me intrusive and shutting me out again. But not wanting to miss a single moment of being near her, I kept her company even at her campus gardening job on Saturday morning; seeing her kneeling with a trowel, I remembered the garden we had made from scratch in Malibu the summer she was twelve, our last mother-daughter project. And I thought too of the small clay pot of dirt her best friend had brought her on her dismal, abysmal sixteenth birthday to remind her of the outside world.

On the flight back to Los Angeles, I was leafing through the Yale Divinity School magazine and came on a boxed quote by a current student: "I believe that we have placed ourselves in the refining fire, in the very breath of the living God by coming here."

I put down the magazine and closed my eyes. *That*, I thought, *is exactly where I want to be.*

8

A LOVED PERSON

[A]nd yet I know we are in this place together.
— Sharon Olds

"Mrs. Melinda? Escuse me for bothering you," a woman's voice said. "I don't know who else to call. I found him on the floor. I am Blanca, and I work for your ex-husband in the house in Malibu. I am calling to you because I know from your children you are a nice lady."

I thought she was telling me Alan was dead.

But then she said she had called 911, and they had to break open the bedroom door to get to him, and now they were taking him by ambulance to Santa Monica Hospital. It is twenty-five miles from the Malibu house to Santa Monica. I pictured the paramedics smashing open that red oak door with the bronze knob.

I called Daniel and Ella at their colleges on opposite sides of the country and made reservations to fly them home as fast as possible. It was February 3, two days after Daniel's twenty-first birthday. He later told me he'd wondered why his dad hadn't called.

When I got to the ER, I checked in at the desk to let them know I was there for updates on Alan's condition. They told me I could go in and be with him. I said I was his ex-wife and thought it best if I stayed in the waiting room, but that I wanted to be kept updated and for them to know Alan had someone there on his behalf. I filled in forms, giving

75

my phone number as a contact and my relationship to the patient as "caring ex-wife."

The way the gurney was positioned in the treatment room, all I could see of Alan from the check-in desk were his bare feet and ankles. But they were so indubitably *his* feet and ankles that something crumpled in me. Later, they covered him with a blanket, and then there was nothing at all to see of him.

It was painfully hard not to go in and be with him, but I felt I had to respect his animosity toward me and keep my distance. Maybe I should have gone in simply to stand beside the gurney. Maybe he would have been too out of it to know I was there or even to know me. But it would have felt like a violation of his wishes at a time when he was unable to enforce them.

A doctor with a clipboard appeared in the open doorway between the waiting room and the ER itself. "You're here for the man in there?" he said, scowling.

There was no one else in the waiting room. "Yes," I said.

"And you're his *ex*-wife?" The way he said it implied I had no business being there if that was the case.

"Yes," I said. "But I care about him."

He waved the clipboard toward the room where Alan lay. "Does this man know he has a brain tumor? The esophageal cancer has metastasized to his brain."

That was when and where and how I found out what kind of cancer Alan had—and where it had spread. It's just as well I hadn't known sooner: only 5 percent of people with esophageal cancer survive more than five years, and given Alan's risk factors—acid reflux disease undiagnosed for decades and forty years of smoking Lucky Strikes—his prognosis could not have been good.

It took nine hours for him to be admitted and taken from the ER to a room. While he was in the ER, I tried to arrange to have him transferred to UCLA Medical Center, where his doctors were. But Alan's oncologist was on vacation until the following Monday, and his internist gave me the brush-off, saying he had not seen him since 1998. Finally, they told me they were taking him up in a service elevator and he would be in Room 625, Bed 2. I went up to the sixth floor and stood by the nurses' station near his room as they got him settled in.

"You can go in, ma'am," a doctor doing paperwork said.

I thanked him but told him I would not be going in—that the patient and I were divorced and my presence would be unwelcome.

His head jerked in surprise. "Then why have you stayed around all this time?"

"Our children are on their way, but until they get here I just want to be sure that his attending physician knows that that man in there is a loved person."

The doctor tilted his head and looked at me intently, waiting for me to say more.

"I think it might make a difference if whoever is attending him knows that he's not just some guy with terminal cancer and no visitors, but a loved person whose children are getting here as fast as they can."

"I see. Thank you. I am his attending," he said, extending his hand and introducing himself.

Daniel and Ella were on their way. But for now there was only me. And such was Alan's power over me, even then, that I did not dare risk entering his room. It occurred to me to breathe a prayer and cross the threshold to go stand at Alan's bedside, not as myself but as Christ's stand-in. I was, by then, a lay Eucharist minister at my church, and Santa Monica Hospital was one of the places I visited on Sundays with travel-size containers of Jesus's sanctified body and blood to serve to our hospitalized parishioners. But I did not enter Alan's room in that guise for one very simple reason: Jesus *never* went barging in where he was not wanted.

I don't know whether honoring Alan's ill-will toward me was the right or the wrong thing to do. All I knew was, had I entered the room and had he been aware of my presence, he would have turned his head away from the sight of me. A proud man, he would not have wanted me to see him so vulnerable. Now, more than ever, letting him be seemed the least I could do.

Two days later, Alan was discharged from the hospital for palliative care. Though I was the one who made the arrangements for hospice and home care, I wished with all my heart that I could have stayed in the guest room and taken care of him myself. But thanks to Blanca, Daniel and Ella had eleven days with him under the blue tile roof of the house that was his pride and joy.

The last time I ever saw him was in December at LAX when Daniel returned from his semester in Norwich, England. He was going to his dad's straight from the airport. I'd come just to say hello and welcome him back, but Alan was late, so Daniel and I were sitting on a bench chatting away when he came striding into baggage claim. His close-trimmed beard was more grizzled and his dark-blond hair had a grayer cast, but he looked just the same in his Levis, white Oxford cloth shirt, and the belt with the silver Navajo buckle; the agitated intensity of his manner was just the same too. Out of sorts at having missed Daniel's arrival, he greeted him hurriedly and rushed him off. He did not say hello back to me.

On Wednesday, February 16, 2000, I got home from the gym at about 1:00 p.m. to find three tearful voice mails from Ella. I called knowing what she was going to say: Alan had died. I felt terrible that I hadn't been home when she'd first tried to reach me. Or the second and third times.

When I rang the bell at the gate—I still automatically reached for my gate opener before remembering I didn't have one anymore—it was Daniel who buzzed me in and came out to meet me. He looked solemn and composed. We hugged. He said Ella was napping and suggested we go for a hike. The rain had let up. He went in the house to get a jacket. I waited outside, uncertain if he'd meant for me to follow him.

My shoes got so caked with mud as we climbed that it was hard to lift my feet. I was ready to turn back, but Daniel wanted to keep going. Just as we reached a ridge overlooking the ocean and the coastal bluff with Alan's house, beams of sun broke through the clouds, looking so holy it was almost cheesy.

"Daniel! Look!" I said, pointing. "Radiant beams."

"Yeah. I know."

The phrase "radiant beams" was a family joke stemming from Alan's attempt to teach them the second verse of "Silent Night" for a Christmas program by pantomiming the line "Radiant beams from thy holy face."

Then, in case radiant beams hadn't gotten the message across, a double rainbow appeared, arching over the cloud with the beams. It was almost overkill, like a *Guideposts* cover.

My hand shot out to grab Daniel's sleeve. "Whoa! Oh my God!"

I knew better than to ask Daniel if he took it as some kind of sign, but I found it impossible not to. Blessed assurance was what I took it to mean: all shall be well.

It was getting dark by the time we got back to the house. A car I didn't recognize was parked next to mine. I left my muddy shoes in the breezeway and went through the kitchen door into the house—my former house, my former kitchen. Ella was right there, in the dark at the breakfast counter, sitting sideways on Guy's lap with her arms around his neck. Her face was bleary from crying. I leaned over to hug her, but it was awkward, and she did not stand up, making it clear that he, not I, was her chosen comforter.

Dark-haired, dark-eyed, soul-patched, a smidgen taller and nine years older than Ella, Guy bore no resemblance to Alan, but when I leaned over the two of them to hug her, what hit me was the deeply familiar smell of Alan himself. I had forgotten the one thing Guy and Alan had in common: they both smoked Lucky Strikes.

The two nights before Blanca had found Alan collapsed, I'd had vivid, deeply disturbing nightmares about him and the Malibu house. All I can remember is that the house was not right, it was not "itself," and yet I knew it was the house. After Blanca found him—"Unconscious?" I asked her. "Not unconscious," she said, "but out of his mind."—those dreams seemed like locater pings from the black box of an airplane downed in deep water. I now wondered if they were distress calls my psyche had picked up, faint, distorted Maydays actually coming from Alan collapsed on his bathroom floor—disoriented, dehydrated, dying—and sending me an SOS.

PART TWO

——

GRACE PERIOD

Now shall I make my soul,
Compelling it to study
In a learned school ...
—W.B. Yeats

9
JOURNEY-PROUD

By faith … he set out, not knowing where he was going.

—Hebrews 11:8

At my last workout at the gym in Santa Monica, my trainer introduced me to a new client, an entertainment lawyer in her midforties.

"This here's Melinda," Jason said, "but don't bother getting to know her. She's going off to be a nun."

"I am not!" I said, swatting Jason's bicep. "I'm just going to Yale Divinity School."

The woman looked stunned, almost stricken. Tears popped into her eyes. "Are you really?" she said. "I've always, *always* wanted to do that."

"What, go to Yale Divinity School?" I said.

"No, just go do something really adventurous and brave and … and *tall* like that."

I nodded my understanding of what she meant. My fear of squandering my life on short-range plans, skimpy hopes, and shrimpy dreams figured prominently into my opting for YDS over convenient local seminaries.

"So you're going to be a priest or a pastor?" she said.

"Nope," I said. "There's no steeple in my future."

"Then, if you don't mind my asking, what made you want to go?"

"My interest in higher education?" I said with a rising intonation and a little laugh.

The woman laughed too, and then she tilted her head to study me. "Seriously, though, what did?"

"God did," I said, shocked by the simple truth of it.

My dog and I were the same age when we set out for YDS on August 13, 2000. Quita was eight; I was fifty-six. Alan had now been gone six months, Daniel was a junior in college, and Ella was nineteen, living with Guy and taking courses locally while on extended compassion leave from her college back East.

My departure day was, appropriately enough, a Sunday, but hoping to get an early start, I skipped church that morning. Even so, it was midday before I finally backed out of my carport and waved good-bye to my friend Cory, who'd stuck around to help me unpack and reload my VW twice to squeeze in everything I thought I couldn't live without for two years.

I had on Minnetonka moccasins, drawstring cotton pants, and a retro shirt with replicas of old-timey travel decals. I had a short new haircut that still surprised me. My heart was light as a feather and my spirit soaring. Quita, riding high in her sheepskin bed atop my yoga mat and a stack of bedding, was a welcome sight in the rearview mirror. A standard poodle but on the small side, she'd once inspired someone to quip that she was a *sub*standard poodle.

My kids' farewell presents made me feel symbolically accompanied by them too. Daniel had sent me a compilation tape he'd made to serve as a thematic sound track for my cross-country trip. Desmond Dekker's "Israelites" was playing as I drove away, and the *bon voyage* rosebud Ella had brought me when she'd come for dinner the night before—we jokingly called it the Last Supper—was sticking out of a seat pocket.

My next-door neighbor had been out front when Ella was leaving and offered to take our picture on the eve of my departure for divinity school. Looking at the two of us, smiling, my arm around her waist and hers draped over my shoulder, you would never have suspected the rift in our recent past or the gingerly footing we were now on: "After great pain, a formal feeling comes."

Despite my tardy departure, I swung by Bellwood Bakery in Brentwood for one last ice-blended latte and a half sandwich on their signature Rodeo roll.

"To go?" she said.

"And how!" I said.

According to MapQuest, the door-to-door distance from my house in Los Angeles to the apartment I had rented in New Haven was 2,893 miles. My itinerary included stopovers at a monastery in Colorado, my folks' house in Kansas City, and a friend's in Chicago. My first night on the road I was staying at a pet-friendly motel in Zion, Utah. Zion, the mountain where God emblematically lives, seemed an apt first-night destination for a divinity school student.

"Journey-proud" is a Midwestern expression for the jittery, insomnia-inducing excitement on the eve of an eventful trip, and I'd had it bad. What made me journey-proud was not the coast-to-coast trip ahead of me but the other journey I was embarking on. Interstates would take me easy as pie from Los Angeles to New Haven, but the spiritual journey requires trailblazing: "Seeker, the path is made by walking." The two-steps-forward, one-back progress of my spiritual path resembled the sort of silt-weighted, goosenecked river that geologists term an "entrenched meander."

My eyes proved bigger than my ears with the religion tapes I'd ordered from the Teaching Company. "God and Mankind" took me across California and Nevada and into Utah. (I particularly appreciated Lecture 1: "Why Nothing Is as Intriguing as the Study of Religion.") I made a pretty good dent in "The Bible and Western Culture" crossing the rest of Utah, all of Colorado, and western Kansas, but by the time I got to "Meister Eckert: From Whom God Hid Nothing," I needed a breather and put on the Neville Brothers. Satirist Ambrose Bierce defined a pilgrim as "a traveler that is taken seriously." Perhaps it's also a traveler who takes herself too seriously. I mean, geesh, what was I trying to do with all those tapes? Cram for divinity school en route?

The large assortment of maps I had on board, from a Rand McNally Atlas to a AAA TripTik, was to reassure my father I wouldn't get lost. He was worried about my making the coast-to-coast drive alone and wasn't mollified when I told him I'd have Quita with me. Daddy launched into a litany of lurking dangers: highway robbers, fake breakdown perpetrators, hitchhikers, rest-stop rapists, etc. Casualty insurance lawyers are natural-born killjoys. My father ruined all kinds of fun for me growing up by reciting case histories of freak accidents involving roller coasters, water skiing, diving boards, convertibles, and trampolines.

Besides, I have come to accept that I am simply someone who gets lost no matter what. There is no GPS in my DNA. In both my writing and my life, I find out where I'm going by going there—*recursively* is a gilded word for it—and invariably get sidetracked and hopelessly disoriented. As Yogi Berra said, "If you don't know where you're going, you'll wind up somewhere else."

Going astray is a subplot of my life through which I enact major themes. For someone who's so big on shortcuts, it's tragicomic how often I wind up going the long way around. There is something not only symbolic but downright mythic about being lost. Setting forth on a journey, getting directions, and ultimately finding one's own way is the classic struggle faced by hobbits and Greek gods alike. Even Gilgamesh, the prototype of Odysseus and all such epic heroes, had to ask for directions.

My mother was prone to losing things; I am prone to losing my way. Dante's hero in *The Divine Comedy* had the same problem:

> In the middle of the journey of my life
> I came to a place in a woods
> Where I could not find my way.

Jesus refers to himself as *the way*, and it is a running theme in a good many of his parables that only by losing ourselves do we find ourselves. Just as a magician uses misdirection to lose us in order to do a trick, God guides me by getting me lost enough to find myself—or to stop and ask him for directions.

I hope that when I die my soul will fly straight to God like a homing pigeon, but in the meanwhile God doesn't hand out maps. "Go from your country and your kindred to the land that I will show you," God says to Abraham. That is typical of God's MO. He led Moses and the Israelites out of Egypt to the Promised Land with a pillar of cloud by day and of smoke by night. God led me to divinity school with a scent, a holy aroma I first caught wind of during my God-smitten, type-A Lent.

Hounds are named for the thing they seek: foxhound, coonhound, wolfhound; I had become a "Godhound," racing along a scent trail with my nose lowered, zigzagging in jagged little vectors, crisscrossing back and forth when the whiff became faint, fearing I might lose it altogether—the precious trace, the crucial clue that would keep me on the trail I was blazing to God. I did not know just what I hoped to find at the end of this cross-country quest. God's fresh imprint in the New England snow? A love note from God hidden in the pages of the Gutenberg Bible in the Beinecke Rare Book Library at Yale?

During my stopover in Kansas City, I paid a visit to my uncle Bud, a World War II flying ace and lapsed Episcopalian. He was dying of lung cancer. Hunkered down in his red leather wing chair in the den, he made room for me to share the ottoman with his cowboy boots and got right down to business.

"Now tell me, hon'," he said, "why is it you want to go off and do this whole divinity school thing?"

Avoiding any mention of holy aromas and *himmah*, I floundered through an awkward spiel about Biblical underpinnings.

My uncle kept nodding vigorously, saying, "Uh-huh, uh-huh," until I finally petered out with a little one-shoulder shrug.

"Probing the mystery!" Uncle Bud boomed, socking the arm of his chair. "Yessiree Bob! Probing the mystery!"

"Shoot!" I said. "*That's* what I should've said at my Harvard interview."

10

BOOLA, BOOLA, ALLELUIA!

Good God, I'm in divinity school!

—September 3, 2000, e-mail

The FTD flowers from my brother arrived the day after I did. The card said, "Welcome home!" I had a moment of stupefied incomprehension that "home" referred to an unfurnished apartment in a Silly-Putty-pink house with powder-blue shutters in New Haven, Connecticut. I had made a quick trip back East in June to line up a place and found this one after ruling out YDS's dilapidated on-campus housing as too depressing.

Even after I painted the kitchen cupboards turquoise and red and got enough furniture from secondhand stores out on Whalley Avenue and an antique fair on Guilford's town green to feel reasonably settled, I still went around saying, "Well, my *real* home is in LA," and "In my *real* life I'm a writer."

Of course everyone at YDS—all 350 of us—had left behind somewhere they were living and something else they were doing. Anne had been at the Folger Library in DC; Steve S. had been an intellectual property lawyer in Los Angeles; Stephen A., after a stint at Goldman Sachs, had been a village school teacher in West Africa for the past ten years; Tay had been a social worker in Chicago; Karen, a bank exec in New Canaan.

I couldn't help noticing, though, that while I continued to speak in the present tense about my "real" residence and "real" occupation as things I would resume after this theological adventure ended, the ordination-track MDivs—those steeplechasers!—spoke in the past tense about theirs. What, then, did that make my life in New Haven? If it was not my real life, then what was it?

Buddhists are so good at this stuff. One time, at an interfaith mysticism retreat, I happened to be sitting behind a Tibetan monk who was the representative of Buddhism, and a woman sitting next to me, whose morbidly huge crucifix proclaimed her religion in no uncertain terms, leaned forward and rudely woodpeckered the monk's shoulder with her index finger—the bare shoulder that his marigold orange robe did not cover—and said, "Where do you come from?"

"Boston, Massachusetts," he said. He was a chaplain at MIT.

"No, I mean originally," she said.

"Ah. Originally." He gave it thought.

"India? Thailand? Tibet?" she said, as if he needed help.

"I don't know," he said at last.

Waking way too early in this place I theoretically called home, I would be hit with panicky anomie, struggling to remember not where I was but who I was—or was trying to become. I would try to round up the islets of my self, the scattered bits and pieces of me strung out like an atoll, and compact them into one coherent self. I had left behind for now the land mass of myself. The continent of Melinda was on the other side of the country: my children, my friends, my church, my community, my hangouts, my world.

But at least I still had Quita. When people at YDS asked if I lived alone, I was never sure how to answer. If I said yes, it omitted Quita. If I added "except for my dog," it sounded measly, as if she didn't really count. If I'd been asked if I *slept* alone, I could have said, "Never! My dog sleeps right beside me."

Quita was my boon companion, and as much as possible, my whither-thou-goest companion. She observed me closely as I got dressed to size up her chances of getting to go with me. She knew which shoes and clothes meant going for a walk and would spring up in the air in a four-off-the-floor joy jump of pure *yes!* When I was out and about with her and would see the sign that says, "No Dogs Allowed Except Seeing-Eye Dogs," I was tempted to blow right by it, and if stopped, explain that she *was* a seeing-eye dog. That's what dogs are all about: guiding us, gladdening us, helping us to "see."

Sometimes, waking way too early and feeling the flotsam of my self dispersed like soggy bread on a duck pond, I would try to get my bearings by tracing the lineage of how it was that I came to be in bed in an apartment on Whitney Avenue in New Haven, Connecticut.

My encounter on the church patio with the two envoys from YDS may have been the inciting incident, but in retrospect, it seemed I had long been drawn to the study of God. Way back in the '60s, as an undergrad at the University of Chicago, I ate lunch every day at the Chicago Theological Seminary. There was something inchoately alluring to me about grad students called "seminarians" talking casually about God while chowing down in an ecclesial cafeteria called a "refectory." What I wanted deep down was not to be eavesdropping on them but to have a place at the table with them.

Ultimately though, the foremost reason I was living with my dog in New Haven was what had happened in the dead of night eight months after Ella got her driver's license: "In the time of my trouble I will cry out to you, and you will answer me."

———

The acceptance letter I'd received from YDS in March had warned me to expect upheaval when I arrived on campus that fall: "As we begin the new millennium here on Prospect Hill, transformation becomes the operative experience." The admissions dean was referring to the divinity school's $39 million renovation, but I hoped transformation would be my "operative experience" as well.

Deferred maintenance had left the Sterling Divinity Quadrangle in a state of woeful and downright dangerous dilapidation. Both aesthetically and philosophically, the divinity school had become something of an embarrassment, and the university had to decide whether to renovate it or shut it down entirely. The philosophical issue was whether Yale, a great postmodern research university and global institution, should even have an explicitly Christian divinity school.

After it was decided to go forward with renovations, the approach taken was to rebuild from the inside out. Some of the div. school's most elegant and gracious interior spaces were sacrificed in the process, but the quadrangle's original footprint remained intact. Rumor had it that Vincent Scully, Yale's legendary professor emeritus of art history and architecture, had threatened to refuse the university the use of his illustrious name if the architectural integrity of the Sterling Divinity Quadrangle's exterior were compromised one jot.

With the Great Hall now a "Hard Hats Only" area, the big enrollment lecture courses were left scrambling for space. Old Testament resorted to the refectory, and New Testament filled the pews of Marquand Chapel. The main entrance to Yale Divinity School was now through the erstwhile ladies' powder room. Despite the foot traffic and the sheepish glances of male faculty, we women still stood shoulder to shoulder at the mirror and, by God, combed our hair and primped. The hammering, upheaval, dust, and disruption were still going strong two years later when I graduated.

Although those of us arriving that fall bore the brunt of the renovation's inconvenience and the campus's constricted usage, I considered myself lucky to have arrived in time to study theology in a place with its architectural character still reasonably intact. I got to eat lunch at long wooden refectory tables in the tall-windowed, elegant, original refectory instead of the downsized, plastic nonentity of a cafeteria that eventually replaced it. I had the pleasure of one year's use of the original ground-floor commons room with its high ceiling, leather couches, soporific armchairs, and wood logs ablaze in the baronial limestone fireplace instead of the new second-floor space, which was about as inviting as the lobby of a Marriott Hotel. My favorite study spot, the YDS library's Day Missions Room with its wood-paneled alcoves and gracious mezzanine, was left unmolested, but many of the div. school's allegedly "revitalized" interior spaces looked as if deadly blandness was the standard adhered to.

One time, heading up a staircase plastered with "Wet Paint" signs, I found myself behind a blind MDiv student and warned him.

"Thanks," Matt said. "I figured as much from the smell."

"Yeah, the smell's a whole lot stronger than the color," I said. "The color scheme committee should've prayed harder for guidance. I don't know what's with all these blah pastels."

"Glad I'm not missing anything," Matt laughed.

The upheaval and inconvenience of being at YDS amid major renovations served as a constant reminder of the "improvements" my own interior needed. The upshot of the div. school's renovation was to improve the utilization of its facilities; the upshot of mine was to improve the deployment of my intellectual and spiritual faculties. I too needed to be fitted for "adaptive reuse" after having my interior taken down to the bare studs by the events of the past five years. The YDS renovation was a noisy, messy process. Mine bore out the monastic wisdom that God's way of working on us is a banging from without and a boring from within.

During orientation, Acting Dean Harry Adams told us, "It is not outlandish to say you have been called by the spirit of God to be here." But he warned us about two temptations we would face: first, the temptation to show off by expounding knowledge before it had been assimilated by reflection—i.e., taking something we'd learned in the morning and by afternoon talking as if we'd known it all our lives; and second, the risk of substituting the study of God for our *relationship* with God.

The second temptation was why I made a no-excuses, come-hell-or-high-water commitment to keep up my Centering Prayer practice while at YDS. I was dismayed—no, shocked!—to find no Centering Prayer group was already in place. During orientation, I had scoped out two other first-years as eager as I for a weekly group. Nothing anchors the discipline of a solo daily meditation practice like a weekly check-in and sit with a group.

Now our fledgling group just needed a quiet place to gather. Taking a peek at the warren of offices and storerooms in the basement of the Berkeley Center mansion, I discovered a ready-made little mini-zendo, complete with incense and cushions, and the three of us agreed to meet at four o'clock on Mondays: a Christian quorum. In Judaism, ten is the minimum number of adult Jews needed to hold a religious service. Jesus trimmed the number for a *minyan* considerably. He said, "Whenever two or three are gathered in my name, I am there."

When it came to my solo practice, I was faithful *ad absurdum.* I counted on it earning me a gold star from God if I simply showed up first thing every morning and sat there for twenty minutes in my Goodwill prayer chair, looking like a model contemplative while stressing over my mental to-do list and thinking about what to have for breakfast. I was like the Pharisees whom Jesus derides for their sanctimonious but vapid observances: "And when you pray, do not be like the hypocrites who love to pray publicly in the synagogues and out on the street corners where everyone can see them. Truly, I say to you, they have received their reward in full."

The next thing Jesus says is the source of Centering Prayer: "But when you pray, go into your inner room, close your door and pray to your Father who is in secret, and your Father, who sees in secret, will reward you."

By "inner room" Jesus didn't mean the drafty, unheated little afterthought of a room I dubbed my "meditation room." He meant the sacred space of my inmost self, the chapel of my soul.

———

My first brush with my downstairs neighbor Ron came a week after I moved in. I went to the basement on Saturday morning to get a load of laundry going—it was way too scary to be down there at night—and discovered that someone had not only used up my new container of detergent but also had had the gall to water down the dribble they left, thinking they'd fool me. I was pretty sure I knew who the culprit was.

Two sets of tenants came with the two-story house where I lived. In the attic were Tom and Mary, strictly roommates, who had been living together for fourteen years in an unheated space that was more of an Anne Frank hideout than an apartment. Tom, a retired janitor with scruffy white whiskers and bed-head hair, was so self-effacing he never presumed to say hi to me first. Mary had been a waitress at a coffee shop in Hamden until she hit fifty and went to work on a factory assembly line to get health insurance.

The two-bedroom, one-bathroom ground-floor apartment was occupied by a chain-smoking, obese battle-ax named Lorna and her disturbingly intense middle-aged son, Ron. Their place was the duplicate of my second-floor apartment except theirs had a sunporch that served as an illicit flophouse for various and sundry family members, including the hulking, sullen teenager I had seen heading to the basement with the overflowing laundry basket.

I made a point of introducing myself and being friendly to everyone in the house so they wouldn't think some snobby Yalie had moved in. Like the bacon you can preview in the little window on the back of the package, I sometimes view myself as being in the position of the representative slice—that is, I try hard to make a good impression on behalf of some larger entity. This time it was on behalf of Yale Divinity School.

But that was not why I didn't complain about the downstairs tenants' garbage and the leaning tower of pizza boxes in my designated trash can, or about their inoperable clunker in my supposed parking spot or about their smelly cooler abandoned in the foyer. It was because the clenched menace in Ron's posture and blotchy face scared me.

Since it was Saturday, I held off knocking until eight thirty. Ron left the house most weekdays at 3:15 a.m. I don't know what he did for a living, but there was a placard in the rear window of his Chevy Cavalier that said, "Emergency Blood Supply," but looked bogus, like a Halloween sheriff's star.

When there was no answer to my timid raps, I winced and rang the bell. After the third widely spaced ring, Ron threw open the door, and there he stood, in nothing but cutoffs. Clearly, I had awakened him, and the bleary rancor on his face said it'd better be for a damn good reason.

"Good morning, Ron," I said, discombobulated at being confronted with a hairy, nearly naked man. "We met briefly the other day. Melinda from upstairs? I'm sorry to bother you like this, but I need to do laundry, and I think maybe someone in your family used up my detergent by mistake." I waggled the Tide container to indicate its emptiness.

Without a word, Ron jammed his hand into his front pocket, pulling his cutoffs to a level that dramatically underscored his lack of underwear, brought out a crumpled wad, and shoved a twenty at me.

I felt as if he'd thrown a punch in money form at my midsection. I recoiled and shook my head.

"That's very generous of you," I said, "but I need detergent."

Without a word, not one mumbled word, he yanked back his twenty, grabbed a dirty T-shirt off the floor, shoved past me, slammed out the door, and drove off with a vengeance.

I was so nervous I didn't know what to do with myself.

Ten minutes later I heard his car and then the back door, and I hurried downstairs. I didn't want him to see into my apartment. We met midway on the narrow, tight spiral of the back stairs.

He handed me a container of Tide two sizes bigger than mine. "Oh gosh, thank you. That's much too much."

"Keep it," he said. "It won't happen again."

Clearly, heads were going to roll; namely, his nephew's, the husky teenager I'd seen heading to the basement with a laundry basket piled yea high. I figured he was the same one I heard at 5:45 a.m. when his mother—Lorna's daughter—tried to rouse him for school, and the two of them engaged in a raw, awful, decibel-escalating exchange of "Get up!" and "Fuck you!" that culminated in the teen's door-slamming exit.

"Just a thought," I said, "but I noticed there are a lot of empties scattered around down there, and maybe it'd be easier to tell when you've run out …"

He glared at me and pivoted to go.

With an impulse prompted by being a new seminarian, I touched his arm as he turned away and said, "Thank you for doing the right thing here, Ron."

His arm jerked and his face just sort of caved in, as if he had never been thanked for anything before in his entire life. The moment suddenly took on stature, elevation, dignity. For a second our "otherness" evaporated. We felt proud of ourselves and of each other for not having let the situation get ugly. I felt guilty for having mentally labeled my downstairs neighbors *riffraff*.

I told my YDS friend Steve about the incident and how it had turned into this golden opportunity for spiritual growth—mine, I mean.

"Melinda!" he said. "Don't try to spiritualize it. Call your landlord!"

11

THE SHINING MEADOW

… why, how,
whence such beauty and *what*
the meaning …
—Mary Oliver

I was constructing a life from scratch. With my class schedule now determined—Looking on Darkness, New Testament Interpretation, Iconography of Christian Art, and Hildegard of Bingen: Monasticism and the Arts in the Twelfth Century—the next thing I needed to figure out was a worship routine. I was, after all, at *divinity* school. I decided that, for starters, I would attend morning prayer daily at seven thirty in the off-campus mansion that housed Berkeley, the Episcopal Divinity School at Yale. What's more, by jogging there and back with Quita, I could accomplish exercise and worship in one fell swoop.

Trusting in the sincerity of Jesus's come-as-you-are invitation, I arrived in sweats with dog in tow and got permission to stash her in the sacristy, a basement room with racks of choir robes, brocade vestments and acolytes' albs, stacks of hymnals, and jugs of Eucharist wine. I experimented with various combinations of streets and byways to find the shortest route for skinning into morning prayer by 7:29½ and the most scenic one for returning home. My discovery of little Autumn Street shaved off nearly a minute.

Then came the September morning when, heading home from Berkeley, I stayed on St. Ronan until, just before its end, I impulsively left the sidewalk to cut across the sloping upper corner of the Eli Whitney meadow. I turned into it quite simply because it was enticing. The lower end of the meadow faced Whitney Avenue, the busy thoroughfare named for New Haven's illustrious inventor of the cotton gin. Since I lived on Whitney Ave., I passed it daily driving to and from campus, and from my car it just looked like a big vacant lot. Unfenced and scruffy, it made a poor showing next to the neighboring Edgerton Park, an elegant English garden with sweeping terraces and alfresco Shakespeare in summer.

Grassy corners often have a path worn across them by kids or those like me who are always in a hurry or who at least need to appear hurried, harried, and busy as can be. (It runs in my family: The commendation on the Hustle Award my brother received the summer he was a batboy for the Kansas City A's reads, "Art never walked where he could run.") But there was no path cutting across this uppermost corner of the meadow, and this time I was cutting across a corner not to save time but to spend it. I like to think it makes God happy when I turn aside to swoon over a dogwood tree in bloom or stop the car to pay homage to a pull-out-all-the-stops sunset or succumb to a sunrise in a meadow.

I cut the corner and landed in a glory-drenched sunbath. The first shafts of light to clear the basalt heights of East Rock Park were, at that moment, hitting only the uphill corner of the meadow's slope. Refracting off dew-beaded weeds and grasses, the slants of amplified sunlight made the upper meadow glow like something supernaturally irradiated, a glowing, angelic light so white it was dizzying. I cut across a corner and wound up witnessing the ho-hum miracle of a brand-new day. Swamped with radiance, I stopped in my tracks, put Quita's leash under my shoe, and facing the rising sun, leaned my whole being into it like a plant on an air shaft windowsill. Atomized by sunlight, I raised my hands in surrender: Beam me up, Lord Christ.

Standing there, I remembered sitting on the front porch of my sister's Kansas farm early one summer morning, drinking coffee in our nightgowns and glasses—it being too hot for robes and too early for contact lenses—when the shafts of light striking the roly-poly hay bales out in the meadow reminded me of that song from *Oklahoma*, "Oh, What a Beautiful Morning!" I started singing it—"There's a bright golden haze on the meadow ..."—and Carole joined in at "The corn is as high as an elephant's eye ..." Then not only were we belting it out but we were swinging around the porch posts, pinching our nightgowns out wide, and then twirling and waltzing out into the bright golden haze on her prairie meadow.

So far in my life two meadows have endeared themselves to me: the prairie meadow on my sister's Kansas farm and the Eli Whitney meadow in New Haven. But of the two, only one worked itself deep into the fissures and fault lines of my soul, sealing them with its chrism of light.

The Eli Whitney meadow was luminous in such an off-the-chart way as to merit a word that, in my opinion, should be used very sparingly, especially by seminarians: *numinous*. I am allowing myself to use it because it is the only word for the nature of that light at that moment. It was radiant with holiness, imbued—no, *charged*—with a sense of the presence of divinity. The light sanctified the meadow as surely as any prescribed religious ritual for making a space sacred by sprinkling it with holy water and anointing it with thumb-drawn crosses of consecrated oil. Anointed by the sun, the meadow gleamed with the sparkling holy water of dew. The radiance suffused the meadow like visual incense, and like incense, it was a sanctifying element.

No chapel, church, or European cathedral has ever made me feel as spiritually saturated as did the light in that meadow. "Take off your sandals," God said to Moses, "for the place on which you are standing is holy ground." The effulgence ricocheting around that meadow made me feel as if I were standing on the outskirts of eternity itself.

The idea bruited about by the scientific community that light is not a physical principle but a transcendent one suddenly made perfect sense to me: that, ultimately, light is consciousness, that to say "God is light" is not a metaphor. Light *is* God. Jesus said, "I am the light and the way." And that morning at sunrise in the shining meadow, I said, "Well, of *course* that's what you are."

After attending morning prayer in St. Luke's Chapel at Berkeley, I now worshipped again in the upper corner of Eli Whitney's meadow. I was in good company: Jesus worshipped in synagogues from Galilee to Jerusalem, but his preference seems to have been for impromptu secular spaces—on the road or on a mountain, in a garden, on a boat, in an upper room. Churches and synagogues can become a substitute for God, while secular spaces like a family dinner table, a hospital room, or a shining meadow can become evanescently saturated—*numinous*—with the true presence of God.

From that very first day I knew that in this shining meadow I had found a place of renewal. I have a small repertoire of them, ways of getting myself back on track when I am feeling derailed for one reason or another, things that provide some lift of the spirit, some steeling of the will, some cleansing of the heart. Sometimes the Holy Spirit intercedes, stepping in with the easy grace of an athlete pulling a teammate to his feet, but usually I have to pick myself up.

Now I had found a new restorative, a place where, when the variables of time and weather aligned, the benediction of sunrise on a frost-stiff meadow could usher in sheer holiness, a brush with ultimate reality. I could be swept off my feet by the ordinary becoming, if only for seconds, extraordinary—enhanced, fortified, transcendent, raised to a higher power—the way that, with a slight shift, the neck feathers of a humdrum pigeon can catch the light and shimmer with an unexpected iridescence. When the opaque becomes transparent, potential exponential, and the mundane sacred, we see things for a moment not as they are but as they *really* are.

Hitting the jackpot of a dazzling new day dawning in the meadow, I felt my soul unfurl, my heart uncrimp, my mind cease and desist its usual riffs. However lonely, tired, weary, anxious, bitchy, downcast, or beleaguered I might have been feeling, or whatever snit or twit I might have been stewing over, as I approached the place on St. Ronan where the row of evergreens ended, the meadow came into view, conferring a renewed sense of possibility on the day. It's not as if suddenly everything was just hunky-dory, but to be immersed in that alleluia of light, slathered with that resplendent psalm *did* create a clean heart within me, *did* restore—if only for a few minutes—a right spirit within me. An intense, spontaneous thankfulness arose in me, springing up with the insistence of a cowlick that refuses to be tamed by a mother's spit.

Its beauty was salvific. And what it had the power to save me from was myself. Because I was alone—alone in the meadow, alone in New Haven, alone in my life—I was highly susceptible to beauty, hyperaware of what a consolation it is. There is a line in the Eucharist liturgy about coming to God's table "not only for solace but also for strength." Okay, fine, fair enough, but I was sorely in need of a good dose of solace.

Far from home and loved ones, I was exhausted from squeaking by on five or six hours of sleep a night, dogged by my same old nameless sadness, and mightily stressed by looming deadlines for multiple papers for which I had not yet even zeroed in on a topic. In the wee small hours of the morning, my roiling, anxious mind would concoct outlandish worst-case scenarios concerning my children, the scary basement, and my ability to chew what I had bitten off by coming to YDS. At stoplights I could get so caught up in my running commentaries and judgments I wouldn't see that the light had turned green. In the shower I'd rehearse what I was going to say to someone or script what I wish I had said until the hot water ran out.

But in the Shining Meadow, mercifully beyond myself, I was all there, right where I was and nowhere else, released from the chronic absenteeism of living in my head, lost in my thoughts, lost to the world. I myself—my identity, my me-ness, my particularity—was rendered gloriously incidental, hilariously irrelevant. Undergoing that light lightened my heart and lifted me out of my ruts.

The connection between beauty and self-transcendence first came to me through a Jacques Lipchitz sculpture on the UCLA campus. Twice a day, coming and going from visiting Ella at NPI, I had trudged past it, a monumental bronze positioned high atop a plinth, never noticing it, downcast not only of gaze but of heart and soul. Then one day, who knows why, I happened to look up, and there it was, what had been there all along but lost on me: *Song of the Vowels*, this earthy, ethereal transfiguration of an angelic human into a seeming harp. The magnificence of it registered at last, defibrillating my heart and shocking it back to life.

Thanks to Looking on Darkness, references to light and dark in scripture and the Psalms now leaped out at me. Whenever the third song of Isaiah was the appointed canticle at morning prayer, I would carry it away in my mind like spiritual take-out food, and when I got to the meadow I would think of Ella as I delivered it aloud, still piping hot:

Arise, shine, for your light has come,
and the glory of the Lord has risen upon you.
For behold, darkness covers the land;
Deep gloom enshrouds the peoples.
But over you the Lord will rise,
and his glory will appear upon you.

The razzle-dazzle happening in that uppermost wedge of the meadow sent my mind joyriding through scripture. I thought of the description of the angel at Jesus's empty tomb: "His appearance was like lightning, and his clothing white as snow." And in Matthew's account of the Transfiguration, he said that Jesus's face shone "like the sun," just as Moses's had after his encounter with God on Mt. Sinai.

The Transfiguration is a pivotal moment in the New Testament, one of the five big moments in the narrative of Jesus: baptism; transfiguration; crucifixion; resurrection; ascension. It takes place when Jesus goes up on a mountain (unnamed but now thought to be Mount Tabor) with three of his disciples: Peter, James, and John. While there, Jesus's appearance takes on a temporary dramatic luminosity witnessed by his disciples; then the prophets Elijah and Moses appear and Jesus talks with them. Peter, wanting to prolong the moment in a manner that Buddhists would call "clinging," suggests they erect three shelters atop the mountain for Jesus, Elijah, and Moses. God silences Peter by speaking from a cloud, identifying Jesus for the second time as his son: "This is my beloved son, with whom I am well pleased; listen to him."

Trappist Thomas Keating says that the primary purpose of the Transfiguration is "to empower us to live in the presence of God and to see the radiance of the presence in all events, people, the cosmos, and in ourselves." The Shining Meadow did that for me in spades: a blinding reminder that even when God seems dimmed down, rheostatted, he *is* present, *is* operative. The Shining Meadow was the fulfillment of the ancient Jewish blessing, "May the light of his countenance shine upon thee and bring thee peace."

Every morning, just like clockwork, as I approached the northeast corner of the meadow, a chubby boy of seven or so and his father would come out of a boxy little house and trudge across the street to wait on the corner of St. Ronan and Blake for the school bus. They kept their backs to the meadow and watched for the bus with identically morose expressions, as if they doubted it would ever actually come. They never talked to each other or joked around, and when the bus did arrive, as it always did, the father just stood there as the boy stepped forward to board it—no high fives, no arm punch, no one-armed hug—until, at the last possible instant, he would reach out and swat his son's backpack good-bye.

Perhaps I should have told them to turn around and take a gander at the Shining Meadow. But I kept it to myself. I hoarded it.

12

THEOLOGY ON THE HOOF

So teach us to number our days
that we may apply our hearts to wisdom.

—Psalm 90

On a cold, drizzly Saturday in mid-November, a dozen of us met up in the parking lot at YDS to carpool on a field trip to a Benedictine abbey. The class we were taking was Hildegard of Bingen: Monasticism and the Arts in the Twelfth Century, and the field trip was to Regina Laudis Abbey—located, coincidentally enough, in Bethlehem, Connecticut. The trip was intended to give us a glimpse of the "lived" theology and practice of a Benedictine abbey so that we might better understand Hildegard of Bingen, the extraordinary twelfth-century abbess, mystic, midwife, artist, composer, and herbalist whom the *Catholic Reporter* once labeled a "spiritual fruitcake" but who has now been canonized.

Giving up on some no-shows, we got under way with me riding shotgun in Professor Margot Fassler's clutter-filled old trooper of a Volvo and a twenty-something student in back. A drive that should have taken just over an hour turned into a two-hour fiasco of missed exits, following the *wrong* red car for half an hour, and the professor suddenly noticing the gas gauge below E and making a panicky exit despite the sign saying, "No Services This Exit." After driving on twisty back roads for what seemed like forever, she coasted on fumes into a Shell station back at the interstate.

"The snake in the garden is passivity," Professor Fassler used to say. "You have to *exert* yourself."

The professor practiced what she preached: planning and executing this extracurricular field trip after months of correspondence with the mother superior; dispatching 4:00 a.m. e-mails to her students; and serving as director of Yale's Institute for Sacred Music while still dedicating herself to teaching with a devotion that was maximal, passionate, and holistic. Professor Fassler's recognition of her students' hunger not only for *logos* (reason and knowledge) but also for *Sophia* (wisdom) made her a standout. She honored the place of wisdom and rued how, as a society, we are far more information obsessed than wisdom oriented.

She "got" that many students engaged in theological studies were, as she put it, "in training to become nothing less than wise." In a piece in the YDS periodical *Reflections*, she wrote, "Academic specialists need not be wise; their careers do not depend upon this quality, whereas those who will succeed in the ministry must be wise. 'Wise' does not test on paper; it is measured only through and by human interaction."

A married mother of two, she once described herself as a "minimalist" as a mother, but perhaps her exertions were simply more focused on her scholarly progeny than her biological ones. Here's an excerpt from an e-mail sent to us at 5:14 a.m.:

Hi,

Let's revisit the definition I gave you of mysticism in the first class and think about it ... [T]he whole subject is troubling to me, and I hope to you! When did all we Christians stop being mystics? When did it become strange, weird even? And why? We have to look to the twelfth century for the answers, I think.

Best wishes,
MF

With her warm smile, energetic eyes, and graying auburn hair in a fetching Dutch boy cut, Professor Fassler—"Margot" to one and all—was engaging, authentic, and accessible, tossing off such endearing remarks as, "We scholars tend to confuse Xeroxing with having actually read something."

But a side effect of constantly exerting herself was that the professor was—how to put it?—just a tad disorganized. A familiar sight at the many conferences, colloquia, receptions, panels, and concerts she chaired or conducted was the envelope or scrap of paper she carried to the podium with her talking points hastily scribbled on the back. Confessing to misplacing papers, she urged us to submit the topics for our term papers electronically: "I'm a loser," she said in the rue-tinged, categorical way a hemophiliac might say, "I'm a bleeder."

I'd wanted to take her class because Hildegard of Bingen was the embodiment of what my spiritual interests skewed toward: the mystical and the monastic. I'd first heard Hildegard's hypnotically entrancing *11,000 Virgins: Chants for the Feast of St. Ursula* on a boom box while walking a labyrinth at a church in Los Angeles. It was the perfect sound track for the "sacred journey" of a labyrinth and spurred my interest in her. A mystic has been defined as one who seeks God without the use of intermediaries, but in Hildegard's case it seemed God sought *her* out. In a letter written in 1175, she describes a vision seen since her early childhood:

> I call it "the reflection of the living Light" … and I see, hear, and know all at once, and as if in an instant I learn what I know. And what I write is what I see and hear in the vision … And the words in this vision are not like words uttered by the mouth of man, but like a shimmering flame, or a cloud floating in a clear sky.

Due at two o'clock, we arrived at the abbey at three—the last car, the one with the professor herself at the wheel. We were an hour late to a place where punctuality is held sacred, where the bell that summons is considered the voice of God.

But Benedictines, thank heaven, are famous for their hospitality as well as their punctuality. *St. Benedict's Rule*, the fifth-century how-to manual of the Benedictine order, instructs monks to greet every guest as if it is Christ himself who's just shown up on their doorstep. Buddhist Ram Dass makes a similar suggestion: "Treat everyone you meet like God in drag." And sure enough, when we pulled up in front of the impossibly charming, fire-engine-red wooden guest house, Mother Lucia greeted us latecomers with smiles all around and the patience of, well, a saint. A saint is someone who is able to focus on the one thing for that moment. And that's what I saw in Mother Lucia: her ability to focus on hospitality, not punctuality, as the one needful thing right then.

Founded in 1947, the Abbey of Regina Laudis is a 350-acre, self-sustaining community of forty Benedictine women of various professional backgrounds. Sisters who have taken their final vows are called Mother. Mother Lucia was a Shakespeare scholar (Yale PhD 1979). Mother Heloise was a costume designer. Mother Dolores was the movie star Dolores Hart who co-starred with Elvis Presley in *Loving You* and *King Creole* and was the recipient of Elvis's first screen kiss. Her last movie before joining the convent was *Where the Boys Are*. Fifty-one years later, she was the star of another movie, *God Is a Better Elvis*, a 2011 Oscar-nominated documentary about the movie career (and heartbroken fiancé) she left behind to become a nun.

Mother Lucia led us to the abbey's blacksmith shop, where a half dozen nuns stopped what they were doing to gather in a semicircle, introduce themselves, and welcome us. They had on wimples, Reeboks, and work clothes consisting of long dark denim skirts with a kind of denim apron overskirt. Atop their wimples they wore all manner of goofy, pom-pommed ski hats and ear-flapped hats with chin ties. Maybe it was just the way the wimples framed their faces, but I was struck by how exceptionally vivid they were—so fully realized, defined, and singular, from the Nordic blacksmith nun of Paul Bunyanesque proportions to a tiny nun whose glasses took up most of her face.

We were welcomed—and put right to work. No tour. No chitchat. Mother Lucia and Mother Margaret Georgina were in charge of our work detail. They set us to winterizing the blacksmith shop with plastic wrap, chopping logs, stacking firewood, and spreading mulch. By incorporating us into the tasks at hand, we were given an opportunity to make ourselves useful to the community. We were instant Benedictines, honorary nuns—men and women alike.

The field trip to Regina Laudis was of particular interest to me, because I was thinking of becoming an oblate of a monastic order. An oblate is a layperson who affiliates with a monastic community and in the midst of their everyday, in-the-world life commits to a realistic, daily spiritual discipline—that is, to creating and living by a rule of life. Monasticism on the modified American plan is how I think of it. For my Hildegard term paper, I was planning to interview an ordination-track MDiv from California who was already an oblate of the sort of Episcopal Benedictine community with which I hoped to eventually affiliate myself.

I climbed into the bed of a pickup truck and handed down logs to the firewood brigade of nuns and students stacking it. After a while, I switched to spreading mulch with Mother Lucia. We chatted companionably about abbey life, but she asked me nothing whatsoever about my own life or how, at my age, I had come to be a student at Yale Divinity School. Despite the cold, working outdoors with a pitchfork atop a hillock of mulch was a welcome change of pace from my academic routine, giving me a sense of accomplishment having to do only with the dispersion of a minimountain of mulch, not how many pages of Hildegard's *Sciviias* or Raymond Brown's *New Testament* I had read.

Benedictines are all about balance, and so our visit was nicely orchestrated into components of work, social time, and worship. At a set time the nuns had us stop working—never mind that, because of our tardiness, we had not yet finished our jobs—and go to the blacksmith shop, where they warmed us up with hot cider and homemade cakes served beside the big old wood-burning stove called an all-nighter.

Then we were taken to the chapel, a beautiful, high-raftered, airy building modeled on the New England barn, for Mother Noelle's orientation talk on Gregorian chant before the vespers service, in which the entire community of nuns chanted the appointed psalms antiphonally in Latin. The see-through metal scrollwork of the chapel's rood screen created a partition between the seated choir and the congregation in the nave. The subtle separation—as of heaven and earth—made the chanting of this ancient sacred music all the more ethereal.

After the service, the prioress conducted a Q and A session with a select few nuns. One of them was Elvis's screen flame, Mother Dolores, in her sixties and so beautiful I found it hard not to stare at her. Professor Fassler beamed with maternal pride whenever one of her star students from YDS's Institute for Sacred Music asked a well-informed, detailed question about psalmody or some other insider musical matter. Her specialty was medieval theology and liturgical and musical practices, but her passion was the Psalms. To her, they were not lyrical or spiritual decoration but lifesaving spiritual equipment, the equivalent of a motorcyclist's helmet or a sailor's life vest. She meant it when she said that if she had her way, every YDS student would be required to memorize the Psalms, all 150 of them, in order to graduate.

After the session, we said our thank-yous and good-byes and, exiting through the gift shop, loaded up on abbey products: honey, handwoven hats and scarves, fragrant soaps, Gregorian chant CDs, and hand lotion. It was eight o'clock on a Saturday night when Professor Fassler dropped me off at YDS to retrieve my car. For her, home, husband, children, and dinner lay across the Quinnipiac Bridge and a half hour farther up I-95 in Guilford.

At Regina Laudis I had entered a parallel universe, been uplifted into a wholly other reality. It wasn't just that it was a picture-postcard-holy farm run by a community of strikingly intelligent, spiritually evolved women living under a monastic rule fifteen centuries old. It was that I had glimpsed just what Professor Fassler had wanted us to: a theology lived out in Reeboks and wimples, with oxen and doxologies—theology on the hoof. I found the theological concreteness of that realm seductively alluring.

"Restore a right spirit within me," the psalm says. And indeed Regina Laudis had done just that. It got me realigned. It acted on me like spiritual chiropractic. It also made me realize how flat-out happy I had been there. Divinity school and the abbey struck me as being like the difference between theoretical physics and applied physics. Perhaps when I came back East I had wound up at the wrong place.

At ten o'clock that night, as I buckled down to study, I thought of the parallel universe of Regina Laudis, where the community had now gathered in the chapel to chant Compline, the last of the seven daily canonical hours set aside for prayer. I was studying God; they were *living* God. I envied them.

13

GOTCHA

Let's have a feast and celebrate. For this
son of mine was dead and is
alive again; he was lost and is found.
—Luke 15:23–24

T he Monday after the field trip to the monastery, I was the
Gospel reader at the daily worship service in Marquand
Chapel. The turnout of YDS faculty and students that day was
about typical: far from packed but not too skimpy. I had been snagged
as a last-minute lector a couple of times, but this time not only had the
chapel ministers asked me in advance, but one of them—Carolyn—
had even called me the night before to give me chapter and verse of the
reading. Which is to say that what happened cannot be blamed on my
being caught off guard.

Far from it: When Carolyn told me that the assigned reading was
Luke 15:11–24, I laughed and said, "You're kidding! The prodigal son?
That's my pericope for my New Testament term paper."

"Pericope" (per-ICK-o-pee) is one of those insider, shoptalk words
divinity students bandy about that makes you feel like a complete jerk
to mispronounce, as I once did. The parable of the prodigal son was
the pericope—the narrative unit—that I chose from a slate of seven
candidates Professor Harold Attridge put forth as term paper topics.
He also gave us a two-page handout of instructions on the purpose,

form, methods, and procedures for an exegesis paper and an eleven-page, single-spaced "Basic Bibliography." I cannot overstate what a big deal was made of the paper for Religion 601: Interpretation of the New Testament. It would count for 40 percent of my grade.

By the time I stood at the lectern in Marquand Chapel to read Luke 15:11–24, I had been marinating in it since September. Ten days before, I had turned in the third of four required progress reports, and the final paper was due in less than a month. By November 13, I was plowing through commentaries, concordances, parallel Bibles, and interlinear Greek-English texts, imbuing myself with methods of interpretation from liberationist perspectives to form criticism, and steeping myself in Joseph Fitzmyer's two-volume *The Gospel According to Luke*.

I had by now so thoroughly picked and poked at the subject of the parable of the prodigal son, I had completely lost sight of why I had chosen it in the first place. Namely, that I had responded to it; I had *liked* it. I hadn't stopped to wonder just what it was about it that had resonated with me.

I also want to say, by way of preface, that I was completely accustomed to switching back and forth at the drop of a hat between academic and religious spheres. There was no clearer enactment of this than the way we shifted, without moving an inch, from Professor Attridge's New Testament class to the community worship service in Marquand Chapel. The changeover that took place between eleven twenty, when New Testament ended, and eleven thirty, when community worship began, reminded me of the way the conductors on the New Haven Hartford Railway would reverse the direction the seats faced at the end of the line. They would merely slide the seat backs, making the fronts of the seats now the backs. The seats don't change, but the direction they're facing does.

The parable of the prodigal son is so well known it has achieved the status of a meta-metaphor. A roster of illustrious painters, poets, dramatists, choreographers, philosophers, and composers have tackled it: Rembrandt, Rudyard Kipling, Balanchine, Prokofiev, Nietzsche, Albrecht Durer, and André Gide. Tobias Wolff, in the last line of his novel *Old School*, says of "these old words" that they are "surely the most beautiful words ever written or said." A Google search reported an astounding 62,400 references to the prodigal son, and I recently came across yet another one in a Jane Kenyon poem:

> There's just no accounting for happiness,
> or the way it turns up like a prodigal
> who comes back to the dust at your feet
> having squandered a fortune far away.

The parable of the prodigal son was so familiar to everyone in Marquand Chapel that as soon as they heard the opening verse—"Then Jesus said, 'There was a father who had two sons'"—they knew what was coming. And so, as I read, maybe they only half-listened, letting themselves drift away a bit, lulled by the parable's familiarity.

My reading of the passage was going fine until I came to this sentence: "But while he was still far off, his father saw him and was filled with compassion; he ran and put his arms around him and kissed him." Up till then, I had been reading the words but focusing on myself. My reading of the text was smudged with ego. Did my hair look okay? Should I hook it behind my ears or not? Was I standing up straight and holding in my stomach? Was I reading slowly and with enough, but not too much, expression?

Then came the moment of rupture. I choked up so suddenly and totally it was as if I had aspirated the Holy Ghost. At the abrupt cessation of my voice, all eyes snapped to attention, galvanized to see the Gospel reader in the midst of a major meltdown.

I was a goner. Tears gushed from my eyes. My voice didn't just get wobbly, it congealed. I stopped reading. I had to. I was unable to read. I looked down at the shimmering, jiggly words of the suddenly illegible text. I kept looking down while my chest heaved with suppressed sobs. I glanced up once and saw compassionate faces glued on me, totally riveted on me.

I was undergoing a *coup d'etat*, a complete takeover, an uprising against all my intellectual hoo-ha. In one split second I went from wanting to do a good job with the Gospel reading—and look good while I was at it—to being at the mercy of the ultimate mystery. God blindsided me. In Buddhist terms, I had gone from small mind to big mind. My rigorously intellectualized understanding of the parable of the prodigal son had vaporized. I was overcome not only with emotion, but with a felt truth.

I was reading my own autobiography in this passage. Situations in it spoke to experiences I had lived through with Ella: adolescent rebellion; estrangement; the joy of reunion; the power of forgiveness. It hit me where I lived. Never mind that mine was a teenage daughter, not a son, who had left home, who had needed to be anywhere but with me. I knew what it was to pine for an angrily absent child.

When Ella stormed out of the house after our escalated fight the summer before her senior year, it turned out she had left home for good. The pain of our abruptly severed relationship was like the phantom-limb phenomenon of an amputee. I could not get over her complete *gone-ness*. A Japanese proverb says, "If you love your child, send him on a journey." It's one thing to send a beloved child on a journey; it's another thing entirely when a beloved adolescent, unable to abide her mother, tumultuously packs herself off, needing to be anywhere but under the same roof with *her*. No wonder I felt abandoned. I was.

I also knew what it was to welcome home a child uncertain of her reception. I knew what it was to run with headlong heart to greet a returning child. I knew what it was to haul out all the good stuff stored in the hope chest of the heart—the sterling silver of pure love, the fine linens of forgiveness, the fragile china of joy. I *knew* the damn-the-cost extravagance of the human heart in a moment of utter celebration.

During the time Ella was alienated from me, God tried to offer me the pain reliever of his attendance, but in my relentless sorrow I treated his solace as if it were the consolation prize, the booby prize. Standing at the lectern in Marquand Chapel in tears, I felt a connection, a point of vital contact, between my soul and a consoling presence—the Paraclete, the Holy Spirit, the Comforter—who had waylaid me, and in public no less, for this very purpose.

Like the prodigal son's father, who had to bide his time, I too had to wait it out—and sweat it out. Sometimes going to the ends of the world is what is right; sometimes sitting tight is. Sometimes a seeking love is called for; sometimes a waiting love is necessary. I had to learn the hard way which was right when.

Stone broke from squandering his inheritance in dissolute living, reduced to scrounging hogs' leftovers in a distant land, the prodigal son comes to his senses and heads for home with his tail between his legs. He rehearses his repentance speech all the way there, but when he arrives, his father's a priori forgiveness makes all his scripted apologies irrelevant.

In Luke's parable, it is the father who is the true prodigal. The word *prodigal* has come to mean a reprobate's sadder-but-wiser return home. But the original meaning of prodigality has to do with a manner of spending, not with leaving or coming home. A prodigal is one who spends or gives with reckless extravagance. In this sense, it is the father who is the prodigal, for the lavish profuseness of his welcome and for the quality of boundlessness in his love for his son.

Recognition from afar is always indicative of ultimate knowledge, of true knownness. The father's recognition of his son *while he was still a long way off* and his unstinting welcome are a kind of consecration as well: the conferring of love upon his son without regard to whether or not he is worthy of it. The father's response to his son's return comes from a heart bursting with love.

A father running to meet a son would have been viewed as highly undignified by Luke's Greco-Roman audience, but this father has far transcended such petty considerations. Upon his arrival home, the prodigal son receives an undeserved loving welcome, accoutrements of status, and an exorbitant celebration. God's love for the lost, Luke says through this parable, is like the father's love for his son. And a mother's for an estranged teenage daughter.

Finally, in a jerky, tearful voice, I finished the reading and sat down. Oddly enough, I did not feel mortified or even particularly embarrassed by my complete and total loss of composure. I had no desire to flee to the ladies' room and lock myself in a stall until the coast was clear. The one time I glanced up during my meltdown I saw the YDS community looking at me not only with riveted attentiveness but with tears rolling down their cheeks, Kleenex dabbing at their eyes, and their faces filled with kindness. In the Confiteor, the Catholic confession, the phrase "an occasion of sin" is a liturgically delicious way of saying that a favorable opportunity for sin came along. It is in this same sense that what I saw when I glanced up was that my unruly, raw, full-strength emotion had provided the assembled community with an occasion of compassion.

I later heard that in Principles and Practice of Preaching the professor used my breakdown, which he had witnessed, as a stellar example of how the unpredictable can sometimes happen in the pulpit. "This morning in chapel," Professor David Bartlett told his class, "there was a student who was reading the Gospel when all of a sudden the Holy Spirit got hold of her."

The Holy Spirit did a *gotcha* on me, all right. And thanks to it, correlations came about, spiritual synapses closed, and deep, ineluctable understandings were reached that had nothing whatsoever to do with anything in *The New Interpreter's Bible, The New Jerome Biblical Commentary*, Fitzmyer, Bultmann, or any other scholarly authority. Whether they knew it or not, those who attended chapel that Monday morning had witnessed not just a catharsis of emotion but a ceremonial healing.

14

THANK GOD IT'S MONDAY

Sitting here resting my bones,
And this loneliness won't leave me alone.
Two thousand miles I've roamed,
Just to make this dock my home.

—Otis Redding

One Saturday afternoon when Quita needed exercise and I needed a study break, I drove to the Spring Glen section of Hamden, the town just north of New Haven, to walk in a pretty neighborhood with flamboyant sugar maples, stately copper beeches, and a brook running through it. Snow showers were predicted for that night, but for now it was a glittery bright autumn day.

A dry, hectic wind was scouring the remaining leaves from the trees and tossing small birds around like chump change. Quita and I were barely under way when a squirrelly gust snatched my cap, and I had to chase it back and forth all over someone's lawn before finally managing to grab it and wave an apology to the homeowner scowling out his window. Dust devils twirled around like gritty swizzle sticks, and I had to yank Quita out of the path of a weird New England version of tumbleweed that came rolling down the street at us.

The glitzy intensity of the sunlight made me feel high-pitched and jangly the way Santa Ana winds in Malibu did. The Santa Anas blow in off the desert, crisp the Southern California chaparral, and create conditions that cause arsonists to fondle their Bics. Even nice, easygoing people get edgy and argumentative during a Santa Ana. It threw me for a loop to encounter a California-style sirocco in Connecticut. The out-of-context familiarity of the wind drove home how far from home I was. Squinting against the glare, I batted at the gritty air with a kind of frazzled despair and began to feel forlorn.

Then came the first stab of flat-out homesickness. I made myself go a couple of more blocks—Quita *did* need exercise, and I *did* need a study break—before my wind-driven longing became voracious, cavernous, catchall loneliness. I fled to my car and sped home, checking my rearview mirror as if escaping an assailant.

Even before this, I'd been depressed as hell that day. I was feeling stressed by six different things I'd been procrastinating over, including something as minimal and dumb as needing to hang the miniblinds I'd bought when I first arrived in New Haven in August. Now, with autumn in full swing and the trees no longer serving as de facto curtains, I had to crouch in a corner of my bedroom to get dressed.

Professor Fassler had told us that when she felt depleted, she picked herself up by imagining the Good Shepherd's crook helping her to her feet and nudging her along. The way I was feeling that day, it would have taken something more along the lines of cocktails and dinner with Jesus at a seaside restaurant in Galilee to get me up to speed.

The loneliness of childhood is intensified by not knowing it won't last forever. At YDS, I had the solace of knowing mine was eternal only until Monday. During the week I had the YDS community, but on weekends I was on my own. Weekends, those vast wastelands of *nada*, were the times I was in the high-risk category for lonesomeness. Like Smokey Bear's fire-threat thermometer, I was in the red zone. Oh, how I welcomed Monday and the return to a peopled life of classes, gossip, and worship!

Monday through Friday I connected with my fellow students and had my particular friends and buddies. My best friend was Steve S. He had been a thirty-something intellectual property lawyer until God intruded on his career path with an insistence he could not ignore. We had gotten acquainted in Los Angeles when I invited him and his partner, Andrew, for dinner a month before leaving for New Haven. I don't know which was harder for Steve: coming out to his Mormon parents as gay or as Episcopalian. Over dinner and a generous amount of wine, we hit it off famously, discussing many important theological questions, such as whether I should get a twin or a queen-size bed for my apartment in New Haven. We unanimously agreed that by the perverse logic of romance a twin bed would guarantee I'd meet a man during orientation, whereas an ample one would cement my celibacy throughout seminary. (The queen-size I got was not meant to seal a monastic fate but to accommodate Quita.)

Monday through Friday I felt I belonged at YDS—the fittingness of it was clear to me. I was part of a community shoptalking about ordination, God, patristics, clinical pastoral education, professors, stressors, and sermons over grilled cheese sandwiches, lousy French fries, and tuna salad in the cafeteria-style refectory. Like a Buddhist *sangha*, the divinity school was both a community of spiritual aspirants and my place of refuge. And the Berkeley Center with its Episcopalian community was my inner-circle *sangha*. The Friday diaspora left me feeling abandoned.

"Have a good weekend!" my buddies would say as they scattered after lunch.

Hey, where's the fire? I wanted to call after them. *Stick around awhile.*

So where did all my weekday buddies go? What did they do with themselves all weekend? Well, Anne hit I-95 right after her last class to be with her grad-school husband four hours away at Cornell; Liz, a drop-dead-gorgeous, erstwhile lawyer from Austin, Texas, was in a hush-hush romance with a YDS professor; "Dollink" was homesick for New York; Noelle and Kevin were young and in love; Steve and Andrew had each other; and ditto for Mark and Pete. Commuters bravely pursuing late-call ordination—Audrey, Roy, and Karen spring to mind—vanished right after class back into the thick of lives with spouses, houses, kids, and jobs. In sum, there were the commuters, the couples, the casual acquaintances, and those whose whereabouts I did not care one whit about.

Weekends were when I asked myself what the hell I thought I

was doing here. Not that there was any question of crying uncle and throwing in the towel, of bailing on YDS. I knew I would not quit. But sometimes, on weekends, I did not know how I was going to last, how I could withstand the loneliness. On weekends I could always find ways to be around people—studying at Sterling Library, or better yet, the law school library, where the stress level was so taut it twanged; going to the British Museum at Yale or the Yale Art Gallery; going to church Sunday morning—but being *around* people isn't the same as being *with* them. Studying at the library and going to museums was akin to the parallel play of toddlers adjacent to, but not interactive with, each other.

My fear of foisting myself off on classmates who might not wish to socialize with someone their mother's age made me reticent to initiate weekend plans. During orientation, a young woman had squinched up her face at me and said, "Ewww, it must be so weird to be here at your age!" In the previous year's entering class, 51 percent had been in their twenties; 24 percent in their thirties; 19 percent in their forties; and 6 percent in their fifties. And my class, I'd been told, was even younger.

Money was also an inhibiting factor. A movie was such a budget buster for some that we had to go to the North Haven multiplex's dollar-off matinee, and afterward, because they couldn't afford to eat out, I'd invite them back to my place and fix dinner. Their gratitude and admiration for a homemade meal served on matching dishes made me feel like a cross between Martha Stewart and a stay-at-home mom. I didn't like it one bit.

It was at divinity school that I discovered—or finally admitted—how much I love being with people. This new yearning for human companionship threw me for a loop. Until Yale, I had been a solitude snob. I had secretly considered myself superior to socially needy beings with low tolerance for aloneness. As a shy, stammering, physically timid, and easily overlooked child, I had made a virtue of necessity and prided myself on my ability to accommodate long stretches of solitude and silence. The lack of partnership in my marriage had further solidified my capacity for aloneness.

When I first arrived at YDS, I did not set out to forge some warm, outgoing self-deployment style. I did not decide to be friendly. I just *was*.

Far more than the official New Year in January, there is such a clean-slate aspect to the start of a new school year that, whether you're six or fifty-six, the sense of a brand-new beginning inherently encourages retooling the self and fine-tuning one's persona. Besides, what did I have to lose? Nothing! What did I have to gain? Buddies! Chums! Pals! Maybe even friends!

At YDS I discovered not only how much I loved being around people but how much I loved hearing and talking *about* them. At divinity school I discovered the joy of gossip—or as columnist Liz Smith calls it, "news in a red dress." In addition to the usual academic and romantic gossip, a juicy tidbit might include who had been rejected where as a postulant; the prejudices of various archbishops; how someone's "process" was getting derailed; who was having doubts about their calling; who was having doubts about their *faith*. A recent book makes the case that gossip is actually beneficial to a community because it implicitly upholds the standards and norms that are violated by those who become grist for the gossip mill. Be that as it may, as DC doyenne Alice Roosevelt Longworth famously quipped, "If you can't say anything good about someone, sit right here by me."

Because of my age and nebulous purpose at YDS, my demographics were "off." There were a few others in my age bracket, but I didn't want to ghettoize myself by hobnobbing with AARP seminarians like the clique of chirpy local Lutheran ladies. I also stayed miles away from the granny auditing Old Testament Interpretation, who kept interrupting the professor's lecture to ask inane questions that made everyone look down at their shoes.

My loneliness was highly treatable. A Friday night Pepe's pizza and video with Steve and Andrew, a good long chat with Deirdre at the deli counter at Romeo and Guiseppe's, Indian food with Liz after yoga, a catty chat with Anne on the sunporch at Berkeley, *tapas* with Hoidra, or an evening at Paula and Joe's in Hamden could plump up my little heart like a squashed pillow briskly poofed back into shape.

I did not take it personally when I heard about get-togethers I had not been invited to. I understood that the age gap created a social gap. Oddly enough though, when I flip through my calendar from YDS,

I see that I did far more than it seemed like at the time: a teetotal dinner party for Steve Smith's Mormon parents visiting from Utah; a married-with-kids couples' Sunday afternoon barbecue; a dinner party or two that I threw; two Easter brunch invitations; the Episco' Disco; a Christmas party; a postchurch brunch in Branford; the gay Scandinavians' smorgasbord, to which I was invited despite being neither Scandinavian nor gay; Steve's partner Andrew's salon to try out his opera-audition repertoire. And once, by some fluke, a kegger thrown by a young Midwestern seminarian with a dog named Grace who slept in the bathtub.

Because I thought of myself as uprooted, like a yanked-out plant with a dangling ganglion of exposed roots, it always astonished me to run into someone I knew when I was off campus. These chance encounters with people from school whom I knew well enough to wave to at a stoplight, say hello to at Shaw's Market, sit next to on a stool at the Yankee Doodle, or have a quick, running-in-place chat with while out jogging gave me a sense of world, of belonging, of having put down new roots, however shallow and tentative they might be. And pigging out on junk food at the undergrad dining hall with my twenty-something pal Stephen G. after our class together on the main campus could not possibly have meant half as much to him as it did to me.

My sense of aloneness took on a whole new dimension the morning I came out the back door and hit a veneer of invisible ice. A flailing grab at the porch railing saved my ass, but that brush with black ice, as I learned it's called, made me so paranoid about falling that from then until the end of April I exited the house in an elderly fashion, hanging onto the railing for dear life as I cautiously skated my shoe on the top step to test the footing. Until then, I had not considered what big trouble I'd be in if I wound up on crutches. How would I manage the steep, tightly wound staircase to my second-floor apartment? How would I take Quita out four times a day? How would I get to class?

That thought led to the realization that with no one keeping tabs on me, no one knew, day to day, whether I was alive or dead. And *that* thought evolved into the fear of a sudden, somewhat ignoble death alone in my apartment. I envisioned it not as an aneurysm or massive stroke but from something stupid on my part, involving the wobbly chair I used for lack of a step stool or being electrocuted by my hair dryer while simultaneously running the water to brush my teeth.

The nice thing about having Quita as a roommate was that she never told me to get to work on my prodigal son term paper instead of taking a nap or to reconsider finishing off the Pinot Grigio as a reward for making flash cards for my New Testament final. The downside of it was that, in an emergency, Quita, even smart as she was, could not dial 911. During bouts of insomnia, lying in the shadowy dark, my mind would go bonkers with doomsday scenarios. As a countermeasure, to make fun of my fear of a long-undetected death, I would make up headlines:

Dead Seminarian Found Semidevoured: Starved Poodle Blamed
Finicky Eater Chows Down on Owner
Umpteen Downstairs Tenants Noticed Nothing Amiss

Observing classmates pairing off, I felt wistful mainly in terms of how it might diminish their availability to pal around with me. I wasn't keeping my eye peeled for an age-appropriate Eli to snag. I was seeking God at Yale, not a boyfriend: "DWF seeking LTR with soul mate." But I did feel pretty ridiculous arriving stag at YDS's Spring Fling. Plus, by the time I got there, the wine had run out, and unlike the wedding feast at Cana, Jesus did not miraculously produce more. To be both solo and stone-cold sober at a dance was more than I could handle: quick like a bunny, I was *outta* there.

The shortest sentence in the Bible is, "Jesus wept." A chapter about my love life at YDS would be just one word longer: *What* love life? I could pad it a bit by saying that, though I did not have a boyfriend at divinity school, I did fall in love several times. In October it was with sugar maples ablaze with autumn; in February it was with a cormorant standing like a folded black umbrella atop a bump of rock poking out of frozen Lake Whitney; in May it was with the blizzard of blossoms on the Branford pear trees; in August it was with the view from poet Emily Dickinson's western-facing bedroom window in Amherst.

But getting back to men. The last seventeen years of my marriage

I'd lived in Malibu. Day in, day out, I had the Pacific Ocean spread out before me like a gigantic blue picnic tablecloth. When I got divorced, I moved inland and went weeks at a time without seeing the ocean—or giving it a thought. Then I'd be driving along Ocean Avenue in Santa Monica or heading down Temescal Canyon in Pacific Palisades, and *whammo*, there it was, its vast blueness all aglitter out there, and I'd think, *Ha! That's right, the* ocean! And that's pretty much the way it was for me about men. I had been celibate for so long—the last three years of my marriage and five years since—I had all but forgotten about sex.

Some of my amnesia stemmed from fear I might fall again for someone like Alan, the sort of wounded man who gets called a son of a bitch. But mainly, in the aftermath of my divorce, romance was not just low priority, it was a nonstarter. I'd had no heart *to* give. Like biblical Martha, I was distracted with worry and upset about many things—most of all, Ella. And it was then that I began to meditate and pray in earnest and that I caught wind of God. Nothing held more allure for me than following God's exotic, intoxicating aroma.

A phone call with Daniel or Ella could always turn my mood on a dime, but I didn't let myself call them nearly as often as I felt like it, nor did they stay in touch with me as closely as I wished. I didn't yet think of e-mail as a breezy way to connect with them and, instead, used it only as a last resort, especially when Daniel would be slow to return my call and I'd worry myself silly thinking about his part-time job as a bike courier.

The main way I tried to combat my weekend blues was by throwing myself into the Yale experience. From the git-go, as soon as I hit New Haven, I had been determined to follow Henry James's dictum: "Be one of those on whom nothing is lost." Calendars of events in the *New Haven Register*, the *Yale Bulletin*, and the *Yale Daily News* were my salvation, offering a raft of academic activities and a plethora of cultural opportunities. Did I want to go to the Yale Anthropology Society's "Cannibal Talk: Dialogical Misunderstandings in the South Seas" or to a reading by Stephen King? How about the biomedical sciences' talk on "Neuroimaging Studies of Pathological Gambling" or Grove Street Cemetery's "famous corpses" tour?

Then there were the guided nature walks in East Rock Park. Those seasonal rambles first thing Saturday morning not only gave me an outing, they equipped me with another variety of theological knowledge: the names of New England's wildflowers, trees, and birds (including the ones amateurs generically termed LBJs, little brown jobs, and LGGs, little gray guys). Like Psalms and verses of scripture known by heart, I gloried in memorizing them and calling them by name when I ran into them: hemlock, wild rhododendron, copper beech, dogwood. And if all that still wasn't enough, just a two-hour train ride from New Haven was the all-you-can-eat buffet of New York City.

Sometimes to get myself over the hump of inertia or to combat aloneness fatigue, I would pretend I was a journalist on assignment. I would take tons of notes and make believe my presence was somehow official. But I didn't have to psych myself up to go to literary events with the likes of Nobel laureate poet Seamus Heaney, playwright Edward Albee, novelists Salman Rushdie and William Styron, and USSR-defector-poet Yevgeny Yevtushenko.

Yevtushenko was a hoot. Wearing maroon polyester pants, a red *guayaba*, a tawdry gold necklace, and a little Greco-Russian tapestry purse hanging on a cord around his neck, he looked like a tacky, wacko pimp. He flung his arms about theatrically, knocked over water bottles, and got very loud and then very soft. For his last poem, "The Land of Yes/The Land of No," an early one written during his first triumphant US visit in the sixties, after the English translation was read, he came down off the stage into the audience and spoke it passionately in Russian to women, me among them. It happened so fast there was no time for me to fear it or wish it. Yevgeny Yevtushenko got right in my face—*What pale blue eyes he has!*—and spoke loudly, eyelash to eyelash, into my eyes.

At a housemaster's tea with William Styron, dozens of undergrads thronged around his wing chair to express their gratitude for *Darkness Visible,* a memoir of his battle with severe depression. Rather than add a mother's thanks for the measure of solace his book had given my daughter, I waited until the youthful crowd surrounding him had thinned and then recalled to him our having met once before at a

Committee for Public Justice event at Hugh Hefner's *Playboy* mansion in Chicago in the midseventies. Afterward, he and some others had come back to Alan's and my place just up the street for drinks. He not only remembered the evening but added a detail or two and was amused that someone at whose house he had once had drinks umpteen years ago in Chicago should turn up in a roomful of kids at Yale as a middle-aged divinity student. I did not tell him—and now that he has died, never shall—that a lasting souvenir of that evening was the ring his glass (scotch, as I recall) left on the arm of our brand-new Italian suede armchair: The Styron Stain, I'd proudly dubbed it.

When it came to sports, I was bound and determined to go to at least one football game at the Yale Bowl. The obvious choice would have been the Harvard/Yale game, but it was at Thanksgiving when I would be in Kansas City with my family, so I went to the season opener. Since I had not yet devised my make-believe reporter guise to help me handle events where it was hard to be alone, the Yale-Dayton game turned into a shining example of what author David Foster Wallace called, "A Supposedly Fun Thing I'll Never Do Again."

First I went to the wrong place—the Coliseum instead of the Yale Bowl—and then I sat in the wrong section. I didn't see the student section until I was leaving, and besides, I would have looked ridiculous in it. I downed a hot dog and a bag of peanuts to try to get in the swing of things. The hype on the game was that if Yale won, they'd be the first college team to have 800 wins. When I left at halftime the score was 21-0.

Then, as if going alone to a college football game weren't bad enough, I went out that night to get a bite to eat. What was I thinking, going solo to Eli's Restaurant at seven o'clock on a Saturday night? Of course there wasn't a table for one available, so I had to sit at the bar. The dreary couple getting drunk just to my left was on their first date after meeting online. They were straining at small talk, but I could tell they'd wind up having sex no matter what. I asked for my check the minute my burger arrived.

But come Monday morning, whenever someone asked, "How was your weekend?" I would never in a million years have responded,

"Miserable! So lonesome I thought I'd die." Maybe it was a holdover of adolescent hang-ups about popularity, but there was something vaguely humiliating to me about my loneliness, a whiff of stigma lurking there, a *sotto voce* hint of something embarrassing.

Yale was a feast, a smorgasbord of events and activities, but sometimes I just could not drag myself out the door. I simply could not rouse myself. There was no rise left in me. "Selfyeast of soul a dull dough sours." Yes, indeed it does.

Sometimes when I was trying to override my inertia I would picture the way my mother used to clap her hands together and say in a sprightly, inspired tone, "I know what! Let's ..." and suggest some activity my sister and I would groan over. Sometimes I couldn't clap my hands and fake-charm myself into doing a damn thing. I wearied of the effort to venture out on my own yet again just to *do* something—the self-help therapy of going out in public—and I would mope around the apartment all weekend, unable to work up the energy to do anything but snack, nap, and procrastinate. Loneliness is a powerful corrosive. Over time it can make Swiss cheese of your will and mincemeat of your spirit.

I wish I had known how to befriend my loneliness with loving-kindness instead of treating it like a subversive enemy or a relative I didn't want to claim kinship with: skirting it, shirking it, stiff-arming it, constantly circumventing or counteracting it. I wish I had known how to enter into my loneliness as if it were a one-room schoolhouse or a wayside chapel, a wayfarer's refuge. I wish I'd had the courage to just let it have its way with me, because, as Sufi poet Hafiz says, loneliness can "ferment and season you as few human or even divine ingredients can."

Loneliness had the muscle to make me feel flimsy, miserable, unworthy, forgotten, and unloved. There were times that, all in all, I felt as if I might just as well have gone and eaten worms. But like the pain of childbirth, the memory of even my most ferocious bouts of loneliness faded with time. What it left behind as souvenirs were faint stretch marks on my soul, ghostly traces of an acute sense of aloneness both endured and survived.

15

A DOLLAR-BILL MADONNA

The two most important days of your
life are the day you were born
and the day you know why.
—Anthony DeMello

It was when a writer friend from Los Angeles came for a visit that the Dollar-Bill Madonna thing first hit me. My friend Betsy had not been in New Haven since she and her late husband had spent their newlywed year in grad school at Yale some forty years before. I happily knocked off all day Saturday and treated her to dinner and the Long Wharf Theater that night, but with a backlog of reading for New Testament and my weekly Looking on Darkness reflection paper due Monday, I had to leave her to her own devices on Sunday.

With a genius for simple pleasures, Betsy slept late, made a leisurely breakfast, and then ran a tub and took a good long bath. It was while languishing in the tub that my friend had an epiphany about the compulsively peripatetic, writing-resistant life she had been leading since her husband's death seven years before. That epiphany led her to leave me a letter on the bedside table that was much more than a thank-you note from a weekend guest. She spoke of her admiration for what I was doing with my life and strongly urged me, "for your sake as well as mine," to stay at Yale a second year and come away with a degree. She told me I was doing something in which she vicariously participated, that what I was doing was important to her because I was symbolically doing it on her behalf as well. She made me feel that I was, in pregnancy parlance, "eating for two now."

I knew just how she felt. I too look to those who remind me of my own sacred duty to continue to grow in stature. After all, isn't that what God or just good old-fashioned self-actualization asks of us? That every year on our birthday when we go stand against the measuring spot, our height will be penciled a little higher up the wall?

I had gone off to YDS not knowing if I was going to stay one year or two. I was conflicted about whether to make it a non-degree-earning sabbatical year or stay two years and get an MA religion degree. Whenever I was homesick or proved incapable of reading more than three pages of Ricoeur's *The Symbolism of Evil* without falling asleep, or was under the gun with a big research paper that hadn't yet come together, I would tell myself *no way* would I sign up for another year of this torture. Every Sunday night as I labored over the paper for Looking on Darkness, due first thing Monday morning—foregoing *60 Minutes*, a second glass of wine, and a decent night's sleep in the bargain—I would get cranky with myself for having thought YDS was such a great idea. To hell with my *himmah*!

In the midst of my ambivalence, I came upon a quote from the Unabomber, Theodore Kaczynski, in which he said that his experience at Harvard was something he had been needing all along without knowing it—namely, hard work requiring self-discipline and strenuous exercise of his abilities. It rattled me that my experience at YDS sounded so much like the Unabomber's at Harvard, but what made all my hard work at YDS *un*like the Unabomber's was, of course, the God angle. What took me to YDS was not just my love of learning but my desire for the *more* of God.

Still, YDS did not seem like part of the journey so much as prep school for the journey. I was at the filling station, not yet on the road. I knew I was furthering myself just by being here, but I did not know what I was furthering myself *for*. It was as if I were at divinity school for an as-yet-undisclosed athletic event. What was I doing here anyway—cross-training?

As I wrangled with the question of whether to stay a second year, there would come these Exhibit A moments that made me feel sky-hooked into an *uber* reality, moments that captured the essence of what felt like an answer. There was my classmate Caleb's chance remark in the refectory between bites of his turkey sandwich that shed pivotal light for me on Platonism. There was a felicitous phrase in a homily that hung in the air above the priest's head like a speech balloon. There was this white guy in the YDS Gospel Choir singing like an honorary brother. There was Harold Bloom suddenly realizing that fifty years ago this very day he had first arrived at Yale as a twenty-one-year-old grad student. There was the sight of Father Chrysogonus Waddell, a portly monk and the world's leading authority on Cistercian chant and liturgy, downing the refectory's lousy French fries with such gusto you would have thought they were the bread of heaven. There was the inadvertent, elegant symmetry of dashing from an Oxford probability theorist's lecture on "The Probability of the Resurrection" on Yale's main campus back to YDS in time for the daily worship service in which the Gospel readings for that day were the accounts of the very witnesses—Mary Magdalene and the travelers on the road to Emmaus—whose testimony had been part of the proof that the probability theorist had cited in applying Bayes theorem to the hypothesis that God did bodily raise Jesus. There was my heartwarming chat in the YDS ladies' room with the goth girl from Looking on Darkness who brandished her face-pierced, black-clad otherness in a way that made everyone a little afraid of her. Such moments left me euphoric—just giddy—with the privilege and the joy of being there: *This is why you must stay. For this very thing.*

Staying for another year felt extravagant, but sometimes extravagance is exactly what is called for. Sometimes it is the very extravagance of a gesture that doesn't just make the point but *is* the point: A celebratory geyser from a shaken bottle of Dom Perignon is a waste of damn good champagne, but it is the waste of it that says it all. I love the story in the Gospels—one of the few found in all four of them—of the "sinful woman" who walks uninvited into a house where Jesus is dining. Without so much as a howdy-do, she pours a whole jar of spikenard, an ancient, costly fragrance, on Jesus while he is sitting at the table and then kneels and wipes his feet with her hair. The disciples, outraged at the waste, calculate how many of the poor could have been fed with the price it would have fetched.

But Jesus says, "Leave her alone. The poor will always be with us." He understood that the woman wanted to send him an all-out, no-expense-spared, damn-the-cost message of adoration, gratitude, and utter devotion, and that a niggardly little dab of nard just would not have done the job.

My friend Betsy's letter not only encouraged me to stay, it gave me a sense of responsibility to stay and graduate with a degree in hand instead of just calling it a sabbatical and heading home empty-handed. I remembered the teary-eyed reaction of the woman at the gym: "I've always, *always* wanted to go do something adventurous and brave and … *tall* like that." Since I considered myself a devout coward, I'd had a hard time grasping that anything I undertook could ever be seen as adventurous. (I hated recess in grade school because it involved balls that might hit me and acrobatic tricks like kick-overs that [a] I couldn't do and [b] would've shown my underpants.)

Above all though, my friend Betsy's letter reminded me of the Dollar-Bill Madonna.

In July, just a month before leaving for YDS, despite having a million loose ends to wrap up, I flew off to Maine to join my brother and his wife for five days in Popham Beach. I almost declined their invitation because of the expense and poor timing of it. Had I not gone, it would have been one of the biggest regrets of my life to have missed out on exploring with Art our family roots in the Popham Colony of 1607 and witnessing what a kick my brother got out of locals' reaction to his eponymous last name.

Before joining them, I spent the night in Boston, and poking around the historic North End, chanced upon an Italian street festival that has taken place the second Sunday of July since 1903. Proceeding from the storefront headquarters of the Madonna delle Grazie Society on Endicott Street—kitty-corner from North Church of Paul Revere fame—three men and a fireplug of a woman shouldered poles running crosswise through a gold platform on which a statue of the Madonna, with baby Jesus face-out in the crook of her arm, was borne aloft.

The mannequin-like Madonna was costumed in a tight-bodiced, gilt-encrusted white satin dress under a blue satin cloak adorned with a gold fabric version of the stock-car decoration called a "flame job." With her brunette ringlets, big boobs, arched eyebrows, hoop earrings, and red nail polish, the Madonna and child looked more like a Mafia prom queen with an out-of-wedlock infant.

Her retinue consisted of a half dozen lackluster musicians and an entourage of stocky matrons whose job was to take the money proffered by curbside spectators and hand over a prayer card as a kind of receipt for their charitable donation. The matron brigade also caught the bills fluttering down from onlookers up in the four-story brick buildings lining Endicott Street, who got a grateful wave of their money instead of a prayer card in return. The money-gathering matrons passed the bills to four preening teens who pinned them onto blue satin streamers attached to the Madonna's cloak and gown.

By the time the parade reached the end of Endicott, the Blessed Virgin's outfit was completely papered with money, mostly one-dollar bills but also a few fervently offered fives and even a couple of miracle-seeking tens. Each and every bill represented an intercessory prayer request. This life-size statue of the mother of the Son of God was plastered with people's hopes, fears, thanks, and pleas for something to happen or not to happen: a pregnancy, a phone call, a job, test results ...

The Madonna delle Grazie, carried among her people to receive their cash-backed prayer requests, was an effigy of hope, a prayer doll, a scapegoat in reverse. In ancient Israel, on Yom Kippur, the Day of Atonement, a goat was symbolically laden with the sins of the people and then literally driven into the wilderness to carry their sins far, far away from the community. The scapegoat bore the sins of Israel the way the Dollar-Bill Madonna wore the prayers of the North End Italian community.

Like the Madonna delle Grazie, I too was an effigy, a bearer. My unwittingly serving as a reminder to my widowed friend of her sacred duty to resume writing now became a sanctifying reason for me to stay a second year at YDS. It didn't matter that I didn't have a clue just what good purpose my being here served, only that I was, in some way, fulfilling my intended purpose—my *himmah.* By staying on, I could, if nothing else, be like that dolled-up Madonna with the dollar-bill prayers pinned to her clothes: a goodwill ambassador of skittish hopes and tall dreams. I would proudly sally forth into any wilderness to bear such sacred cargo.

Shortly before Christmas vacation, in the midst of final exams, I pulled into a parking lot in New Haven and found myself facing a big hand-lettered sign on the attendant's kiosk: "No Grace Period!!! *Don't Ask!!!*"

I read that refusal to grant even a minute's reprieve, and all at once, clear as day, I knew that was exactly what my time at YDS was: a gift of time, a respite from ordinary time and regular life to immerse myself in theology, the study of God, to the nth degree. On the spot, right then and there, I committed to staying a second year to earn an MA religion degree. I granted myself a one-year extension of my grace period.

16

PHARISEE ME

Wake up, my spirit.
—Psalm 108:2

I decamped for Christmas vacation right after my Iconography of Christian Art exam. In a matter of hours, I went from following a salt truck in a blizzard to the exotic shock of Southern California "winter."

Ella met me at LAX. It took me a moment to recognize the redhead in a Jeep. I'd pictured her blonde and in a Volvo. Though officially still on compassion leave from her school back East, she was preparing to transfer to a West Coast university.

I had rented out my house in LA for a pittance in exchange for the tenant, a recently divorced contractor, agreeing to vacate it for two weeks at Christmas and one week in the summer. This was my first time home since I left in August, and I had not factored in that, since this was now *his* home, I would be faced with photos of his kid on my refrigerator, his clothes in my closet, condoms in my bedside table drawer, and my furniture rearranged to make room for macho pieces like his eight-foot leather couch. It was discombobulating.

I hit the ground running to get a tree up and the house decorated before Daniel arrived, but nothing could change the fact that this was going to be a hard Christmas, their first without their father. Ella's boyfriend, Guy, was a welcome addition to our usual family activities,

133

but, of course, the *usual* was not the same without their father, a man who, despite his saturnine temperament, never exhibited one iota of "Bah humbug!" at Christmastime.

I spent New Year's Eve in Ojai with friends, where another dinner guest, upon hearing I was studying at Yale Divinity School, said, "Oh my *Gawd*! Don't tell me you believe in *Gawd*!"

I returned to New Haven with Daniel and Ella's assurances that they would come visit me during their spring breaks in March. The hope of a family get-together while I was at YDS was precisely why I'd gotten a two-bedroom apartment.

I arrived the day before classes started and found out that, five days later, on Saturday, the Reverend Canon Eugene Sutton from the National Cathedral in Washington, DC, was coming to lead an all-day Centering Prayer retreat for the YDS community. It was to be held at St. Thomas Episcopal Church in New Haven. Since I attended church there on Sundays, I was familiar with its elegant, ample hospitality room.

I panicked. A measly turnout would be mortifying—for YDS and for me. After all, I was the one who had started the Centering Prayer group at YDS, and I was now its weekly convener as well as the go-to person for anyone wanting to know about it.

But the main reason I papered YDS with flyers and pleaded with people to come was because I knew the Reverend Canon Gene Sutton personally. We had struck up a friendship at a Franciscan monastery in Malibu when we were both in training with Father Thomas Keating to become emissaries of his method of Centering Prayer. One afternoon when Gene wanted to ditch the isolated mountaintop monastery to check out Malibu at sea level, he approached me because he'd heard I used to live there. We swapped autobiographies with the ease of instant friends, and it was clear as day that this charismatic, drop-dead-handsome African American Episcopal priest was going to be a superstar. Now, just three years later, here he was, a canon at the National Cathedral.

I was enlisted to show our esteemed presenter around Yale on Friday, and then I was to deliver him to the Union League Café on Chapel Street for dinner with the Berkeley Center brass. The Union League Café was the university's go-to spot for wining and dining distinguished guests. I once fell in behind Maya Lin, the designer of the Vietnam Veterans Memorial—an undergrad project at Yale for which she received a B+— as she was being squired to the café by Yale's legendary art historian emeritus Vincent Scully.

I did not tell Gene I was worried sick the turnout at the retreat might be puny, but I tried to drop a few hints by mentioning pressing schedules and various other activities slated for the weekend. I couldn't cite the crushing workload, because the semester was barely under way and had not yet had time to become brutal.

But come Saturday, they showed up. My cohorts came through. Scads of seminarians—and on a Saturday, no less! They overflowed the couches, chairs, piano bench, and window seats and had to sit on the floor. I was beyond relieved; I was downright proud of the turnout on that oh-so-cold January morning. Some YDS faculty even came. I could not believe my eyes when the much-revered Rev. Dr. Marilyn McCord Adams, my History of Christian Thought professor, came—and stayed the entire day.

Gene began the retreat by asking us to introduce ourselves and briefly say why we had come. As we went around the room, it got to be funnier and funnier that the vast majority said they were there because I'd said I'd kill them if they weren't.

By the end of the day, as we debriefed after a final twenty-minute sit, I could tell that three of the attendees had "gotten" the prayer with the same no-question-about-it intensity that I too had experienced my first time. A good number of the others said they were willing to give it the one-month trial that came with Gene's "full satisfaction or your money back" guarantee. (Never mind that the retreat was gratis since the Annand Program had underwritten it.)

After the retreat, for a while there, our little prayer group had a few more chairs in the circle at four o'clock on Mondays. But as the semester progressed, except for one newcomer who continued to show up regularly, the rest fell by the wayside. Dropouts would sometimes sidle up to me and say how much they wanted to be there and how badly they needed just what the prayer offered: resting in God.

"Faith and intellect" is the slogan of YDS. Like "brains and beauty," it's a winning combo, but the pursuit of both the knowledge *and* the love of God ain't easy, and it's a sad irony of seminary that the spiritual life of many seminarians gets put on hold—shot to hell!—while they are pursuing ordination to priesthood. The "and" becomes "or" as the rigor of studying God drives the sense of connection with God into hibernation.

Rule of Thumb #28 in *What They Don't Tell You: A Survivor's Guide to Biblical Studies* states: "Faith is not like dominoes. When one part falls, it doesn't mean that all of it will fall." But for some seminarians it did all come a-tumblin' down like the walls of Jericho. The definition of theological education I heard most often around YDS was medieval theologian St. Anselm's "Faith seeking understanding." But there were some whose studies wound up undermining the very thing that had propelled them to divinity school: their faith. The attempt to integrate it with understanding proved too daunting.

One young MDiv, just a prince of a fellow, confided to me that when he opened his acceptance letter to YDS he'd felt more scared than happy.

"Scared of what?" I asked.

"That God would become academic."

17

STICKS AND STONES

I will arise and go now, and go to Innisfree,
And a small cabin build there, of clay and wattles made …
And live alone in the bee-loud glade.
And I shall have some peace there, for peace comes dropping
slow …

—W. B. Yeats

On February 16, 2001, the first anniversary of Alan's death, I went with Quita to pay a commemorative visit to my former husband's hometown. In honor of the occasion, I wore a cashmere turtleneck sweater he had given me for Christmas a long, long time ago. I thought of the trip as a kind of pilgrimage and was astonished to discover it was only twenty-five miles from New Haven to Southport, Connecticut.

Driving there, I remembered how Alan used to claim I was "afraid of the East." I always spluttered indignantly at the absurdity of it, but I had known what he meant by it—and that he was dead right. As a recovering Midwesterner, I did feel like a semibumpkin around preppy, Ivy League New Englanders. I did feel like an outsider whenever we went to Southport and saw old friends of his, whose country-club wives lived in tennis dresses, had boarding-school nicknames like "Bunny" and "Muffin," and referred to their mothers as "Mummy."

Southport is a picturesque village of two thousand people. I had not been there since the Bicentennial summer of 1976, but it was so unchanged that, without even trying, I located Trinity Episcopal, where Alan had sung in the boys' choir growing up. With its spire encased in an exoskeleton of scaffolding for restoration work, I almost didn't recognize it at first.

Leaving Quita in the car, I entered the sanctuary and slipped into a pew near the back. A lone workman up front nodded to me, slid shut his metal tape measure, and with a little salute left me there alone. The memory of the last time I had been in that sacred space was so sharp I felt short of breath: Alan's father's memorial service in March of 1973.

Trinity Episcopal Church had been packed to the rafters: a solid phalanx of black-clad mourners filling the pews both on the main floor and in the balcony. Alan's mother, entering the sanctuary with the family from a side door, was momentarily overcome to see the massive turnout. Her hand flew to her heart, and I heard her breath catch. It was the size of the turnout, not any one dignitary in particular whom she had glimpsed, that caught her by surprise: ambassadors and former ambassadors; current and past US senators; a former vice president; past and present university presidents and provosts; board chairmen; trustees; art museum people; corporate heads. Late one night, after a requisite number of martinis, Alan's mother, a Connecticut Yankee from way back, batted the air disparagingly and confided to me, "These big men! These big men! They're all so *small!*"

As I sat there now, slammed by the memory of my father-in-law's standing-room-only service, complete with a quorum of the Trinity Boys' Choir rounded up, despite the diaspora of spring break, to sing in fulfillment of his widow's sole request, I thought of Alan's simple, minimal service in the chapel at St. Matthew's a year before. The contrast could not have been starker—or have more accurately reflected the vast difference between father and son: the public servant versus a very private man.

There had been so few people at Alan's service that a chapel that seated at most thirty was not full. Of course, the measure of a life is not taken by the number of people who show up for a funeral; it can be measured by the depth of its impact on a few chosen dear ones rather than by the circumference of a circle of shallow acquaintances. Even so, I'd felt sad for Daniel and Ella's sake that there were so few there to mourn their father's passing. Two members of Alan's family came: his one remaining sister and one representative niece. One member of my family came: my brother, Art, from Tacoma. We sat in the second row. As the ex-wife I wasn't "allowed" to sit in the front row with my children. Nor did decorum permit Guy to sit beside Ella.

Alan's service had offered no consolation, and worse still, no humor. There was no fond laughter at a remembered trait or foible in the priest's eulogy or in Ella's remembrance. How could there have been? The priest had never met Alan, and Ella was eighteen and grief-stricken. Her remembrance was eloquent, honest, insightful, and loving, and she herself was bravely poised. Daniel did his father proud with a thoughtful reading of "The Lake Isle of Innisfree" by Yeats, his dad's favorite poet. But the poem itself was almost *too* perfect in its poignant evocation of a man longing for seclusion and "some peace."

As for me, I was numb with incredulity that Alan, *Alan*, was gone. Because I had not gotten to say good-bye, Alan's death lacked reality and the force of truth and still remains for me what psychologists term "an ambiguous loss." During the service I was also distracted with worry about my brother's diabetes being out of whack from travel and about people who had not yet arrived due to bad weather delaying their flights. I was worried about needing to run to the car for orange juice for Art and about the priest starting without the latecomers—and eventually she did. And then I worried about that.

I don't know whether Alan would have wanted a memorial service. I think he just vaguely assumed I would step in to make sure that, like Daniel's official baptism, it was "done right."

From Trinity Church I found my way to Sasco Hill Road, and at the very end of it, the house where Alan had grown up. Houses on Sasco Hill Road used to be identified only by the owner's name; now the mailboxes had numerical addresses on them.

A Range Rover pulled up to the mailbox at the end of the cul-de-sac just as I arrived. I put down my window and introduced myself to the attractive thirty-something woman behind the wheel.

Then I said, "Today is the anniversary of my husband's death, and I was hoping I might just walk down to the point to pay my respects at the family's memorial stones." I didn't say former husband, because I thought she might find it odd for an ex-wife to care enough to show up.

"Oh, I'm not the owner," she said. "I'm just the nanny. But go right ahead. I'm sure my boss wouldn't mind."

I thanked her, asked her to thank the owner, and said I would leave my dog in the car.

It was a raw, windy, overcast day. The grounds looked ill-kempt, with sticks and limbs from recent storms littering the sweep of land between the house and the bluff overlooking Long Island Sound. Dreary clumps of leftover snow clung to the wan, winter-weary lawn. The clay tennis court midway down the expanse of lawn was gone, and the redwood tree that Alan's mother had planted as a sapling, saying, "I can't wait till it's big enough to drive through!" now towered over the pines. Until then, I had never realized how much the site of Alan's boyhood home resembled the site of our Malibu house: a sloping sweep of lawn to a bluff overlooking an expanse of water.

Standing there, I recalled a photograph of him as a toddler sitting, barefoot, cross-legged, on this very lawn in front of this very house: an adopted baby boy in a plaid sunsuit inspecting at close range a wispy little flower clutched in his fist. Something about the bemused concentration of this fair-haired child puzzling over, pondering, *querying* a flower with such pensive intensity had always been haunting to me. I think it was because the photo captured Alan in an Edenic, all-too-ephemeral state of untrammeled wonder and innocence.

Three boulders brought from the beach below had bronze plaques affixed to them for Alan's father in 1973; his mother in 1974; his sister Charlotte in 1999. The newness of Charlotte's plaque looked garish beside her parents' weathered ones with turquoise patina weeping down the stones. Charlotte died just months before Alan—and without knowing her little brother was dying too.

On May 30, 1999—coincidentally, Alan's fifty-seventh and last birthday—I had gone to say good-bye to Charlotte as she lay wheezing with emphysema in a Phoenix hospital's telemetry unit. My once self-described

"Rubenesque" sister-in-law now weighed an alarming eighty-five pounds. At the end of our visit, as I leaned over to kiss her good-bye, my dangling cross caught her eye: a small silver cross with a slightly asymmetric wobbliness. Charlotte reached up and touched it; then she pulled up from inside her nightie the stamped silver Navajo cross she had always worn but always out of sight inside her A-line executive dresses. She lifted her cross to mine, and we clinked them in a kind of toast to eternity.

"See you later, Charlotte," I whispered.

"Till then," she wheezed.

There was no stone for Alan. I had known when I went to Southport there would be no plaque-bearing rock to commemorate him, yet even so I found it upsetting. Its absence felt glaring, like an exclusion, a shunning. I had to remind myself he wouldn't have wanted to be there "with" them anyway.

In the Jewish tradition, this first anniversary would have been the time for the unveiling of a memorial tablet, the *Yahrzeit*, the Hebrew anniversary of the person's death. There is great wisdom, I think, in the tradition of waiting a year, of going through one complete cycle of the holidays, the loved one's birthday, and all the other hard days before facing the finality of the memorial tablet.

Standing in front of the stones, I tried to think of a prayer or psalm to recite from memory. I started to say the 23rd Psalm, "The Lord is my shepherd, I shall not want," but it felt like such a default cliché, the equivalent of singing "Kumbaya" at a vigil, I stopped out of sheer embarrassment. Why the hell hadn't I thought to bring along my *Book of Common Prayer*? I had arrived empty-handed—no flowers, no prayer book, not even a pebble—and I suddenly felt just terrible about it.

One of the most ancient of Jewish traditions is the placing of a pebble to mark a visit to a grave. There was no stone for Alan on which I could have left a pebble of visitation, but why hadn't I thought to bring along a little stone, a nice flat skipping stone like the kind he used to throw with the kids at the beach in Malibu, just to leave there in the grass to mark my anniversary visit? And why didn't I think to pick up two sticks from the lawn and make a cross in front of his sister's stone in memory of how we had clinked our crosses to our eventual reunion?

Had Alan and I still been married when he died, I would have brought up a rock from the sea cave under our headland and placed it on the bluff beside our ocean-facing "cocktail rock," and I would have gone with our children to spread his ashes somewhere out in the Kofa Mountains in Arizona's Sonoran desert where we used to camp in springtime and where he was more at ease in himself—and with us—than anywhere else in the world.

I was grateful that my children had let me be the one to collect Alan's ashes from the mortuary. It was located way out in the Valley, and on the long drive home, I rested my hand on the container and talked to the memory in my heart of the man I had loved, bidding him farewell and *adieu*, the good-bye which, like *adios*, means "to God." The holiness of that drive with Alan's mortal remains was as apparent to me as when I drive from the Sunday service with my hand steadying the Eucharist box with Jesus Christ in sanctified take-out form destined for a hospitalized or housebound parishioner. I only wished that my children had let me stand on the shore to read the Burial Sentences from *The Book of Common Prayer* while they went into the ocean to scatter his ashes. But they'd felt it necessary to exclude their mother in order to honor their father, who had died without having ever forgiven me for leaving him.

I married the man I loved—and was passionately attracted to. Happiness was not a priority for me. Happiness was not something that Alan—that deeply pensive, adopted toddler pondering a wispy flower as if it held the ultimate answer—had emerged from his childhood knowing much about either. As for what and whom Alan loved, I would say he loved his children; his privacy; his oceanfront house; well-designed, fast cars; and the Southwestern desert. If he loved me, he kept it too much to himself.

As I crossed the open lawn in Southport heading back to my car, I raised my arm high in farewell to the house and in thanks to anyone who might be watching from a window. Then I drove back to New Haven, where, as it turned out, it was I, Alan's ex-wife, not his kids, who had followed in his footsteps to Yale.

18

HOLY SPIRIT MOJO

Is not life given to us to become richer in spirit?
—Vincent van Gogh

I waffled when my YDS friend Deirdre asked me to volunteer at STEP, an after-school tutoring program run through the New Haven Public Library system. I knew I had it easy compared with MDivs with 3-D lives that included real-world jobs, commutes, spouses, partners, at-home kids, hospital chaplaincies, residencies in local churches, and upcoming General Ordination Exams; but even though my full-load academic life was comparatively one-dimensional, I felt hard-pressed and stressed by it.

Still, it felt weird not to have a community-service component to my life. I'd tried to volunteer for the Spiritual Life History project at the Masonic Geriatric Center in Wallingford, but they turned me down. They wanted MDivs who had completed Clinical Pastoral Education. In my opinion, which I kept to myself, any seminarian with a pair of ears, a ballpoint pen, and a willing spirit ought to have qualified.

What prompted me to accept Deirdre's invitation two days after she first asked me was the call I made to a phone number I'd been carrying on a scrap of paper in my wallet for almost a year. I apologized to the person who answered for calling on the nurses' station line and asked if I might speak to Nevaeh.

"I'm calling from Yale to wish her a happy birthday," I said.

I name-dropped Yale because I thought it might help cut the red tape. But in the confusion that ensued as the message got batted around various extensions, "Yale" became "jail." I wasn't surprised at the mix-up. It made far more sense that someone would be calling Nevaeh from jail than from Yale.

Three days after my birthday call from "jail" to fourteen-year-old Nevaeh at an adolescent treatment facility in Long Beach, California, I drove to a derelict strip mall where a liquor store and the Dixwell Branch of the New Haven Public Library were the only places still in business. Old men with bloodshot eyes leaned against the bashed-in fender of an old clunker, passing around a paper-bagged pint. I debated with myself whether or not to greet them on my way into the library. When I did, the way they ducked their heads, touched symbolic hat brims, and mumbled, "ma'am" made me feel embarrassingly white and schoolmarmish.

I pinned on my STEP badge and made the rounds of the tables and computer stations trying to drum up business. By and large, the boys were goofing off on the computers while the girls were using the time to get their homework done. Shantay let me quiz her on her vocab. I complimented Octavia on the cover she was drawing for her book report. I got no other takers on my first pass, so I went around again. This time I offered to swap jokes or play tic-tac-toe. It felt simply wonderful to take a breather from theology and morph from nose-to-the-grindstone grad student to free-range, impromptu tutor.

Volunteering at STEP reminded me of when I was a volunteer at Hollygrove in Los Angeles. Hollygrove was where I met Nevaeh. Founded in 1880 as the Los Angeles Orphans Home Society, Hollygrove is a facility for abused, abandoned, and neglected children ages five to twelve who have been removed from the custody of their families and placed there by court order. Hollygrove was where Marilyn Monroe lived during a stint of family upheaval, and legend has it that the movie studio she could see from her window—Raleigh Studios—was what set young Norma Jean daydreaming about movie stardom.

Hollygrove strives for the children's reunification with their own repaired or reconstituted families, or failing that, for foster home placement. Short of that, they try to pair a child with an adult volunteer, called a "special friend," who commits to a long-term relationship that involves spending one day a week with the child. And then there were the weekly volunteers like me who just provided a little extra TLC through on-site enrichment activities like Book Bugs.

The STEP program combined the same two basic ingredients as Book Bugs—a library and some elementary school kids—but the similarity ended there. At Dixwell, parents or older siblings came to collect the kids from the after-school haven of the library. I saw kids whose faces lit up at their moms' or dads' arrival, or just as wonderful, kids who took a family member's arrival for granted and barely glanced up. In any case, at Dixwell, at the end of the day, every kid went *home*. At Hollygrove, at the end of the day, every kid went to a single-sex, age-grouped on-site residence euphemistically called a "cottage."

But I did not meet Nevaeh through Book Bugs. Participation in it was an earned privilege, and she'd always racked up too many demerits. I met her when Cathy, coordinator of volunteers, asked if I would consider coming to Hollygrove once a week just to hang out with her and give her a one-on-one experience with someone outside the system—neither caseworker, judge, therapist, teacher, nor staff. Nevaeh was three months from turning thirteen, and since Hollygrove's upper age limit is twelve, she would soon have to leave the place she called home and go to a group home for adolescents. The idea was that as a parting gift in her final months I would be *hers* in a free-floating, spontaneous relationship completely focused on her, a relationship in which she got to be the center of attention without having to act up or act out. I said yes to Cathy, because I was flattered to be asked and because it was for only a short while. Little did I know that three months would become three years.

Nevaeh and I hit it off right from the start. We got along splendidly, this aggressive, destructive twelve-year-old and I. Blocky and bulky as a refrigerator, Nevaeh was obese in a packed solid rather than a jiggly loose way. Her skin was the glossy brown of an M&M shell. She had small, even teeth. She lavished far more time on her hair than on her hygiene. Grime was deeply embedded in the fat creases on her neck and wrists. When she would hold out the flat of her grubby palm to offer me an M&M—reds were my favorite, oranges hers—I would accept it almost sacramentally, counting on God to protect me from all the germs on it. "Take, eat," Jesus says to his disciples at the last supper after he himself has knelt down and washed their feet.

Ours was a devotional relationship. Once a week, as her thirteenth birthday drew nigh, I devoted my time and total attention to Nevaeh. A little child, desiring the mother's undivided attention, will take the mother's distracted face in both her hands and turn it toward herself and hold it there. With Nevaeh, that's the way I was all the time: beamed on her, 100 percent hers, 100 percent of the time.

She had never been a candidate for foster-home placement because the hope, though similar to a snowball's in hell, had been for reunification with her fiasco of a family. Her mother, a drug addict and chronic rehab dropout, was a lost cause. It all hinged on the father, but it was her father, egged on by his live-in girlfriend and mother of two of his six children, who had asked the court to place Nevaeh in a facility.

"I didn't leave him no choice," Nevaeh told me. She always defended her father for having thrown in the towel on her, but it was plain as day how painful and humiliating it was for her that, of all his kids, she alone had been banished from home.

I never met him. Every time I was supposed to, he flaked. A perennial no-show, he did not come to the Halloween, Thanksgiving, or Christmas/Kwanza celebrations, which he had sworn he would attend. Shortly before her deadline birthday, Nevaeh and two other girls put an act together for a talent show, and she invited her father and me to come see her swan song performance at Hollygrove.

When I arrived, I caught her eye and waved to let her know I was there, and then I watched as she kept anxiously scanning the audience for the face that mattered most of all, the one that would have really made her day. She kept saying he'd come, that he was just running late, and begged to go last on the program so he wouldn't miss her performance in the lip-synching trio of girls all dolled up in sparkly dresses, blue eye shadow, and glitter in their hair. As usual, he later claimed car trouble, but it was a failure of love, not a car, that kept him from keeping his promises.

Once the security guard buzzed open the gate, I would drive into Hollygrove's fenced compound and stay put with Nevaeh inside of it. Because of her behavior issues, she could not be taken off the premises except by staff. She blamed all the trouble she got into on what she called her "natural-born curiosity." The only time I felt physically afraid of Nevaeh was when it was time to leave. I always had to remind her to please not squeeze the stuffing out of me. The first day, she hugged me good-bye so hard she lifted me off my feet and made my ribs ache.

Nevaeh and I just hung out together on-site, talking and twirling on the swings, sitting on a bench playing I Spy, moseying around the softball field, climbing the jungle gym to sit side by side atop the double-wide slide, chatting and eating M&Ms. Proud to have something to share, she handed out the M&Ms I brought her to anyone who asked. As we approached a group of girls, she would link her arm through mine and put on a superior air.

"This is Melinda," she would say. "She's *mine*."

Nevaeh's proprietary pride reached its zenith when I finally gave in to her plea and brought Quita to Hollygrove. Since she knew that I was exclusively hers, she considered my dog, by extension, hers as well. She took charge of Quita's leash and made herself the boss of whose turn it was to get to pat her.

Letting go of the leash and seeing her besieged by a raft of hyped-up, clamoring kids jockeying and shoving to touch her and grab the leash made me nervous. Poodles can be picky about people, and Quita's demeanor toward strangers was cautious and standoffish—i.e., *French*. I was always careful to keep her out of range of toddlers, who squealed rapturously on sight of her and reached out to grab her curly brown mop, and I always asked adults not to pat her until she had a chance to sniff their hands.

But that afternoon at Hollygrove Quita was self-transcendent. She allowed abandoned, abused, and neglected kids not only to touch her but to fawn over her. She "suffered" them in the same sense in which Jesus says, "Suffer the little children to come unto me; do not stop them." That afternoon, in her blasé equanimity with hordes of amped kids, my Quita was a virtual golden retriever, a veritable Lassie. That day I found out Holy Spirit mojo works on dogs too.

A number of the kids at Hollygrove had gruesome, flagrant scars. Given their histories of physical and sexual abuse and severe neglect, I knew better than to ever inquire how they had gotten them, but the first time Nevaeh wore a sleeveless blouse and I saw the nasty scar on her upper arm, I blurted without thinking, "Oh, sweetie, what happened to your arm?"

She clapped her hand over the scar and looked away. "It was an accident," she said. "Jason's knife—it slipped."

"Who's Jason?" I said.

"My big brother," she said.

Nevaeh's two favorite topics of conversation were candy and babies. She wanted lots of both. She told me she couldn't wait to have babies but that she'd never get a dog because a dog was way too much responsibility. What she loved to do above all else was to sit on my lap and sing duets. I taught her lullabies and old-timey, perky Patti Page and Perry Como songs like "How Much Is That Doggie in the Window?" and "When the moon hits your eye like a big pizza pie, that's *amore*." We conflated two of her favorites into a medley: "You Are My Sunshine" and "I Love You a Bushel and a Peck."

Holding her on my lap—this almost-thirteen-year-old who outweighed me by a good seventy-five pounds—I sang her lullabies and songs about a world of love she had never known, a world that was a far cry from her drug-addicted infancy and violence-riddled childhood, a world of prayers for peaceful sleep all through the night, and a world where, "When you awake, you shall have cake and ride the pretty little horses."

Though we made a ludicrous sight, with me smothered and squished beneath this humongous girl sprawled on my lap, no one, neither kids nor staff, ever laughed or so much as chuckled at the spectacle of us. It was clear as day that, odd though it looked, it was not the least bit funny. It reminded me of when five-nine, sixteen-year-old Ella had curled up in my lap at the Taizé service just the way she had as a toddler.

When I was with Nevaeh I experienced myself as a blissfully, blessedly emptied vessel. It seemed so elegantly symmetrical and fitting to me that since Christ emptied *himself* to become one of *us*, I, in turn, had to be blessedly emptied of *myself*—of ego, of big *M* Me—to do *his* work in the world. When I was with Nevaeh, I felt the way I had trick-or-treating on Halloween for UNICEF: doing good *and* getting candy.

My visits were a revocable privilege, and since impulse control was not Nevaeh's strong suit, sometimes when I showed up she wasn't allowed to see me. In the daily assessment in which merits and demerits were tallied up and discussed, she frequently came up short. So I just assumed it was the privilege-loss thing again the Monday in January when I came for my usual visit and someone on the staff apologized for my wasted trip.

But it turned out Nevaeh was not even *there*. She had been taken from Hollygrove by ambulance in the middle of the night.

On Sunday evening, Nevaeh's father had returned her to Hollygrove after an overnight home-visit. He had finally gotten his act together and followed through on coming. At some point that evening she told someone in her cottage that she had been raped by three boys under an outside staircase at the back of her father's apartment building.

Staff did not believe her. They saw it as one of her attention-getting tactics, a real grabber this time, a lollapalooza, that's for sure, but her demeanor just did not resemble that of a rape victim. Faced with dismissal of her claim, Nevaeh freaked out. She became hysterical, completely, uncontrollably hysterical. Finally, at 1:00 a.m., staff called 911 for an ambulance, and Nevaeh was taken to a children's psychiatric facility.

I think what happened is that when Nevaeh returned to Hollygrove from her home-visit she panicked. Her birthday was now looming large, and the thought of having to leave Hollygrove made her freak out. I also think she was worried that her family might lose track of her and never come to visit her at the group home. I think she could not bear to be uprooted a second time from a place that was home to her—first her father's and now the safe haven of Hollygrove. Rather than be evicted when she turned thirteen, she got herself kicked out a few days shy of it. Rape was the pretext she invented for a hysteria that was real. Or maybe she thought that one way or another she *had* been raped. Or at any rate, screwed and violated most of her life.

I got the name and address of the facility where she had been taken.

It was to hell and gone out in the San Fernando Valley. I was going to go straight there to visit her but was told she was in the intake phase, and since I wasn't family, I would need to wait a day or two.

It all came back to me: *Oh yes, that's right, the intake phase.* I never could have foreseen how my daughter's hospitalization in an adolescent psych ward could have ever stood me in good stead, but now my firsthand familiarity with the procedures, routines, protocol, security issues, and rigmarole of visiting such a place was precisely what gave me the courage to tackle visiting Nevaeh. Instead of being scared off by the daunting, heartbreaking idea of entering a Bedlam for children, I felt well prepared, girded, able-hearted.

The adolescent unit at UCLA's NPI was forthrightly institutional—a locked ward with steel-mesh window coverings—but it was a country club compared to this dive. The whole setup of the place was jail-like, starting with the staff, who spoke through a microphone and buzzed me in from a booth behind bulletproof glass like a late-night gas station attendant. It was obvious from the downtrodden appearance of the facility and the demographic of its patients what this was: a bottom-of-the-barrel institution for poverty-level, predominantly Hispanic and African American kids who had gone off the deep end so profoundly and urgently as to require hospitalization here. This facility was a place where—to borrow Robert Frost's rock-bottom definition of home—"when you have to go there, they have to take you in."

The parents, grandparents, and older siblings who came during visiting hours seemed ill at ease and embarrassed, as if stigmatized to be seen in such a public space with a family member they did not know what to say to or how to act toward or how to even be around in this institutional setting. The atmosphere was befuddled, awkward, and strained. Family visitors sat clumped around communal tables in the cafeteria with these traumatized, severely damaged children—some semicatatonic, or screaming, cowering, whimpering, or scared out of their wits; some were so little their legs dangled from their chairs. A staff member who looked as if he might moonlight as a bouncer patrolled the room, glaring at visitors who spoke loudly, jabbed their fingers, or yelled at their children to sit down or shut up.

I was Nevaeh's only visitor. Her father had *said* he'd come but didn't. Her mother was in rehab again. Her brother Jason had yet to come. We played cards—hearts, spit, and old maid. Two people can't play old maid, but we did. We chitchatted. She sat on my lap and we sang our lullabies and medleys. But she was not the same. There were these gaps, these lacunae in her being, like threadbare places in the weave where you could see daylight you shouldn't have been able to.

Nevaeh never returned to Hollygrove. By the time she got out of the hospital, she had turned thirteen. She went straight from the children's psych hospital in the Valley to the locked side of an adolescent treatment facility in Long Beach: "Go directly to jail. Do not pass Go. Do not collect $200."

I visited her in Long Beach for eight months. Every single time I signed in on the clipboard in the locked entryway and called the nurses' station on the house phone to get buzzed in, there was a sense of skeptical amazement that Nevaeh had a visitor.

"Nevaeh? You say you're here to see *Nevaeh*? What are you, family? What's your relationship to her?"

"No," I would say, "I'm her friend."

During the times I visited Nevaeh, I watched her go steadily downhill. She was often so heavily medicated she was woozy. She had no spark, no spunk, no "natural-born curiosity." Junk food and sleep were all she craved. Like a lifer explaining the ropes to a rookie, she liked to bandy insider lingo about privileges and punishments.

"Code Green. Now that means get your ass out in the hall *stat* or else you be put in confinement."

"Have you ever been put in confinement?" I said.

She rolled her eyes at the stupidity of my question.

Just before leaving for divinity school, I drove down to Long Beach to visit her one last time. She was still on the locked side. Still hadn't made it to the group home. I made a farewell party of it, bringing cupcakes, lemonade, and gift-wrapped surprises as well as everything she had asked for: shampoo, conditioner, a disposable camera, a big bag of M&Ms, and two decks of cards. She sat on my lap and we sang our duets, but her eyes were listless and her heart wasn't in it.

That last day, as I was leaving, she insisted I show her that I still carried in my wallet the scrap of paper on which she had written down her father's phone number and that of the Long Beach facility. She used to conduct spot checks to be sure I still had it. Now she asked me for a pen and added, "Jan. 21—My birthday! Call me!!!"

On January 21, when I called from Yale and the staff misheard it as "jail," Nevaeh finally came to the phone. I sang "Happy Birthday" to her, and though she added, "And many more on Channel 4," her voice was sadly robotic. It did not sound as if she was having a happy birthday.

"I know what!" I said, striking an excessively chipper tone that reminded me of my mother's. "Let's sing our duet long distance."

Nevaeh remembered not only every word but every last one of our idiosyncratic intonations in our medley version of "You Are My Sunshine" and "I Love You a Bushel and a Peck"—the places where we'd speed up or slow down and let our voices swoop and slide from one phrase to another. After we sang, she was eager to hang up so she could go boast about my call. She liked having been called even more than the call itself. In an adolescent treatment facility, a phone call is a treasured status symbol—and a long-distance call all the more so.

One year later, on her fifteenth birthday, I once again called the Long Beach facility from "jail" in New Haven and asked to speak to Nevaeh.

"Who?"

I repeated her name.

"Oh, yeah. Her. She *gone*."

"Gone where?" I asked.

But they would not divulge her whereabouts until a series of increasingly senior staff had queried me about the nature of my relationship to, connection with, or interest in Nevaeh. I explained over and over again about having been assigned to spend "quality time" with her at Hollygrove until she turned thirteen, how it had been about letting her get to be the center of attention for once in her life.

"Huh!" one staff member said. "That girl was a *fool* for attention."

I was finally connected to Nevaeh's former social worker, who, after vetting my explanation, told me that Nevaeh had been transferred to an adolescent facility near Redmond, California.

"Why way out there?" I asked.

"It's near where her father's moved. We thought that if Nevaeh were more accessible, he might visit her and take more of an interest in her. Perhaps eventually even provide a home for her."

"Dream on," I said.

In spite of how forsaken Nevaeh was by her family and how *God*forsaken she sometimes seemed, whenever and wherever I was with her—even in the heartbreaking children's psych hospital—the way we were together felt utterly sacred, like an enactment of the Hindu greeting *namaste*: "The divine light in me bows to the divine light in you."

19

PARADISE LOST

> They paved paradise
> And put up a parking lot.
> —Joni Mitchell

Short wooden stakes with fluorescent orange ribbons were the first warning signs of what was to come. For a while, I ignored them, pooh-poohed them, played dumb about them—those surveyor's stakes with their garish ribbons sticking out of the ground like *banderillras* from a bull's pierced hide. I considered yanking them out but then thought better of it. Ecoterrorist divinity student? Not me. Besides, I told myself, I'd be long gone from New Haven before whatever development or "improvement" those fluorescent ribbons were precursors of had come to pass.

Then came the string line for the straw-lined trench for the concrete footing for a solid wall. Then came the fence posts, and—oh my Lord!—they were twelve feet high. Then came the backhoes, Bobcats, and ditch-witches and the hard hats to operate them. Now there was no denying what was happening: The meadow I had reverently trespassed across for the last six months was about to be walled off. The Shining Meadow was about to be defrocked of its *Shekinah* glory.

Finally, a sign was attached to the padlocked chain-link fence along the Whitney Avenue side of the meadow that told me why:

Water Supply Land
No Trespassing

A new reservoir—that's what it was all about. And all the dirt from the excavation for the reservoir was being dumped up in the meadow's northeast corner, my morning corner. This was not some conical dirt pile where kids could play king of the mountain, and this most certainly was not "the mountain of the Lord" in Micah's prophecy. No, this was a man-made mountain with its top flattened to a mesa to accommodate the endless procession of dump trucks delivering still more dirt to it week after week, month after month.

I felt like suing the Water Supply Board for desecration of a sacred place. In ancient Jewish law, three witnesses were required to substantiate a charge or a claim against someone. Could I have produced three credible witnesses to the glory of God's presence in the meadow? Not the father and son pessimistically awaiting a punctual school bus and missing a solar benediction. And not the skinny old man and his arthritic old black lab shuffling down the sidewalk, seemingly unaware that a celestial hello was taking place not twelve feet away.

To casualty insurance companies, there are acts of God and acts of man. When it came to the northeast corner of Eli Whitney's meadow, I knew who was responsible for the beauty and who was at fault for its demise. It's an old story, isn't it? Paradise lost.

What does it mean that I cared so much about some place getting fenced off where I used to spend maybe ten minutes a day? Is it a bad sign when "insignificant" things signify? What does it say about me that the fencing off of a meadow should have the force of *event*, a kind of eco-spiritual crisis? The loss of the meadow was not world shattering or tragic; it was just another encroachment, another minidiminishment, another little shock to shrug off: *Hey, no big deal.* Compared to losses by death, depletion, attrition, or enmity, this was small potatoes indeed. Yet they do add up, these little losses. They are cumulative. They take their toll. They count, they *matter*, these quiet, personally meaningful places that you don't own but that belong to you while you are there, because it is your truest, holiest self you bring to them.

Why did the upper northeast corner of Eli Whitney's meadow mean so damn much to me? What made it so consoling? Why was I so grateful for it?

It lifted me out of darkness and brought me into the light, that's why.

When Baby Jessica fell down that well in Texas in 1987, the rescuers couldn't go down the shaft she was trapped in, because they might cause it to cave in on her. They had to dig a new shaft parallel to and of the same depth as the one where she was, and then tunnel in from the side to reach her. Those two shafts of equal depth—the disaster shaft and the rescue shaft—signified the night and day of holy hell and the shining meadow. The darkness of the holy-hell years drove my heart into the ground: Alan's and my entrenched, icy silence; Daniel's premature absence from home; the prolonged divorce proceedings; my mother's sudden death; Ella's treatment-resistant depression; the anguish of her estrangement from me; Alan's illness and death. The radiance of the meadow spoke those ancient words to me: *Sursum corda*, Lift up your heart.

The Shining Meadow loosened my attachment to myself. Michelangelo prayed, "Lord, free me of myself so that I may please you." The light in the meadow did just that: it granted me respite from myself. And, oh, how welcome a thing it was, being relieved of the burden of myself.

I once rode a sweet little donkey up a steep Greek mountain. I thought it would be fun, but it was terrible. I was the cargo this poor beast of burden bore up a mountain while the man who came with her beat her with a stick to keep her going. When I begged him to stop, he laughed in my face. The donkey taught me what Jesus means when he says, "Take up your cross." It is none other than my very own self. What else could it be? What is harder to have to bear up under than the thick, hard, unwieldy, ego-laden, self-protective shell of my same old, same old self? I ask you: What is harder to have to carry up the mountain than that?

20

THOSE BENEATH ME

You hypocrite, first take the log out of your own eye, and then you
will see clearly to take the speck out of your neighbor's eye.
—Luke 6:42

D
ashing into Berkeley at 7:28 a.m., I stashed Quita in the
sacristy, squeaked into the chapel just ahead of the priest *du
jour*, and was dumbfounded to hear myself summoned to the
observance of a holy Lent. I had clean forgotten it was Ash Wednesday.

I got down on my knees, and the priest imposed a cross of ashes on
my forehead with his thumb as he uttered those most formidable words:
"Remember that you are dust and to dust you shall return."

There I was, down on my knees at *divinity* school, without the
slightest idea of what I was going to "do" about Lent. What would I give
up for the next forty days: wine, movies, popcorn, *Jeopardy*? Or what
practice would I take on: double sits of Centering Prayer? memorizing
psalms or scripture?

Reciting the Great Litany of Penitence, I felt guilty this year, the same
as every other year, of every item on its confessional checklist: "the pride,
hypocrisy, and impatience of our lives; our self-indulgent appetites and
ways" (long naps, wine of any color); "our exploitation of other people;
our anger at our own frustration; our envy of those more fortunate than
ourselves" (certain insanely gifted writers who shall go nameless); "our
intemperate love of worldly goods and comforts, and our dishonesty in

daily life and work; our negligence in prayer and worship, and our failure to commend the faith that is in us" (what, me evangelize?); "our blindness to human need and suffering, and our indifference to injustice and cruelty; our waste and pollution of your creation, and our lack of concern for those who come after us; our prejudice and contempt toward those who differ from us, our false judgments and …" (wrapping it up, blindsiding me with a sucker punch) "our uncharitable thoughts toward our neighbors."

"Uncharitable thoughts" was a gross understatement for the roiling, boiling, hands-on-hips, unchristian thoughts, epithets, mental commentaries, and mock speeches I spewed in my head day in, day out about my downstairs neighbors. These included not merely the chain-smoking matriarch and her middle-aged son, but the whole motley, whack-a-mole horde of illicit occupants: divorce-refugee relatives, grandkids, romantic interests, and fishing buddies. My "uncharitable thoughts" toward the sum total of them featured phrases such as "selfish disregard," "reckless endangerment," "thoughtless assholes," "think they own the place," and "congenital slobs."

The word *neighbors* came at me one more time in the Ash Wednesday service that morning, and once again, it leaped out at me as if I had underlined it with my fluorescent yellow Hi-Liter: "We have not loved our neighbors as ourselves." Jesus once told a lawyer to love his neighbor as himself, and the lawyer retorted, "And who is my neighbor?" Jesus told him the parable of the good Samaritan. That shut him up but good. No wonder Jesus went around saying, "Woe to you lawyers!"

I had been breaking the Great Commandment right and left with my downstairs neighbors: "You shall love the Lord your God with all your heart and with all your mind and with all your strength and with all your soul; and your neighbor as yourself." But it was that line in the Great Litany of Penitence about "uncharitable thoughts toward our neighbors" that just nailed me.

So on Ash Wednesday, having given no thought whatsoever to a Lenten regimen, I went overboard, as we are wont to do when caught flat-footed, and in a burst of penitential extravagance, I gave up uncharitable thoughts toward my downstairs neighbors for Lent. I promised God that I would fast for forty days with my mind, mouth, and heart. I would do this not only by not speaking critically about them or muttering under my breath as I tripped over their clutter in the hallway, waded through their empties littering the laundry room floor, and removed their Styrofoam containers, pizza boxes, and fast-food trash from my designated garbage can, but also by refraining from even harboring judgmental thoughts about them. "Oh God, come to my assistance! Oh Lord, make haste to help me!"

Did I ever have my work cut out for me! Nothing brought out the worst in me faster than off-leash dogs and the downstairs tenants. But as Buddhist nun Pema Chodron says, "Without the inconsiderate neighbor, where will we find the chance to practice patience?"

The downstairs tenants violated basic courtesy and common decency so flagrantly and frequently that every time I uttered the line in the Lord's prayer, "Forgive us our trespasses as we forgive those who trespass against us," I'd picture them and get to thinking about their trespasses against my trash can, my parking space, the hallway, and the staircase (though never again my detergent). But worse still, according to Jesus, not only was I supposed to forgive them, I was supposed to *love* them. He must have meant business because he said it no fewer than nine times: "Love your neighbor as yourself."

They left their shoes strewn in the narrow entryway for me to trip over. They left a bucket of dirty water with a string mop in it right at the foot of the stairs for eight days straight. (Damn right I kept count: eight days.) The mangy Christmas tree they pitched into the front yard at the end of January was still there on Ash Wednesday. They were the incarnation of entropy and the apotheosis of thoughtlessness.

Now I would have to find a way to get over my contempt for the ground-floor horde. Now I would have to quit keeping track of their trespasses. Now I would have to refrain from uncharitable thoughts about them. I like the word *refrain*. It implies a chosen restraint. "Above all else, we admonish you to refrain from grumbling." I would have to guard my mouth, my mind, and my heart. I would have to catch myself before my heart hardened against them and my thoughts took off running about them. Thoughts matter. Thoughts *count*. Thoughts, after all, are the point of origin of actions.

All day long, everywhere I went—except, of course, YDS—well-meaning people kept discreetly telling me I had dirt on my forehead, thinking they were sparing me a spinach-in-the-teeth-type embarrassment. Being reminded all day of the ashes I was wearing also served to remind me of my rash, eleventh-hour Lenten renunciation. Why had I committed to such a thing? Should I ask God to allow me a do-over?

In psychological terms, my Lenten agenda would be called "cognitive restructuring." In Buddhist terms, it was about overcoming small mind. Buddhist teachings seem so much more down-to-earth and user-friendly than daunting Christian directives such as St. Paul's to "put on the armor of light." But whichever one, letting go of thoughts is the basis of transformation in all religions. My Lenten task involved, first of all, awareness of my judgmental thoughts about my downstairs neighbors—catching myself criticizing and critiquing them—and secondly, letting go of the thoughts instead of going off on a mind-binge of negativity. Sometimes, even while sitting in my little meditation room in my Goodwill prayer chair and entering the inner room of my being where Jesus said to go when we pray, I'd catch myself itemizing their stuff sprawled in the hallway and inventorying their vehicles hogging the parking apron.

Unlike me, my attic neighbor Tom didn't need Lent to put a cork in his mouth. Try as I might, I was never able to lure him into bad-mouthing the ground-floor tenants. But Tom's roommate, Mary, and I loved to swap gripes and grievances. So Mary couldn't understand what had come over me when, after listening to her spout off about their latest violation, I would mumble something conciliatory. I couldn't tell her what was going on, that it was a Lenten thing. Jesus made it very clear on several occasions that conspicuous piety is a serious no-no: "Beware of practicing your piety before others in order to be seen by them; for then you have no reward from your Father in heaven."

The magnitude of my annoyance and indignation at those beneath me garishly revealed my own smallness as a person. Theologian Frederick Buechner got it right: "The more I dislike my neighbor, the more I'm apt to dislike myself for disliking him and him for making me dislike myself, and I am continually tempted to take out on my neighbor the dislike I feel for myself."

I read somewhere that it takes thirty days to change a habit. Lent gave me an extra ten in which to nip my judgmental thoughts in the bud and completely retool my thinking about them. Mind you, I did not have to think highly of them; I did not even have to think well of them. I didn't have to *like* them—or their leavings in the hallway, their cigarette butts on the stoop, and their sprawling trash. I just had to love them as myself. Given the bouts of self-loathing I was prone to, it wasn't really asking all that much.

Abstaining from griping about them got me in the habit of keeping my trap shut and my mind and heart more open to them. I came to see that they weren't *bad,* they were beleaguered, swamped, on the ragged edge. I reached a kind of delicate, tippy neutrality. I learned how to turn on a kind of white noise machine in my head when thoughts of them arose. Neither static nor music, it simply drowned out the traffic noise of negative thoughts.

By the time Easter finally arrived—*alleluia!*—unless they did something exceptionally flagrant or egregious, I was able to shake my head with something resembling benign amusement. Thoughts of them would arise—habit is, after all, the yeast of most of our thoughts—but I would catch myself getting snagged and choose to let the thought move on: "git along, little dogie."

This Lenten discipline that had come from a line in the Great Litany of Penitence—that hefty, magnificent, catch-all confession with no loopholes, no escape clauses, no ifs, ands, or buts about it, that comprehensive checklist of our all-too-human faults, flaws, and frailties—had worked so well that now I barely noticed their trespasses and squalor. Once I had given them up for Lent I never could work up the same head of steam again. That last-ditch, eleventh-hour Ash Wednesday resolution of mine had, by God, actually *worked*.

———

The year after I graduated, I went back to visit YDS and stopped by the house on Whitney Avenue to say hi to Tom and Mary in the attic and to Stephen A., the YDS friend who had taken over my apartment. When

I crested the steep, still-potholed driveway in my rental car and saw the parking apron cluttered with the exact same assortment of vehicles, plus a ratty Toyota pickup on the flagstone patio of yore, I had to laugh. The downstairs tenants had proved as immovable as their two junkers. And when I went in the as-ever-unlocked back door, sure enough, their hip boots, boathook, bucket, and cooler were still in the hall.

When Stephen A. had first expressed interest in renting my apartment, in a spirit of full disclosure I told him all about the horde of illicit tenants downstairs and their heedless ways and rude usurpations. Now, backslider that I was, hoping for some juicy anecdotes and good gossip, I asked him how it was going.

"Oh, just fine," he said. "You know, I never could figure out why you warned me about them. They're perfectly nice people."

21

ZEN IN THE SHELL

Don't open the door to the study and begin reading!
Take down the dulcimer.
Let the beauty we love be what we do.
There are hundreds of ways to kneel and kiss the ground.

—Rumi

After our History of Christian Thought exam, our *final* final, a bunch of us went to Viva Zapata's to celebrate with pitchers of midday margaritas and Aquinas-inspired riffs on "transubstantiated" tequila and tortillas. We had survived our first year of seminary and were now officially on vacation.

But with my house in LA rented, I couldn't just go home for the summer and hang out, seeing Ella and friends and having Daniel come for a visit. Besides, as promised, my kids had visited *me* at YDS in March. Quita went nuts at their arrival. It was so strange and wonderful having my daughter beside me in Theological Aesthetics and my son at the seminar table in my Old Testament TA group, and to be flanked by them in Marquand Chapel. Sitting around the kitchen table in my apartment in New Haven, with Daniel driving hard bargains in Monopoly and Ella beating the pants off us at Scrabble, I felt as if we were right back home in LA at my long old farm table.

As if by tacit agreement, Ella and I had tabled all troubling topics. Their five-day visit had flown by with pizza, Ping-Pong, canasta, classes, the British Museum, the Ivy Noodle, the Yankee Doodle, a movie, and worship services galore. I *loved* being with my kids in my YDS world—watching guys do double takes over Ella and hearing Daniel engage in cosmological repartee. It was as if I'd suddenly revealed this amazing secret I'd had all along: my two perfectly delightful, simply brilliant adult kids!

Right after summer vacation started, I made arrangements to collect Ella's belongings from the college in New York, which she'd left in a rush when Alan was hospitalized. On compassion leave since his death, she was in a grief group and grief therapy, but what anchored her to LA was her relationship with Guy.

The bandy-legged old maintenance man who escorted me to the storage area on campus avoided eye contact as he helped me carry open cartons and loose armloads to my car. He must have done this for other parents whose daughters had never returned to school. It was startling—almost eerie—to see family photos and familiar shoes and scarves of Ella's tossed helter-skelter into boxes that had sat unclaimed for eighteen months.

"Thanks so much for your help," I said, shaking hands and handing him a folded twenty when the last box was loaded. "Just so you know: the reason my daughter left school so fast was because her father was ill, and he'd taken a sudden turn for the worse."

The relief on his face showed what he'd been thinking about those abandoned belongings: that my daughter had either been expelled or committed suicide.

"He passed away a year ago. But my daughter never returned, because her boyfriend is back home in LA."

The old man wiped his sleeve across his eyes. "Well now," he said, "I sure appreciate you telling me that. It's most always something else."

Being out of school and off duty in New Haven was bewildering. I'd swing by Atticus Bookstore to pick up some literary light refreshment, but instead of coming home with the latest Robert Parker or Sue Grafton I would be lugging some theology tome I hadn't gotten around to reading during the school year. I would go to Best Video to rent a movie, but instead of coming home with a rom com or a thriller, I'd have a stack of heavyweight documentaries that I would then take notes on while watching. The night I caught myself watching a 1958 documentary about theologian Paul Tillich and hitting pause and rewind over and over so that I could write down a long quote verbatim, I decided it was high time to put a stop to this busman's holiday and kick back for a while.

School had been out just over a month the Sunday morning that Quita and I came on the turtle. By then I had gotten the hang of being on vacation. I had spent a few days in Massachusetts at my friend Carol's, where, starting in right after breakfast, we would put on Palestrina and play canasta all morning, move to Scrabble in the afternoon, take our dogs for a walk in Borderland State Park, fix gin and tonics, and eventually dinner, then talk our heads off till bedtime, and do it all over again the next day.

The turtle was trying to get through a rusty old fence that ran along the marshy backwater of Lake Whitney near the Davis Street Bridge. It was very big, and the fence consisted of row upon row of little wire squares. Its head fit through a square just fine. Its body was the problem. After sticking its head through a wire square a couple of rows up from the bottom, it would then drive its shell forward against the fence like a hunched lineman pushing against a blocking sled.

At first, Quita and I were both really excited. I had to reel in her Flexi leash and hold her back by her collar. Pretty soon, though, she was ready to move on, but I made her wait because I wanted to see if I could figure out some way to help the turtle. It had been trying to get through the fence for such a long time that its sharp-clawed hind legs had dug two good-size holes: the terrapin equivalent of spinning your wheels and getting in deeper.

Since the top of the fence came to my armpits, I couldn't just lean over it, reach down, pick up the turtle by the edges of its shell, and deposit it on my side of the fence. But I was game to try to get this stymied creature on its way. I didn't have much else to do. It was because of the burdensome idleness of my summer that I could let myself get worked up over a determined turtle. I knew perfectly well that if I had been in the midst of midterms, term papers, or finals I wouldn't have paid the slightest attention, much less made its plight a cliff-hanger drama I wanted to get involved with.

But being at loose ends, with not a blessed thing I absolutely had to do except lose the twelve pounds I'd gained stress-snacking during the school year, was a luxury I could now afford. To splurge my attention on a *turtle* after the relentless anxiety and stress I'd gone through over my daughter spoke worlds to me about how dramatically changed my circumstances were. Besides, I couldn't have devoted myself to Ella that summer even if I'd wanted to. She was in India with Guy, and the only way I even knew what medications she was now taking was that after her cosmetics bag slid into the toilet in their hotel bathroom in Agra, she'd called me in New Haven to contact her doctor in Los Angeles to have her prescriptions faxed.

Every time the turtle drove forward, its smooth-skinned head would strain on its elongated, stringy neck; then it would recoil and withdraw its jutting head to just a nubbin peeking from wrinkled folds that looked for all the world like an uncircumcised penis. As for its actual gender, with turtles, it's mighty hard to tell.

But I'm sure it was a *she*, because a few days earlier, I had chatted with a naturalist in Borderland who was in the process of hand-carrying pregnant turtles from a pond to the place where they instinctively returned to lay their eggs. Their dilemma was that their route crossed one of the park's busiest trails. It reminded me of the turtle trying to get across the road in Steinbeck's *The Grapes of Wrath*, where it symbolized the Okies of this world being knocked around, beaten back, and obliterated by high-speed, oblivious big shots. This turtle sure could have used a nice moving man like that naturalist to get her where her instincts were screaming she needed to be.

The fence at the spot where she was trying to get through came clear down to the ground, but not five feet away was a place where the bottom of the fence was curled up enough for her to easily crawl under it. I chafed with hectic frustration at the futility of her effort—all that squandered energy!—as well as my inability to help her because of the height of the fence. I felt so sorry for her, watching her give it her all but all to no avail. I had no way of telling her she had slightly miscalculated her exit spot and that it was sheer folly for her to persist. I could not get through to her turtle brain that all she had to do was scoot over a few feet and she'd be under the fence and on her way.

I itched to play *deus ex machina* with her. If only I could have vaulted the fence, picked her up, and positioned her at the place with the gap! Failing that, if I could have taught her to meditate, she would have discovered how sitting still loosens your hold on the illusion that there's somewhere else besides right where you are that you need to go. Observing her stubborn refusal to adapt and reconsider her adamant belief that she was at the right spot, I could not help but wonder if God sometimes itches to give *me* a nudge, to scoot *me* the scant inches that would make all the difference. Does my poor reckoning drive him nuts? Does he give it a little body English when he sees *me* struggling? Does God itch to play God with me?

I must admit I have a soft spot for turtles. There is something so downtrodden, cumbersome, lugubrious, and thanks to Aesop's fable, legendarily persistent about them. Lord knows there's nothing electrifying or flashy. They are primordial plodders, primeval slowpokes, so dawn-of-time they remind me of the way God is addressed in Daniel's prophetic vision as "the Ancient of Days." But there is also something endearingly reminiscent of *Star Wars'* Yoda in their wizened, wise, goofy faces.

Really though, it's the self-protective way that turtles withdraw into their shells that gets me. In my first novel, a psychological fantasy mercifully out of print (sales were brisk among my family), I dubbed the heroine's father the Enormous Tortoise. Though I adamantly denied it at the time, he was, of course, based on my own emotionally retracted father, a man constitutionally incapable of responding to "I love you" with anything other than "Likewise." He signed greeting cards "Love, Daddy" in faint pencil so the card could be reused, but I worried it might be his love that was faint and erasable.

I was, at any rate, very partial toward the Lake Whitney turtle. I was all for her. I wished her well with all my heart. With her purblind determination and all-out devotion to her objective, how could I not be pulling for her? She had a biological appointment to keep, and by

God, nothing was going to get in the way of her keeping it, including a wire fence too high to climb over, too low to belly under, and too small-squared to wiggle through. She was instinct incarnate.

I found—no, I *invested* in that mud-encrusted zealot of a turtle something fraught with meaning. I identified with her sense of urgency and her belief in the critical nature of her task and also—truth be told—with her flawed vision, her failure to grasp the need to adjust her course and see that there was a simple way around this obstacle.

As I stood there contemplating the turtle's dilemma, a police car stopped at the light at Davis Street and Whitney Ave. It was just after seven o'clock on a Sunday morning. The streets were empty, and there was, for the moment, no crime to fight, so I waved to them, held up a wait-a-minute finger, and approached their patrol car. The two cops exchanged a quick *now-what* glance and eyed Quita and me with wary apathy.

The light turned green, but they waited. I smiled, bid them good morning, and pointing to the turtle behind the fence, explained the situation: how her slight miscalculation was keeping her from returning to the place where she was programmed to lay her eggs.

"You know, like salmon swimming upstream to where they were born," I concluded.

The cop behind the wheel laughed and jerked his thumb toward the backseat. "So, what, you want us to put it back there and drive it somewhere?"

"Maybe even turn on the siren?" the other cop chimed in.

I heh-hehed politely and then explained what I thought they could do: lean over the fence and, by employing their nightsticks like chopsticks, move the turtle over to the place just a few feet to her right where she could crawl under the fence. The cops rolled their eyes at each other.

"Ma'am, believe you me, that turtle's better off staying on the side of the fence it's on. Alls it's gonna do is get itself kilt out here in the road."

I hate being called ma'am except when I'm in Texas.

"Yeah," his partner said, providing backup. "It gets out in the road, it could cause an accident too. Someone swerves to avoid hitting it."

"Hitting *her*," I said. "It's because she's pregnant that she has to get where she's going."

The two cops glanced over at each other and shrugged *whatever*.

"I feel sorry for her," I said. "I'd hate to think of her spending the rest of her life trying to get through that damn fence."

"We'll check it out, ma'am. Just as soon as we can," the driver said.

I cocked my head at him: *yeah, sure you will.* He gave me a snappy, mock salute and gunned away on a red light.

What on earth was I thinking? That they'd be like the nice policeman in *Make Way for Ducklings* who stops traffic to let the mother duck and her ducklings cross Commonwealth Avenue to get back home to the pond in the Boston Commons? Why, for that matter, didn't I think to go back home myself and get the snow shovel or the push broom from the garage and scoop her up or sweep her along to the spot with the gap under the fence?

The next day, first thing in the morning, I went to check on her. It lent my day a rousing sense of purpose—a somewhere to go, a something to do. I tried to fire up Quita with it too.

"Hey, Quita-teeta, wanna go see if the turtle's still there? Come on, girl. Let's go see!"

The turtle was still there and still hard at it. She had moved a couple of feet closer to the gap under the fence and gouged two new holes in the dirt beneath her hind legs. Not only was she not a quitter, but she would not even take a breather. There was something absurdly noble—a kind of Don Quixote pathos—about her all-out effort.

I wanted to make contact, to connect with her in a manner that would convey my good will. But showing affection to a turtle is awkward. They're hard to pat. With her head withdrawn and her shell insensate, a front leg was my only choice. I studied one closely as I worked up my nerve. I had not noticed until then that the leg had random, triangular scales on it like the triangles on an asparagus stalk. I slid my hand sideways through a wire square low in the fence and slowly reached out to touch her left front leg with the tip of my index finger.

What happened next was as fast and unexpected as a car in your blind spot. At my touch—my almost touch—her jaws flew open as suddenly as steel-trap jaws slam shut. What had been a flat line of mouth suddenly became a gaping, gargantuan maw. This beaked, whitish red astonishment of a mouth lunged at my finger with such aggressive, instantaneous intensity that I very nearly pulled back a stub. That's when it first occurred to me that this might be a snapping turtle. Shaken by my narrow escape from a friendly overture, I bolted for home.

Early the next morning when I went with Quita to check on the turtle, she was nowhere to be seen. But I knew she had not given up and retreated into the marsh, because *outside* the fence, on the sidewalk and in the grass, was a succession of gloppy green "plopids." (Thanks to Ella's onomatopoetic childhood word, "plopid" is enshrined in our family lexicon for one unit of poop.) Without exaggeration I say that I rejoiced over those turtle turds. And Quita, who had spent just as much time as I with the turtle—albeit in less rapt contemplation—sniffed every single one of those plopids with spellbound intensity. Then, with lowered nose, she backtracked along the trail to the curled-up place at the fence's bottom edge where the turtle had at long last sailed under with nary a gouge in the dirt.

In a way that is elusive but completely valid to me, my encounter with that turtle was not only a high point of my summer but part and parcel of my theological education … the extracurricular, improvised one that had nothing to do with divinity school or organized religion. (Turtles fare far better in Taoism and Hinduism than in Judaism and Christianity. The turtle as such is not mentioned in the Old or New Testaments. The biblical "turtle" is the turtledove. But in the Taoist scheme of things, the tortoise supports the world on its dome, and in Hinduism, the turtle supports the elephant whose back supports the world.) My absorption in the turtle may show I didn't have enough to do that summer, but it also shows how enthralling the commonplace can become when one takes a brief sabbatical from self and lets it have center stage. There was a time when I would not have considered the contemplation of a pregnant snapping turtle the highest and best use of my time. But tell me how better to spend a summer morning than praising God to the skies for setting in motion a universe that could produce such an oddball, ancient, cranky, stick-to-it-ive critter?

My summer job in New Haven was to be a student of such mundane miracles and minor accidents, those spiritual fender benders that are collisions with grace itself. My job was to pay attention, to be on the qv for peripheral visions of the holy, to not get lost in the bland absences, and to never *ever* summarize a day by writing in my journal what King Louis XVI wrote in his on the day the Bastille fell: *Rien.* "Nothing."

I was glad a turtle's determination could steal my heart. My response to nature was a way of taking my vital signs. It was in the theology of nature that I felt most thoroughly grounded in God. Nature broke open the holy for me. If I were to lose my capacity to delight in the overnight wonder of a surprise lily, become blasé about cacti, quit being enchanted by creeks, not be enamored of goats, not be delighted by the very notion of hedgehogs, and not be wowed by a turtle's tenacity, please kick me out!

Even in the midst of gritty New Haven I found snippets of nature, toeholds of litter-free, untrampled ground. There was one certain semisecluded, modest little boulder on the slope around the corner from my apartment that I made friends with. Settled on its congenial, molar-tooth surface, I could play with a twig, mull things over, and replenish my soul.

God's graffiti was scrawled all over the place in illegible little scribbles of cloud; the elegant calligraphy of a rock-strewn creek; the artistic, slapdash streaks on alstroemeria petals. The stutter of light along the silken filament of a spider's solitary line—the *dit-dit-dash* of fragments of light skittering back and forth along it—always made me feel as if God was sending me a holy hello in that Morse code of light. Walking into a spider line always served as a wake-up call: Hello! You have just been clotheslined by God.

The question, as always, was what would enable me to go beyond myself and, as St. Paul says, "come up higher." The traditional ways "up" are through knowledge, love, work, and contemplation. I had some of each in my spiritual toolbox, but my means of ascent was a Rube Goldberg device that was temperamental as hell, slow as molasses, and sabotaged by ego. It gave me fits, and sometimes, to be honest, I felt like giving up and calling it quits on the whole business of getting to God by means of such a chewing-gum-and-baling-wire device.

Besides, the perception of beauty—intentional attentiveness to it—was every bit as much a means of ascent as any of those others. When my antennae were up—when I had ears to hear and eyes to see—my enhanced receptivity made me aware of God's presence in a volitional, deluxe way. Thoreau writes in his journal, "We are as much as we see." Indeed, when all is said and done, the spiritual life comes down to just that: consciousness of the sacred in the ordinary, an enhanced, exponential awareness of the vestiges of God filling the world.

By the end of the summer, I had day-tripped with Quita around New England and ferried to Martha's Vineyard with Carol. I had put myself through the wringer at Yale's Gothic cathedral of a gym and lost the twelve pounds. I had seen my novel *Skywater* come out in a new edition but failed to follow through on my intention to write daily. I had driven with Quita from New Haven to Kansas City to visit my family, stopping in Kentucky to pay my respects at Thomas Merton's grave at the Abbey of Gethsemani. A ninety-three-year-old monk had died that morning, so that evening, instead of vespers, I attended the Service for a Departed Brother, the exact same service Merton was given when his mortal remains arrived from Bangkok in December 1968.

In July, as agreed, the tenant in my house in LA decamped for one week, and Daniel came from Oregon for a visit. Ella and Guy were back from India, and the four of us played Trivial Pursuit, an ideal game for a conflict-averse mom grateful simply to have both her kids under her own roof.

I'd made a pilgrimage to Amherst, Massachusetts, to visit Emily Dickinson's home and stood in the kitchen where she had made her signature ginger snaps; in the parlor where the family dead had been laid out; in her bedroom where she had written her dash-strewn poetry at a humble little table and had no mirror to see her red hair and eyes "the color of the sherry that the guest leaves in the glass"; and in the cemetery where her headstone reads simply: "Called back."

While in Amherst, I'd happened inadvertently upon the college, and the pit of my stomach clenched with PTSD as I remembered the call I'd received when Ella was three nights into a high school summer program on the Amherst campus that her NPI doctor had cleared her to attend. The call came while I was waiting in the wings at a friend's in Chicago before returning home. The program director informed me they were evacuating my daughter as "dangerously unhappy" and "too risky" for them to allow her to stay. They put her on a plane in New Hampshire, I met her at O'Hare, and we flew back to Los Angeles together. I say "together," but she did not utter one word during the entire trip, and after takeoff, went to sit at the back of the plane with a blanket over her head. A flight attendant came to ask if my daughter was all right. I said yes. She expressed "concerns" and kept a wary eye on her. As did I.

I also visited Deerfield, Massachusetts, a picturesque village where citizens dressed in Colonial costumes and where Alan had been sent to boarding school and our son would have been too had I not made it a Rubicon. Having lunch at the Deerfield Inn, where generations of visiting parents and students have dined, I felt like a voyeur of the road not taken.

A summer in which I'd had nothing to do proved abundant after all, starting with turning aside—like Moses for a burning bush—for a pregnant turtle stymied by a fence. As my brother, Art, used to say, "Sometimes the interruptions *are* the work."

22

DIV. SCHOOL DOG

The eyes of the French poodle can shine
with such an unalloyed glee and
darken with so profound a gravity as to
disconcert the masters of the earth,
who have lost the key to so many of the simpler magics.

—James Thurber

If Quita'd had a bumper sticker on her rear end in New Haven, it would have said, "So Many Squirrels, So Little Time." If Quita'd had a Latin motto, it would have been: *Toti sciuri sunt boni*, "All squirrels are good." If Quita had become a Christian in Connecticut, she would have had to give up squirrels, because repentance means to change the direction in which you look for happiness.

Connecticut is the squirreliest place on the planet, and given her squirrel fixation, Quita, off leash in New Haven, squirrel capitol of the world, would not have lasted five minutes. Though she deemed cats worthy of pursuit, they couldn't hold a candle to squirrels. Quita went bonkers over every single one of them. It was especially hard on her being eye level with the ones zipping along the tree branches and telephone wires right outside our second-floor apartment. She would sit at the window and moan. When I meditated I was like Quita with squirrels: my mind chasing squirrel thoughts, straining at the leash, heedless of my master's tug to bring me back, to make me heel and show some self-discipline. This thought came to me, of course, while I was meditating, and I couldn't wait for the timer to go off so I could write it down.

The only place I ever let Quita off leash was in the fenced play yard next to the Berkeley Center. Loopy with freedom, she would do her Crazy Lady number, hunching up her back and running in circles, snatching grass left and right, and fake growling. Watching her tear around made me wonder if heaven might not be a bit like that: an off-leash place—but limitless!—where you are free to roam and chase squirrels and not get creamed by cars or trucks.

The other reason Quita had to be on leash was that she was fear aggressive with other dogs. She did not consider dogs playmates; they were the enemy. It was my fault. As a puppy, she nearly died of lupus. The lupus went into permanent remission, but almost losing Quita made my natural tendency to be overprotective kick into high gear. As a dog owner and, far worse, as a parent, my biggest mistake was to prize the safety of my loved ones over their free-range, off-leash yearnings. Unable to bear seeing my dog or my children at risk, I put a premium on my own sense of security. It pains me to admit it, but Quita caught her fearfulness from me.

Her single biggest wish was that I would never go anywhere without her. When left behind, she registered her disappointment and displeasure by raiding wastebaskets, her coping mechanism for separation anxiety, boredom, and loneliness. During final exams, she let me know in no uncertain terms that her outings had gotten far too skimpy and went for what she knew was my jugular: books and papers. Instead of making the rounds of wastepaper baskets, she now shoved books off tables, pulled them from bookcases, and then chewed and tore them to pieces. She consumed the entire back cover of *Signs and Symbols in Christian Art*. To appease my goddess of destruction, I planted envelopes, junk mail, and other paper trash for her to strew and browse through to her heart's content. The goddess had to be propitiated.

Once Quita had reached her limit, she would trick me into taking her out by acting as if she had to go pee urgently—pacing and pawing at the door, batting at my arm. Then when I would take her out, she wouldn't go—meaning I would have put on hat, coat, gloves, and boots and gone out into the freezing cold all for nothing: a *faux* pee. I'd get so mad I would yank the leash hard and swear at her; then I would feel guilty and ashamed of myself.

I don't believe in winter clothes for animals, but I did worry that Quita, a California girl, would be cold in Connecticut, so I left her unclipped. By April she looked like the Woolly-Woolly in *Babar*. Her appearance caused quite a stir at the New Haven groomer's, where I finally took her in April. I wanted her to have a simple puppy cut, nothing sculpted or froufrou, but they said that, in her state, the only option was shaving her down to one inch all over.

The two things in New Haven that gave Quita boundless joy were squirrels and my return home. As soon as I came through the door, she would pop a wheelie, flash me a goofy grin, and run to grab a fleece man for me to toss for her. She had three fleece men: Young Man, Middle-Aged Man, and Old Man. I had no man. Not even a fleece one with a squeaker.

Dorothy Parker used to threaten her husband—I forget which one—that if he didn't shape up she'd send him to military school. I sometimes worried that Quita thought of being carted off to seminary as that kind of punishment. But then I would remind myself that the real punishment for her—and for me—would have been for us not to have been together.

23

UNLEASHED

The clearest way to see your own energy reflected back is to look at the
behavior of the animals around you. If we
can learn to read [their] energy …
we all can become better human beings.

—Cesar Millan

My calendar for Wednesday, August 22, 2001, shows that I
had an appointment with Nino at four o'clock for a haircut
and was due for dinner at Paula and Joe's at six thirty.
Written small in faint pencil in the lower left corner of the box for
August 22 is the notation "ERP," an intentionally cryptic, after-the-fact
reminder of what else happened that day besides getting my hair cut and
having dinner with friends: the East Rock Park incident.

East Rock is New Haven's oldest park and by far the largest. Before
it became a park in the 1880s, Yale cut timber there. The park's four
hundred acres boast athletic fields, walking trails, a ranger station, the
Pardee Rose Garden, a playground, a river, a waterfall, a marsh, the
Giant Steps, birds galore, and woods so woodsy you'd never dream
you're in a medium-size city with a major university until you reach the
summit with its sweeping view.

I first stumbled on East Rock Park by way of a historic, impossibly
charming covered bridge, just the sort of thing that convinced me I
really was now living in New England. Two men jogging out of the park

by way of the bridge stopped to advise me to not go in—not alone, not this close to dark. Because of their warning, from then on I had a sense of latent danger lurking in the park.

But I wasn't about to forego it. This was a place of respite from academia, and exploring its trails with Quita helped assuage my guilt for her on-leash existence. The guided nature walks on Saturday mornings not only acquainted me with the park's innards but also taught me, if only fleetingly, the geology, flora, and fauna of my new surroundings. Whether it's a forest or a room full of strangers, learning names is square one in getting acquainted, and those guided nature walks were to my new surroundings what name tags had been during YDS orientation.

East Rock Park has several entrances. My usual point of entry was the covered bridge off Whitney Ave., but sometimes I entered at Orange Street or down the subtle path across the street from St. Thomas Episcopal Church. I had never gone in the back entrance off Davis Street in Hamden until the end of my first year at YDS, and I didn't go in very far that time. Once I got past the Pardee Rose Garden it had started to seem rather forbidding, so I went just a little way past the fork in the road and down an abandoned roadway before turning back. Something about the woods gave me the willies and made my imagination take off running.

This time, though, around 9:00 a.m. on Wednesday, August 22, I went in by the Davis Street entrance in search of the shady woods in the deep end of the park. The radio at breakfast had said it was going be a scorcher, so I went in with Quita because I thought it would be pleasant in there, and when I got to the fork in the road, I purposely took "the one less traveled by."

The farther in I went, though, the more I regretted that I had not taken time to study the big map at the entrance. I had no idea if the path I was on made a loop or where its many offshoots went. In total ignorance of where I was going, I just kept going. The one thing I knew for sure was that I was not on the road to the summit. That road allowed vehicles. This one didn't.

The deeper in I went, the eerier it seemed that I had not seen one single solitary soul. Finally, after walking an hour, I saw the first sign of another human: a sleeping bag in the undergrowth just off the path. Crumpled beer cans, half pints, a faded plaid shirt, and one sock were scattered around it. I don't know if I was more afraid at the thought of a live person or a dead one being in the sleeping bag. I tiptoed past, pulling Quita in close and wishing she were a kickass Doberman, not a thirty-eight-pound, *sub*standard poodle. I reviled myself for my stupidity in coming so far into the park alone.

The illicit sleeping bag in the undergrowth—camping was not allowed in the park—roused the memory of Sub-Zero Man, fanning my fear by citing a precedent for it. One summer in Malibu I was hiking with Daniel and Ella, then seven and five, along a deep arroyo in Trancas Canyon, when we came on a Sub-Zero refrigerator carton blocking our way. Daniel gave it a couple of aimless kicks before starting to go around it. A colossal man shot out of it like a monstrous Jack-in-the-box and grabbed at Daniel. Red-faced, red-haired, bloodshot-eyed, beer-bellied, reeking, this giant burst from the box on all fours, reared up in our faces, and grabbed at us.

I heard myself scream, then I scooped Ella onto my hip, gripped Daniel's hand, and fled. The man chased after us, lurching like Frankenstein's monster and bellowing drunkenly, "Come back! Stop! I'm not gonna hurtcha. I wooden hurtcha!"

At that moment I did not see him as just some homeless guy who'd lucked onto a castle of a carton and dragged it into the arroyo to sleep. Sub-Zero Man was the bogeyman incarnate. And now that the sleeping bag in the undergrowth had reminded me of him, I was completely spooked. The sleeping bag also reminded me of how big city parks are an "attractive nuisance" for all sorts of crimes and misdemeanors. Worst-case scenarios began running through my mind—dry runs for disaster, rehearsals for catastrophe. I got myself thoroughly primed for something bad to happen. I conjugated hideous what-ifs in the conditional, future, and future perfect tenses. All at once I was every bit my father's daughter, the one he had taught to fear all manner of things. Suddenly I was afraid, "sore afraid," as the Bible would say.

What I now feared was not just some off-leash pooch in the park getting in a scuffle with Quita but an out-of-nowhere stranger lurking in the deep end of the park in hope of just this: *me*, a lone female with a harmless-looking doggie. On city sidewalks or along a road within shouting distance of houses, I did not have to size up the threat potential of an approaching male; I just had to decide whether or not to nod and say hi. A few times, though, I had suddenly been overtaken in the park by a hard-breathing man on a sound-muffling dirt path, and with a jolt of adrenalin spurting through my body, had whirled around to see which it was: jogger or mugger.

"Diminished capacity" is a good description for what happens when, under extreme stress, reality becomes opaque. Fear makes reality murky. What I am trying to say is that even before anything happened, reality had taken on a certain viscosity for me. I had become thick—stupid— with fear.

By the time I reached the park's densely overgrown back entrance, I was a nervous wreck. I looked down from atop a high wall onto a street where traffic was swirling around a crew of four orange-vested Street Department workers. I had no idea where I was. I was like an explorer who did not know what land she had landed in, only that, having crossed a vast ocean, she was grateful to see any solid ground at all.

During a lull in the jackhammering, I called down to the workers, "Hello! Excuse me! Hello? Where *am* I?"

They did double takes of amazement and exchanged glances and shrugs before one of them posed the question asked of an alien creature, "Where the hell did *you* come from?"

"Davis Street," I said. "I came in at Davis Street."

All four of them eyed me as if I were nuts. "*Davis* Street! You come all that way through the *park*?"

"I didn't mean to, I just sort of kept going. Is it shorter if I take city streets back?"

"Depends. Where you tryin' to get to once you're out of the park?"

"Whitney Ave. At the New Haven-Hamden line."

They guffawed with incredulity and shook their heads some more; then they agreed amongst themselves that it would be faster—by miles—to go back through the park.

But one of the men shook his head worriedly and said, "I don't know. I ain't been in *that* part of the park you just come through since I was a kid. But me and my buddies? We wasn't up to no good in there, lady." He shot me a glance. "If you catch my drift."

I nodded that I did but gave a little one-shoulder shrug to mean I didn't see that I had much choice. Then I thanked them, waved good-bye, and went back through the stone pillars of Bishop's Gate. I felt forlorn and a little bit doomed, as if I were passing through Dante's gate, inscribed, "Abandon hope, all ye who enter here."

Though I still had no idea where I was, I did not consider myself lost. After all, all I had to do was go back the way I'd come. Nonetheless, I berated myself for what I had gotten myself into—going so far without knowing where I was going, getting myself in over my head, scaring myself. It felt familiar, typical.

To contain my fear over kids and men "up to no good," I cultivated anger. I let my mind free-range over actual and imagined incidents with out-of-control, off-leash dogs and their *laissez faire* owners. In the course of my first year in New Haven, I had become, shall we say, *disproportionately reactive* to unleashed dogs. I had had it with unleashed dogs. I had become a leash-law Pharisee, a martinet who could cite chapter and verse of city codes regarding the necessity of dogs being on leash. Given my adamant stance on leashes, it's ironic that the one I used on Quita was called a Flexi leash.

Quita and I had now spent a year on leash in New Haven, and in the course of it I'd had to constantly modify our routes to accommodate dog owners' cheery disregard, cavalier contempt, or belligerent scofflaw attitude toward leash laws. To them, exercising their dogs meant exercising freedom from leash laws. I could map whole areas of Hamden and New Haven, sticking pins in the map to mark encounters and hasty about-faces based on sightings of oncoming off-leash dogs. I could color code the pins to reflect the severity of the encounter from mild (owner contains off-leash dog until we pass by) to over the top (owner fails to heed my request to control his off-leash dog, claiming he's friendly, and his dog attacks Quita when she rebuffs his invitations to play).

I memorized off-leash dogs: where they lived, what their schedules were, and where and when impromptu doggie play groups met for off-leash romps. There was the footloose Newfoundland on St. Ronan Street; the Welsh corgi at 8:10 a.m. on the Orange Street Bridge; the doggie gang at Edgewood Park from 6:00 a.m. on; the old black Lab snuffling among the cypresses on Blake Street; the two bichons frises tearing off the deck on Deepwood … I was running out of safe streets. My leash had grown shorter and shorter.

I was more than halfway back to civilization—having already tiptoed warily past the sleeping bag in the undergrowth and converted my fear of it to further fuel my anger—and had, by now, worked myself up into quite a mental state, my mind being, let's remember, the only place where any of this was happening: the memories of past incidents; the imaginary future ones. Then suddenly two real live, here and now, off-leash dogs came trotting jauntily around a bend in the trail, and seeing Quita, perked up and sped up. A few moments later, two young women of nineteen or twenty—Ella's age—came strolling around the bend, their dogs' leashes dangling down their chests.

Now, you would think I would have welcomed the sight of two such harmless humans, but by now my anger had become the equal of my fear, and as you may recall, I was *sore* afraid. "Sore" not in the sense of "very" but in that of "angry, hothead."

So I yelled at them, "This park has leash laws! Get your damn dogs on leash!"

They stopped, traded stunned looks, and did nothing. If they'd been chewing gum, it would've fallen out of their mouths. I repeated what I'd said, inserting several obscene adjectives to modify the words *dogs* and *leash*.

Meanwhile, though the girls had stopped, their dogs kept coming. They were the kind of small, furry, self-important dogs that get spoiled rotten by their owners. Quita was straining toward them, barking and carrying on in her usual way.

I told the girls a third time to get their dogs on leash, and this time one of them did that world-weary adolescent thing of rolling her eyes, putting her hands on her hips, and as if addressing someone simply too dumb for words, said, "*God*, lady, relax. They're *friendly*."

I ask you, is there anything more infuriating than being told to relax when you are completely bent out of shape? "Well, mine *isn't*," I said. "So, for the last time, call your fucking dogs and get them on leash!"

Throwing me dirty looks, the girls took the leashes from around their necks and called the dogs to come. The dogs turned their heads to see if they were serious, and after a couple of playful feints, let themselves get nabbed.

Crisis over. Yes?

No. Once the girls had their dogs leashed, I unleashed myself on them. "What's the matter with you? Can't you read? Are you illiterate? Is that it? The signs plainly say, 'All Dogs Must Be on Leash.' I am so sick and tired of you people who think you're the exception to the rules, who think the rules don't apply to you!"

The girls exchanged reared-back looks—*Whoa, what's with her?* Then the one who had adopted the insulting adolescent stance made the mistake of saying "*sor*-ry" in that sarcastic, heavily two-syllabled way that is the opposite of contrition. It so enraged me that I proceeded to download yet another dose of my suppressed rage, making them the symbolic, composite culprits for every woodsy walk where I'd felt vulnerable and jumpy; for every off-leash dog that had rushed at Quita while I shouted at the owner, "Excuse me, hello? Sorry, but will you please put your dog on a leash till I get by?"; for every time I had apologized for the inconvenience of their having to leash their dog, because *I don't care if your dog is friendly, I don't care if your dog gets along with other dogs. Mine doesn't, so dammit, would you please just leash your dog for a minute?*; for all the times Quita had been charged by these "friendly" dogs, and I had gotten tangled, bruised, and knocked around in dogfights around my legs.

In New Canaan, Connecticut, dog owners wanting exemption from the town's leash requirement sought to use the American Kennel Club's Good Citizen Test to prove if their dogs were off-leash worthy. The test's ten requirements are: accept a friendly stranger; sit politely for petting; welcome being groomed and examined; walk on a loose leash; walk through a crowd without appearing overexuberant, shy, or resentful; sit and stay on command; come when called; react without going after another dog; react to distractions such as noises and joggers without giving chase; and behave for a handler other than its owner.

Now I ask you, how many *people* could pass that test? Lord knows I couldn't. Do *you* come when called? Sit politely for petting? How are *you* at walking through a crowd? And just how accepting are you of friendly strangers?

But the thing is, though I had been the one belittling them, I was now the one who felt small. My tirade at the hapless girls left me shaken, molten, jangled, flinching at the image of myself in my own eyes—never mind theirs—and cringing at the utter sham of myself as the God-seeking divinity school student.

But the girls turned out to be only the pregame warm-up.

It happened ten or fifteen minutes after they left. The man was sitting a little way into the wedge of woods at the juncture of the two roads, the one that allowed cars and the one that didn't. He was eating a sandwich. He had his dog with him. The dog was off leash, nosing around in the underbrush.

Oh no, I thought. *Not again.*

What did the man look like? Nothing special. A sandy-haired, nice-looking, midthirties guy in jeans and a short-sleeved plaid shirt. A carpenter, a contractor, an electrician. Someone you'd let in your house to fix something without a second thought. A guy with a white Explorer and a big, solid, black-and-tan dog. The one thing I registered above all else about him was that he did not look like someone to be afraid of. Unlike Sub-Zero Man in Malibu and the maybe-man in the sleeping bag deep in the woods, he wasn't the least bit scary to me. Plus, I was almost out of the woods. I was almost in the clear. That too may have emboldened me.

"Hey, mister!" I yelled. "Would you please hang onto your dog till I get by with mine?"

The man stood up, holding his sandwich away from his face. *Who, me?* his startled expression said. Like the girls, he was taken aback by my request, but he recouped more quickly. "It's okay, he's friendly."

"Well, my dog isn't good with other dogs. So will you just get your dog?"

"Sure, no problem."

Just then the snub-nosed, stub-tailed bruiser of a dog raised his head, saw Quita, and came trotting intently toward her.

"Jesus! Get your dog! Call your dog!"

The dog sped up. The guy yelled the dog's name twice and then made calm-down motions at me. "Lady, it's okay, it's okay. He's *friendly.*"

Those famous last words. I had heard them one too many times. It infuriated me, enraged me. Quita, picking up on my emotion, barked, snarled, and strained against the leash. His dog kept trying to sniff her rear end, and she kept wheeling and whirling around, frustrating his efforts to reach her. Sure enough, a dogfight broke out around my legs. I tried to knee his dog away, but he kept ducking around me to get at Quita.

The man threw his sandwich aside and came running out of the bushes. He kept calling the dog's name as he came. It's weird I can't remember it. He shouted it repeatedly, trying to get it to come. Was it Calvin? Cal?

I tried to escape with Quita. But she and the other dog were whirling and snapping around my legs. The man grabbed for his dog and missed.

"God, I've never seen him like this," he said.

Then his dog's head rammed hard into my knee, and a spew of rage came out of my mouth. I exploded like an espresso machine when a stuck steam valve suddenly lets go under the built-up pressure. I went ballistic. I came unglued. I loosed myself on the man who could not get his dog to come and could not catch his dog and was mystified by his dog's behavior. It was the one-too-manyth time I'd had a run-in with an off-leash, allegedly friendly dog charging Quita and me. His dog was the last straw. My encounter with the girls and their off-leash dogs had left me revved up. My safety was off, and my trigger finger was itchy.

With self-righteous indignation, using every noun, verb, adjective, adverb, and participial form of every obscenity I knew, I berated the man and his dog and all such stupid, selfish people like him with their uncontrollable off-leash dogs. I consciously refrained from calling the man *himself* an asshole, jerk, son of a bitch, or bastard, but how I managed to stop short I do not know, because I was on a tear.

All the time I was yelling at the man, he was yelling at his dog. He tried to grab its scruff. He snatched at its hindquarters. He became furious at the dog for evading and eluding him and not obeying him.

The man's inability to capture his dog humiliated and thus infuriated him. He had, after all, declared "no problem" when I had first asked him to get his dog. Now, having shown himself incompetent at controlling his dog, he was ready to kill him.

I kept trying to escape, but everywhere I turned, his dog lunged at Quita, and she would whirl around and the man would try to grab his dog, but the dog would elude him. At last the man got hold of his dog by a leg, threw him down on his side, and then, having no collar to grab, picked him up to lug him over to his SUV. I heard exertion, stress, and fury in the man's hard breathing.

Meanwhile, all the while, in some other part of my mind, I knew that my spiritual life was nothing more—and nothing less—than my ordinary life, this life right now, at this very moment. "A life," says Merton, "is either all spiritual or it is not spiritual at all." And I knew I was flunking mine, an abject failure who deserved an F.

I fled, keeping Quita close beside me as I ran along the narrow strip of dirt on the right-hand edge of the road. The drop-off was steep, and there was no guardrail. I had slowed to a brisk walk when I heard him coming. I was still in the woods, but a couple more bends would put me in the clear out by the Pardee Rose Garden.

He roared up behind me and then braked hard when he was abreast of me, slowing to a crawl to stay even with me. He leaned way over to say something to me out the open passenger window. His SUV yawed, the side-view mirror nearly grazing my left shoulder. I had nowhere to go. I was trapped between his vehicle and the drop-off. I was afraid he meant to crowd me over the edge. In the backseat, his dog was so thoroughly chastened it did not even stick its head out the open window to bark at Quita.

His vehicle crept ominously along beside Quita and me, almost bumping us. I kept walking, walking, walking, head down, eyes down, glad for the bill of my cap acting as a kind of blinder, glad my cap said only YDS, not Yale Divinity School.

The dynamic had shifted; it was almost palpable. It was his turn now. But when he first spoke there was something compassionate, almost pastoral in his voice.

"What is *wrong* with you?" he said. "Tell me. I just want to know. What is *wrong* with you?"

The way he asked left no doubt there was something seriously wrong with me; the only question was just what it *was*. But he sounded genuinely inquisitive, as if he really cared to know, was truly desirous of learning the diagnosis of my condition, the way if you asked a blind person how she'd lost her eyesight, she might say, "Macular degeneration" or "Diabetic retinopathy." At first he sounded as if he thought I really could explain what was wrong with me, as if he were worried about it. It almost made me cry, the seeming concern in his voice, the way that for a moment I felt profoundly *known*.

"No, really," he insisted, "what is wrong with you?"

He kept asking, and I kept my head down and kept walking. I did not glance over at him leaning across the passenger seat. I did not answer him, and I did not shake my head to mean I was not going to answer him. I was nonresponsive, nonreactive. I steadfastly ignored him.

And it drove him up the wall. By the fourth or fifth time he asked me what was wrong with me, the note of concern in his voice was gone. He yelled it at me in a demanding, accusatory way, not at all how you'd ask a blind person about the nature of her problem.

"What the *fuck* is wrong with you? No, really, what's your problem? You stupid cunt, what is your *problem*? Answer me, you fucking bitch, answer me!"

The thing is, I knew he was right. A stranger had unearthed my shameful secret: I did have a problem. There *was* something seriously wrong with me, this me that he had revealed. The jig was up. All these years I had tried so hard, had gone out of my way to be—or at least to be *thought* of as being—a thoughtful, nice, caring, decent person. All the years—a lifetime!—that I had worked so hard to keep my self-approval rating high had just been shot to hell. I had been shown up as a fraud.

He assailed me with his ruthless question a few more times and then, with a last furious spate of obscene epithets, gunned away. I moved in from the brink of the road, relieved he had not pushed me over the edge. But, of course, he had.

When I came out of the woods he was waiting for me. Engine off. Nosed in at a parking spot overlooking the Pardee Rose Garden. Laying in for me. He got out of his Explorer and started toward me. His dog paced agitatedly in the backseat.

Trying to give him a wide berth, I left the road and started up and across a grassy slope.

"Ma'am?" he said, following me. "Ma'am?"

Oh, yes, ever so polite he was now. Quite a change from "cunt" and "bitch." I kept angling across the slope.

He followed me a little way up onto the mowed slope and spread his hands as if to show he was unarmed. "Ma'am? Ma'am!"

Maybe he figured he'd better make nice in case I'd memorized his license plate. I couldn't see it while he'd crept along abreast of me, and when he drove off I was too rattled to notice it. Was he afraid I'd report him to the police? Report him for *what*? Leash-law violation and name-calling? Or who knows, maybe he wanted to apologize. I had no idea why he had changed his tune. But somehow his deferential "ma'am" made me feel close to crying and terribly, terribly sorry for myself.

Sooner or later I would have to come down off the slope. He stood between me and the way out of the park. If he kept following me, he could cut me off from it. But he stopped. He put his hands on his hips and stood still on the grassy slope while I came down the slope and walked on the road toward the exit onto Davis Street. Whatever he had planned to say when he got out of his Explorer and tried his new approach—the tactic of politely accosting me with "ma'am"—went forever unsaid.

Then it occurred to me that maybe he had let me go because he planned to follow me once I was out of the park. Formulating escape plans from fantasized danger is something I excel at. If he followed me, I would make a beeline to the Whitneyville Market, where Johnny, the butcher, could scare him off with a cleaver.

But he did not follow me or drive past me on Davis Street. I did not have to implement any of my baroque plans. When I reached Whitney Avenue, I went straight home. I had been gone over three hours and, foolishly, had not taken water for Quita or myself. Sweaty, dehydrated, sullied, I got in the shower as soon as I got home: "Gonna wash that man right outta my hair."

While I was showering, I thought about how what had happened to me in the park was a lot like what once happened to a family in Chicago. For years there had been a horrible smell in their modest house. They all smelled it, they all complained about it, but they just kept telling themselves that a rat or a possum or a stray cat had gotten trapped in the walls and died and that sooner or later it was bound to stop smelling. This went on, as I said, for *years*.

Then one night while they were having supper at the kitchen table the wall gave way, and the whole family was inundated with excrement. Turns out that, years ago, the pipe from the upstairs toilet had become disconnected, and all those years the walls had been filling up with shit, their very own shit. It was, I thought, an exquisite metaphor for what had happened to me in East Rock Park: the wall within me had finally buckled, inundating me with a lifetime of my own reeking shit and facing me with an immured Rapunzel who had finally knocked down the wall, let down her hair, and let the shit hit the fan.

While I was in the shower, the phone rang. I jumped a mile at the irrational thought that somehow it was *him*. On the third ring I got out of the shower. I had to. I had to know who was calling me right then.

It was my brother. Art began the call by asking me if I was all right. I asked why he was asking. He said he didn't know, just that he'd sat down as usual at nine o'clock to write his column for the paper but kept getting the feeling he should call me. It was now nine thirty in Tacoma, twelve thirty in New Haven. I did not plan to tell Art about what had happened, how badly I'd behaved, how ashamed I was of myself, how alarmed I was by the explosive force of my rage, how astounded I was when the wall collapsed and the flash flood of my accumulated shit hit me.

But the next thing I knew it was pouring out of me, the whole story. My brother, as always, was a good listener. He did not interrupt me, not once. I concluded by saying in a fake perky voice, "But, hey, let's look on the bright side here. I guess all that time and effort I put in at the Cathedral of Sweat this summer paid off. I mean, he didn't call me a *fat* bitch."

"That's not funny, Melinda," he said in a pained voice. Art, who had been so amused at the nickname of Yale's Gothic gym, and Art, who loved a rueful laugh at his own expense more than anyone I've ever known, did not find my attempt at humor amusing.

"Okay, okay, I'm sorry. But I've just got to find *some*thing funny about it," I said. And then I burst into tears.

That night, at 1:05 a.m., I woke up with my skin prickling and the soles of my feet aching with fear from a bad dream about my house in LA. I dreamed I did not know my own house. There were things about it I had not known before. There were lights I did not know how to turn off. The front door was open, but it had a barred security door on it. I was trying to put my house to bed. It was later than I had meant for it to be. Quita kept coming back downstairs to see what was taking me so long. At one point she brought me a little candy cane. It was ominous how smart and devoted she was. I was a little afraid of her. She knew my house better than I did. I couldn't get one light to turn off. She took care of it.

When I woke up from the dream, I thought I was in my house in LA and was terrified there was someone in it—I mean someone besides Quita and me. Then I remembered I was in my apartment in New Haven, but I was right about there being someone else there besides Quita and me. I did not know who it was until two years later.

In the meantime I tried telling myself that I just wasn't myself that day. But there's no such thing as not being yourself. Who else is there to be? I was myself all right that day in the park—but it was a self I did not want to own up to.

Most of the time I go around on the default setting of myself—the one that says I'm a very *nice* person. Thoughts matter, all those judgmental, gossipy, mean-spirited, one-down, depressing thoughts I have, but they don't count against me—against my self-image, I mean—the way what I *do* does. When my behavior doesn't jibe with my narrative of myself, when I cannot reconcile my presentation of myself, my self-deployment style, with who I think I am and am at a loss to account for myself, when I do or say something out of whack with my image of myself as that nice person, I might think, *Wow, where did that come from?*

But what happened in the park was so discordant, iconoclastic, and out of alignment with my basic notion of myself that my automatic-pilot persona could not play dumb about it. What happened in the park left me deeply shaken and asking myself, *Who* was *that? Was that my* true self?

I did not discover who it was in the park and in my "dream" house in LA until two years later when I came across Jung's concept of the shadow self and felt a *click* of recognition, the way when the last tumbler falls into place on a combination lock, it isn't so much a sound as a telltale sensation in your fingertips. I read Jung's definition of the alter ego and instantaneously *got* that my confrontation in East Rock Park, first with the girls and then with the man—but especially with the man—had been, in actuality, a confrontation with my shadow: "that which we have no wish to be."

"There is no light without shadow and no psychic wholeness without imperfection," Jung says. "To round itself out, life calls not for perfection but for completeness; and for this the 'thorn in the flesh' is needed, the suffering of defects without which there is no progress and no ascent." Jung recognized in St. Paul's *cri de coeur* a man doing battle with his shadow:

> I cannot understand my own behavior. For I do not do
> what I want, but I do the very things I hate ... I can
> will what is right, but I cannot carry it out. For I do not
> do the good I want, but the evil I do not want is what
> I do ... What a wretched man I am!

That day in East Rock Park my shadow took control, staged a *coup d'etat*, hijacked me, commandeered me. My shadow enveloped me, casting a long, dark shadow over my allegedly nice self: outweighing, outgunning, and outsmarting it. My shadow overshadowed me. It beat me up and robbed me of myself. I got mugged in East Rock Park. The assailant was my own disowned self, that foisted-off reject I wanted no part of because she didn't square with my self-image.

All I had intended to do on that hot August morning was go for a walk with Quita in the shady woods of East Rock Park. The collision that day of ordinary, everyday, opaquely sacred circumstances with Jung's concept of the alter ego resounds in the tagline of the popular radio series of the 1930s and '40s *The Shadow*: "Who knows what evil lurks in the hearts of men? The Shadow knows!"

It is my shadow self, "that which I have no wish to be," that makes the cross Jesus wants me to take up so damn heavy. And the intensity of my wrath in the park goes to show it only gets heavier with age. My shadow remains feral, but I now leave the back door ajar for her. I am willing to own her, to let her in. I have to: she is part of who I am.

Sometimes, growing up, my sister and I would call each other by our first names spelled backward. It was astonishing to me how strange, how *other*, something as familiar as our names sounded when simply reversed. I think of my shadow as being like that. Melinda and Adnilem: so opposite, so one.

24

MY DIV-ERSITY

One of the many ways I describe YDS to folks
is that we are a "changin' same."
—Emilie Townes, academic dean

T he message on my voice mail was so hesitant and vague I had
no idea what Elizabeth, the orientation co-chair, was calling
about. I only knew it had something to do with plans for a
diversity panel during BTFO. At YDS, where I was about to begin my
second year, orientation is called BTFO. It stands for Before the Fall
Orientation.

When I returned her call, Elizabeth rattled off whom she had lined
up for the panel: George for Hispanic; Christine for Asian; Terence
for African American; Stephen and Sharon, co-heads of the Gay and
Lesbian Coalition; and she herself for religious diversity.

"Great!" I said. "Sounds like you've covered all the bases. Want me
to bring a batch of brownies for refreshments afterward?"

There was an awkward pause. "Well, um, actually ..." Elizabeth
said.

My turn came third, after George, the Hispanic, and Sharon, the
lesbian. Like them, I began by introducing myself in standard YDS
fashion: name, where from, what denomination, and which degree.

"I'm Melinda from Los Angeles, Episcopalian, MAR. In case you're
wondering what I'm doing up here, I, as a grad-school geezer—what

is officially known as a 'mature learner'—am here to represent age diversity."

I was gratified it got a laugh but felt that revealing my age would be pushing my luck.

"I want to read you an excerpt from something by Merton," I said. With this crowd, it went without saying that this meant Thomas Merton, Trappist monk, Zen sensei, theologian, and social activist. I opened my tattered little pocket edition of *Thoughts in Solitude*.

> My Lord God, I have no idea where I am going. I do not see the road ahead of me. I cannot know for certain where it will end. Nor do I really know myself, and the fact that I think I am following your will does not mean that I am actually doing so. But I believe that the desire to please you does in fact please you. And I hope that I have that desire in all that I am doing. And I know that if I do this, you will lead me by the right road though I may know nothing about it.

I closed the book and looked out at 145 shiny new seminarians, the majority of whom were less than half my age.

"If Merton's words resonate with you," I said, "if you too have no idea where you are headed, or whether you belong here, or who your true self truly is—then guess what? I'm just like you! However 'diverse' our ages, we are kindred spirits.

"You're here for orientation, and so am I. I too am disoriented. You probably think that by my age I ought to have it all figured out—who I am, where I'm going, what I'm doing here—but the fact is, all my life, one way or another, that's pretty much what I've been up to: trying to get my bearings, trying to figure it all out, trying to penetrate the inner sanctum, that holy of holies, of *getting* it.

"As for just what this broad-spectrum, all-inclusive 'it' I'm so hell-bent on figuring out might be, all I know is that coming to YDS pertains to it and is of a piece with my lifelong search for some Rosetta stone or decoder ring that will make everything fall into place. The mystery will be solved—once and for all!

"Okay, that's me. I can't wait to find out what brings *you* here. Welcome aboard!"

25

THAT SUDDEN TUESDAY

*theodicy: the justification of God's goodness
in light of suffering and evil*
—*Westminster Dictionary of Theological Terms*

T he Red Cross representative who came to the hastily arranged memorial service late Tuesday afternoon on the eleventh put out a plea for MDivs with Clinical Pastoral Education to come to their New Haven headquarters. Crowds of people had shown up there simply because they did not know where else to go and the Red Cross is synonymous with disaster. Overflowing the parking lot and double-parking along Whitney Avenue, they were just sitting in their cars in shock. She was looking to YDS for people to come and sit with people in their cars: "Feed my sheep. Tend my lambs."

On Wednesday, September 12, I went to Old Testament Interpretation in dire need of whatever psalm, prayer, theological interpretation, or grace-filled insight the professor, an Irish Roman Catholic and renowned Old Testament scholar, would bring to bear on yesterday's cataclysmic events. I was stunned when, without so much as a moment of silence, he launched into his lecture, picking up where he'd left off on Monday, two days ago in the former world.

On Thursday the thirteenth, in my seminar on the main campus, even the notoriously outspoken Harold Bloom ("I am both well hated and well loved") was mute about it, the "it" that had made normal unimaginable. *The Odyssey* was that week's assigned reading, and Bloom saw to it that our discussion stayed hermetically sealed. It felt surreal, like being in a parallel universe in which what happened had not happened, as if word of the Twin Towers had not reached the occupants of the ivory tower.

On Friday the fourteenth, YDS students were notified by e-mail of a vigil on Yale's Cross Campus cosponsored by the Islamic Student Alliance and the Hillel students from the Joseph Slifka Center. We were beseeched to "please attend even if you are 'vigiled out.'"

The university segued quickly from vigils to panels, from dirge to discussion. A panel of distinguished historians and former presidential cabinet members was convened in Battell Chapel to discuss the topic "Faith Reflections on Mass Violence." A panel at YDS discussed "Theological and Ethical Responses to Violence." Panels were how the university processed "that sudden Tuesday." Panels were its forte. Panels were in its comfort zone.

The university's vigorously intellectual response was par for the course, but I'd expected the divinity school faculty's to be more pastoral, especially since a number of them were ordained priests and pastors. Perhaps the uniform failure of my YDS professors to even acknowledge the cataclysm hit me so hard because of what I had experienced in the immediate aftermath of another national tragedy.

I was a sophomore at Mills College when JFK was assassinated. At lunch in my dorm that fateful November day, it was announced that all afternoon classes were cancelled *except* Miss Sargent's Seventeenth-Century Poetry and Literature. I was taking it and was outraged that she—she alone!—was holding class. I blamed it on her being a stiff-upper-lip, tweedy Brit determined to "carry on" despite the staggering tragedy.

At two o'clock, without preamble, Miss Rouselle Sargent began reading John Donne's holy sonnet "Death Be Not Proud." Through the poetry of her beloved seventeenth-century poets, sonnet after sonnet, verse after verse, Miss Sargent eulogized John F. Kennedy and shepherded our desolate sorrow with language at its utmost reaches. Thanks to her courageously uncanceled class, by the time she closed the textbook and said, "Class dismissed," I came away not only with a radically altered opinion of Miss Sargent but with my dumbfounded grief having been lent eloquence.

That was what I'd hoped my YDS professors and even that self-described "old dinosaur and exhausted monster" Harold Bloom would have provided. Professor Bloom had told us he considers the King James Version of the Bible the finest thing ever written in English. Why, then, couldn't he have just read us a psalm or two of consolation from it?

26

ALTARPIECES AND ACADEMICS

Why carry a whole load of books
Upon your back
Climbing this mountain,
When tonight,
Just a few thoughts of God
Will light the holy fire.

—Hafiz

After the "No Grace Period" sign in a New Haven parking lot sparked my decision to stay a second year and get an MA, I declared a concentration in Religion and the Arts. It became my Eurail pass to Yale University—and liberated me from having to take Systematic Theology, a core course at YDS I feared and dreaded. Many of the course offerings at YDS made me drool—Augustine and Jung as Pastoral Theologians, Ascents to Heaven in Antiquity, Classics of Spiritual Poetry, Cosmos, Rupture, and Mimesis—but there were others, such as Systematic Theology, that might have made me sympathize with the students who, according to legend, stabbed to death with their pens the medieval theologian Eriugena for making them think too hard.

The only stipulation for YDS students taking courses in other schools and departments of the university was that the course material had to be "processed theologically." No problem! That, after all, is what the spiritual journey itself is all about: processing the raw material of one's life with awareness of the divine mystery within it. God gave us the nature to experience God, but it's up to us to endeavor to notice God's presence—and to make the connection. As the sign in a priest friend's office says, "It's the burning bush, dumb-ass!"

I was all over Yale's main campus, taking courses such as Power, Art, and Magic in the Renaissance, Zen Buddhism, and Medieval and Renaissance Manuscript Illumination. The zenith of my academic career was my "theological processing" of Emily Dickinson's poetry in my term paper for Harold Bloom's Genius and Genius seminar. With a theological lens through which to view her poetry, I focused on Dickinson's theology of time and sanctification of the quotidian: the way her father's house in Amherst was her holy ground and domestic activities, such as making her father's daily bread, were sacramental acts shot through with the divine for her.

I considered framing the page with Harold Bloom's handwritten—ink, not ballpoint!—comments:

A/Honors

Exquisitely conceived; eloquently expressed.
      Like your novel, this both holds you and allows you to learn through it.
I am grateful for having read both.
Phone me in the new semester, if you are around, and come to tea.

Honored though I was to be invited to tea by arguably our greatest living literary critic, I did not take him up on it for fear teatime might prove as awkward as the dismally ill-at-ease interval before class got under way when, hunched over the seminar table in his baggy black V-neck sweater, with his lugubrious baggy eyes, Professor Bloom would attempt to make small talk with us.

Taking hard-core courses at YDS like History of Christian Doctrine, I always found the biographical tidbits I gleaned about the theologians themselves far more alluring than the theology itself. As a novelist, I wanted to know about the formative experiences their theology may have been rooted in—their biographical backstories. I wanted to put flesh and blood and human warmth on the bare bones of their theology. I wondered, for instance, if the migraines and visions that twelfth-century abbess and mystic Hildegard of Bingen experienced from childhood might have originated from the trauma of separation from her family when, at the age of five, she was given to a nunnery as a "tithe child," the tenth child.

And then there was Thomas Aquinas: kidnapped as a teenager and held captive by his family for two years to try to prevent him from becoming a Dominican monk, with his own mother sending a prostitute to his chamber to tempt him. (It failed: Aquinas kicked her out.) His theological pondering made me pray for an *Aquinas for Dummies*, so imagine my delight in learning that, after having a direct experience of God near the end of his life, Aquinas abandoned his arcane life's work, saying, "All that I have written now seems like a pile of straw to me."

All *I* know is that I cared more about what happened in their lives—in the incarnation of God in the events of their lives—than about whatever theological "truths" they deduced from those events. It ought to have served as a tip-off to where my true interest lay that, shortly before coming to YDS, doing research for my screenplay about the Middle Ages' star-crossed lovers Heloise and Abelard, I had devoured Abelard's autobiography, *Historia Calamitatum: The History of My Misfortunes*, but skimped on researching the twelfth-century Scholastics' theological philosophy. The focus of my "costume drama" was not Abelard's theology but this charismatic teacher's illicit affair with his brilliant, beautiful private pupil Heloise, which resulted in her pregnancy and his castration and monastic sequestration.

I came to YDS to acquire formal knowledge of the God I had come to know ad hoc. I'd felt I needed theological ballast to offset my decidedly mystical tilt. I came to Yale intellectually starstruck and thinking that the study of theology would enrich the dimensions of my spiritual life and deepen my love of God. Just being there was a kind of intellectual *darshan*: a contact "high" that comes from simply being in the presence of a great teacher. But the academics were just that: *academic*. I found the study of theology heady but not "hearty" or soul filling.

My encounters with the holy did not come from theological knowledge but from my extracurricular spiritual experiences: the theology of Eli Whitney's meadow; the sacrament of spreading mulch at Regina Laudis Abbey; the revelation from my run-in with off-leash dogs in East Rock Park. For me, knowledge of God was experiential, not intellectual. The ongoing events and struggles in my life were the context of the spiritual.

Keen as I was to know about theologians' personal histories, I had resisted the idea of my theological studies nosing around in *mine*. I'd discovered, though, that whenever an assignment like the Looking on Darkness paper or a Gospel reading like the parable of the prodigal son triggered my past, it was often accompanied by a transformative, analgesic insight that lent the memory a healing aura, a sense of elegiac coda. I now found myself seeking *out* opportunities to create personal connections with my academic work.

That was why I knew immediately that the topic for my art history paper on an "antiquities issue" would be the fragmented Fra Angelico altarpiece I had seen in the Yale Art Gallery. The fifteenth-century panels had recently been confirmed as having belonged to a triptych by the Renaissance master Fra Angelico. Two of the panels belonged to Yale, and two belonged to the J. Paul Getty Museum in Los Angeles. I relished the fact that the altarpiece, like me, united LA and Yale. The exhibition at Yale had brought the panels together for the first time since their separation by a carpenter's saw centuries ago. The fragmentation of early Italian altarpieces was a lucrative and common practice in the late eighteenth and early nineteenth centuries. The prerequisite for it was the secularization of sacred images. Once altarpieces became dissociated from their original sacred function, they became simply aesthetic objects, works of art, not objects of veneration.

The fragmented Fra Angelico altarpiece not only made an ideal candidate for "theological processing," it also intertwined with my personal history in two meaningful ways. First of all, it was a reminder of the Fra Angelico panel with the "literary" angel that my sister had FedExed to me when Ella was first hospitalized, claiming it was a last-minute birthday present when what it was, in truth, was an act of pure compassion.

The other personal connection I had with the fragmented Fra Angelico at Yale derived from a piece that Ella had created in a summer weekend workshop at the Brentwood Art Center in Los Angeles when she was sixteen. The workshop was restricted to adults, but she'd gained entry to it by permission of the instructor, who was familiar with her work from previous classes.

By the time of the opening-night reception in September, Ella had been readmitted to NPI and was not able to go. But I went, curious to see the range of creative results from a dozen artists dealing with the same time constraints and required materials, including a forty-inch-by-thirty-inch fiberboard. I went alone and, snagging a glass of wine, decided to make a circuit of the exhibit to take a quick look at all the pieces before zeroing in on whichever one was Ella's.

One piece had spectators thronged three deep in front of it, exchanging raised-eyebrow looks and wide-eyed *whoas.* Through a slight gap between onlookers, I glimpsed a child's nailbrush and knew the piece was Ella's. I approached it with a mixture of pride and apprehension. A viewer stepped away, somberly shaking his head. I took his place.

It was not just the blue piggy nailbrush I recognized. *Everything* on the piece was familiar to me: swags of fabric cut from an evening gown of my mother's; my father's handwriting on a strip torn from a letter; a vertical column of plastic med cups from the NPI dispensary with "Ella" written in black marker on each; photos of the sentinel cypresses along our driveway and of the arched bridge over the water lilies at Monet's Giverney, where Ella and I had stood together the summer before last; the cloth name tag in the lower right-hand corner, her first use of the signature that became her trademark. I knew not only the sources of these things but the resonance these images, textures, and words had for her: cherished places, cherished words, cherished people.

The entire surface of the fiberboard was densely, *intensely* covered with photographs and painted-over photographs, layer upon layer of newspaper stamped with stenciled letters, and collage strips torn from letters to her and poetry by her.

Mounted on a hinged flap within a large black rectangle was a photo of Ella as a towheaded cutie pie of three in pink high-top sneakers, a pink tutu, a string of beads on her bare chest, and arms raised to crown herself with a sparkly cardboard tiara. Looking at the photo of my giggly little sprite in a tutu and tiara surrounded by the poetry of my anguished teenage daughter writing about wanting to "unfinalize" her "paraphrased presence," something inside me buckled under the weight of her pain.

I leaned in close to read another of the poems framing the photo just as an onlooker reached past me and lifted the hinged flap to see what was underneath it.

Until that moment, standing in a crowded art exhibit, I had not known a Polaroid existed, an "after" photo she had taken of herself the Sunday afternoon three weeks after her first discharge, when she had tried to stop one kind of pain by inflicting another kind on herself. The Polaroid showed a vulnerably lovely, pallid, sixteen-year-old Ella with her long hair dyed black, pushed back from her face, and her head turned slightly away and tipped back to show a Modigliani length of neck with thin red lines across it.

I had left her home alone for one hour in broad daylight while I went somewhere not ten minutes away. Coming home, I turned into my cul-de-sac, and my heart seized at the sight of the black Camaro parked haphazardly in front of my house. Ella's NPI doctor had made several house calls since her discharge—but never before on a Sunday.

I ran into the house, shouting, "Ella! Ella?"

Her doctor was standing at the foot of the stairs. He was unshaven and in a sweatshirt and jeans. He looked so unprofessional and scraggly that his presence in my house felt off base.

"Where's Ella?" I said. "What's happening?"

"She's okay," he said. "Meet us at the ER. We were just leaving."

"What *happened*?"

"She took a bunch of Benadryl, cut herself, got scared, and called me," he said.

"How much?"

"Probably not enough to have to have her stomach pumped."

I ran upstairs. Ella was standing by the windows in her crimson room. I was struck by her height against the light. When had she gotten so tall? Then she turned toward me, and I saw what she had done to herself—the cuts on her face and neck and arms and legs. But it was her eyes that scared me the worst. Ella was alive, but her eyes were not.

I had read enough about self-cutting to know that it is not about suicide. The purpose it serves is to create a temporary distraction *from* pain. The physical pain of the cutting mitigates the far greater emotional pain. The cuts were deemed superficial by the boyishly young ER doctor who assessed *how deep* and *how many*, but the sheer number of cuts Ella had inflicted on herself—117—gave me a heartsick sense of the unsustainable volume of her pain.

It went without saying that she would be readmitted to NPI straight from the ER. Her doctor told me just to drop off her stuff on the ward and not try to see her today. I nodded my understanding: *I am her mother. I upset her.* It also went without saying that NPI's assessment of my daughter's safety—the major criterion for her release—had been wrong.

I hovered by Ella's piece with the protective instinct of all mother creatures for their young. What I was seeing on exhibit was so forceful, raw, and personal an iconography of pain and darkness and yearning that I wanted to stand squarely in front of it with my arms outspread to block it from view.

And as I stood there, it came to me that if there were a Lourdes for adolescents in distress—a pilgrimage site for afflicted, angst-filled, miserable, food- and/or mood-disordered, suicidal, anxious, alienated, stricken adolescents—there could be no more fitting and honoring altarpiece at its shrine than this untitled masterpiece with its idiosyncratic but universal iconography of the consolation of beauty and the pit of despair.

Since I did not identify myself as the mother of the artist, the comments I heard from viewers were uncensored. I did not want to leave it, but I could not bear to remain beside it any longer, watching strangers wince, shake their heads, and softly gasp, "Oh my God!"

When the show ended, I went to the Brentwood Art Center to pick it up. The mother of one of Ella's K–8 classmates was at the reception desk. Our kids had whacked piñatas at each other's birthday parties. I greeted her and told her I had come for Ella's piece. The way she lowered her eyes said she knew which one it was. Perhaps it was in reaction to that mother's obvious discomfort that I brought home my daughter's altarpiece and hung it like a *mezuzah* by the door I use coming and going from my house.

I alone knew that the academic paper I wrote on the fragmented Fra Angelico altarpiece in the Yale Art Gallery had personal reverberations, linking me to my sister's compassionate fragmentation of another pair of Fra Angelico panels and to my daughter's creation of an autobiographical altarpiece.

27

SHOW AND TELL

Then you shall call, and the Lord will answer;
you shall cry for help, and he will say, Here I am.

—Isaiah 58:9

"Wow," I said, halting a forkful of scrambled eggs midway to my mouth. "Do you think people will be ready to open up and talk about that right after breakfast?"

It was one week before graduation. Last evening, twenty or so of us Episcopalian "middlers," second-year seminarians, had arrived for a weekend retreat at Wisdom House in Litchfield, Connecticut, the town with the most photographed church in America. The retreat leaders were the head of the Annand Program for Spiritual Formation and my Looking on Darkness professor from my first semester at YDS.

At the Friday session, the professor held forth fireside with a lengthy, lofty, formal presentation, complete with a flip chart. It was hardly what we had envisioned as our evening's entertainment. It was after ten o'clock before we had a chance to get into the wine and snacks. My friend Anne and I carried brimming plastic cups of red wine straight up to our room, got into our jammies, gossiped awhile, and conked out.

Now, after going through the breakfast buffet line, I'd sat down across from the two leaders, and just by way of conversation, said, "So! What's on the agenda for the morning session?"

"The topic for the morning session," the professor said somberly, "is 'Your Experience or Image of God.'"

That's when my fork halted in midair, and I felt my stomach fist with instant resistance to the idea of being asked to spill the beans to a roomful of people, some of whom I barely knew and one of whom I couldn't stand, about my one and only direct personal experience of God.

One week before graduation, the selfsame professor who, in my first class on my first day at YDS, had sent me into a tailspin by assigning a paper on a personal encounter with darkness as our point of entry to his class, was now going to ask us to tell about a personal encounter with God. The symmetry of it was like a pair of brackets encompassing not only the temporal span from my point of entry to my point of exit at seminary but its spiritual arc as well.

Maybe it is perfectly legit to ask seminarians on retreat to reveal their experience, if any, of God, but it struck me as spiritually prurient on his part, the equivalent of springing the topic "My Best Sexual Experience" on a panel of sex therapists. The topic seemed all the more heavy-handed in light of the ponderous formality of his evening session not having created the atmosphere of closeness and trust that such a personal topic requires.

It was snowing like crazy when we gathered after breakfast. The mid-May storm raging outside and the fire ablaze in the fireplace created the sort of cozy, cut-off-from-the-world encapsulation that makes storytelling ideal. But when the professor announced the topic, "Your Experience or Image of God," a palpable frisson went through the room, followed by nervous laughter, lame jokes, and quick exchanges of oh-shit glances.

Hoping to get the ball rolling, the co-leaders each recounted a personal encounter with the holy. The professor's had occurred while he was driving alone on a rural highway and he suddenly had an intense sense of enclosure, as if bubbled, with the presence of God; the Annand Program director's had happened during his wife's obstetrical crisis. Each had experienced what the ancient Celts spoke of as "a thin place," a spiritually porous place where the membrane between the human and the divine worlds is exquisitely permeable, a sacred space, a holy milieu.

Then they opened up the topic to us, and a long, loooong silence ensued. You'd have thought they'd just asked us to violate some YDS "Don't ask, don't tell" policy about seminarians' autobiographical accounts of God. Until that retreat, I'd had no idea what varieties of religious experience, if any, my seminary compatriots had had. Despite what folks may think, seminarians really don't sit around the refectory swapping stories of divine interventions.

Until that retreat, I had exchanged "experience of God" stories with only one person at YDS: my friend Steve. After a winter hike while on retreat together at Holy Cross Monastery in West Park, New York, we sat in my car with the heater running to finish a conversation, which led, in turn, to our confiding in each other.

It was Jenny who ended the long, awkward silence—the one I would have voted "least likely to go first." Gentle, self-effacing, forty-something Jenny with the blue clogs, the blue corduroy jumper worn like a school uniform, and her dishwater-blonde braid hanging down the back of her Norwegian ski sweater offered herself as the icebreaker; and the session I thought would never get off the ground got off to a flying start as she told us in a quiet, quavery voice how she had thought she could never love anything or anyone as much as she had loved her Johnny Walker. But now, she said, a God better than even the finest single malt scotch permeated her stomach and chest and all her insides with the same comforting warmth. Jenny had just revealed to a roomful of seminarians that she had once been an alcoholic but was now inebriated with God.

Thanks to Jenny, we started to tell our stories. They ran the gamut from hers about God *replacing* scotch to Robert's about *having* a scotch with Jesus at 2:00 a.m. in his pj's and bathrobe as he wrestled with a big decision. That snowy May morning at Wisdom House, I heard stunning, deeply moving, unquestionably authentic stories of visual, acoustic, olfactory, sensory, and thermal experiences of God: visions, voices, smells, sensations of warmth and of touch "like a hand gently turning my cheek."

Every single one of us who'd had a personal encounter with God had come away from it feeling not just blessed but humbly honored, and in some way, divinely favored. ("Fear not, Mary," the angel Gabriel says to the Virgin Mary, "for you have found favor with God.") Theologian Karl Rahner's description of the effect of God's "self-communication" is that it alters our relationship to our horizon, to the mystery that surrounds us. God's one-time mystical "intrusion" into my consciousness altered mine so radically it was no longer a matter of my believing in God but of trusting my own experience of God.

The "Image of God" topic was intended as the alternative for those who had not yet had an experience. There was not a whiff of stigma attached to those who told about their image or idea of God. After all, an instance of divine favor is by no means a requirement for admission to seminary—or for that matter, to the priesthood. It was, by and large, the young seminarians, who had not yet experienced life's more solemn joys or the hard blessing of sorrows that bring you to your knees, who exercised the Image of God option. One young woman told us how, as a child, she had imagined God coming into her room with the warm air from the heating vent. Another woman said she imagined God as the safe place her mother's lap had been while she was being held and read to within her mother's encircling arms.

As always when a roomful of people is randomly taking turns, there was the matter of deciding just when to chime in. I tried not to start scripting in my head what I was going to say, but my daughter's pivotal role in the experience I was going to tell made me anxious to reveal as few specifics as possible. What I was hoping was that someone else's experience would dovetail enough with mine to let me get away with "Ditto!" and a highly abridged account.

The common thread running through nearly all our stories was that a personal experience of God was intimately linked with a personal encounter with darkness: it emerged from it, came *of* it. It was when we were *in extremis*, our lives brought to a beveled edge, that God had graciously manifested himself to us in some indubitable way. Our mystical encounters had not happened in some nebulous void but in direct connection with crisis and pain. The depths of despair were the heights from which we encountered God, the lows of life, our spiritual highs.

With just three of us to go, I lucked out, getting to ride the coattails of a guy whose experience bore striking similarities to mine. His crisis had to do with his calling. Mine involved Ella and a Volvo.

28

A GLINT OF GOD

Why is it that when we talk to God it's called prayer,
but when God talks to us it's called psychotic?
—Lily Tomlin

The first thing Ella wanted to do after her final discharge from NPI was get her driver's license. Having missed out on that rite of passage eight months before on her sixteenth birthday, she was now impatient to join the ranks of the licensed and pooh-poohed my suggestion that she take a couple of brushup lessons from the driving school she'd attended with her learner's permit. She declared herself ready.

"Well, okay then," I said and took her to the Santa Monica DMV.

Ella didn't even get to the driving part. She flunked the written test. I was stunned. Straight-A Ella flunking a multiple-choice test on traffic laws?

As if it were a fluke, she retook the test a few days later—and flunked again. Now I was really worried. Was she not even bothering to study? Or had her illness—or the slew of medications and procedures aimed at treating it—left her incapable of passing a simple test?

Since she'd have to wait some period of time to retake it if she failed on her third try, she decided to take the brushup lessons; then she squeaked by on the test with exactly the permissible number of misses. Ella got her license, and I got her a Volvo that was the same age as her brother: nineteen years old.

One week later, Ella rear-ended a Russian masseuse in a strip mall in Hollywood. (What she was doing there I never knew—Ella, not the masseuse.) I handled it out-of-pocket to keep her exorbitant teen-rate car insurance from skyrocketing further, but we got taken to the cleaners by the Russian's sleazy, gold-chain-wearing boyfriend.

On her seventeenth birthday, Ella asked to go over to a friend's for a little while after dinner and have her cake later. The friend lived nearby, so I said okay. Ella called an hour later.

"I'm okay," she said, "but I had an accident, and my car is totaled."

"I'll be right there," I said. "Where are you?"

"On Sunset," she said.

"Where on Sunset?"

"In front of the Beverly Hills Hotel."

The Beverly Hills Hotel is not in Santa Monica, where her friend lived.

"Is Jane okay?" I said.

"I'm not with Jane," she said. "I'm by myself."

"I'll be right there."

When I arrived at the flare-lit scene, cops were directing traffic around the wreckage, waving along gawkers, and sweeping glass from the Volvo's shattered windshield out of the intersection in front of the flamingo-pink hotel with the famous Polo Lounge. Ella's stalwart Volvo was so demolished it made me queasy to think of her having been inside it, but she was unscathed, and as it turned out, the accident was not her fault.

Ella *was* at fault, however, for lying to me about her whereabouts, and driving home from the scene of the accident, I asked her what she had been doing in Beverly Hills.

"None of your business!" she screamed.

We rode in silence the rest of the way. Passing through the kitchen, she cut a hunk of her birthday cake before I could light the candles and sing "Happy Birthday" and took it upstairs to her room to eat while on the phone with Jane, the friend whom she had not gone to see.

Six weeks later, while I was in Kansas City visiting family, she called to tell me she'd hit a car with the right-of-way at the intersection behind the Starbucks in Brentwood. She said she was fine, but the front of the like-new, five-year-old Volvo I'd just gotten her was "sort of all bashed in."

First thing after returning to LA, I went to the body shop to see the damage and authorize the repairs. I came home in a foul mood and called Ella downstairs to tell her how much her lousy driving was going to cost me. An ugly fight erupted in the kitchen. Ella came unglued. She exploded in my face like an IED. I had never seen her like this. She stormed out on foot with just her purse. I did not know she had just found out her father had terminal cancer and that he had issued a gag order to tell no one—especially me.

A week later, the rookie priest inadvertently informed me of it. By then, I'd already asked him to provide a home for her. Had I known about his cancer, I would have thought it too much, under the circumstances, to ask of him. But as it turned out, the time she spent living with her father in the last year of his life was an enormous gift—to both of them.

Right after moving to Alan's in Malibu, Ella quit therapy. She had now fired both her mother and her doctor. She was virtually on her own. She was living with her father, but under his present circumstances and based on history, she'd have precious little oversight.

In August, two weeks before the start of her senior year, heading into town from Malibu, Ella came around a curve on Pacific Coast Highway, and blinded by sunlight hitting her dirty windshield, saw, too late, that traffic had come to a dead stop directly in front of her. That was the end of car #2, the spiffy cream puff with the brand-new grille, front bumper, and bodywork. No injury to anyone: God bless Volvos!

After it was declared a total loss, Ella wrote me a formal letter in turquoise ink on three-hole notebook paper in which she laid out with what she considered impeccable logic her rationale for why it was absolutely necessary for me to buy her another car, the third in eight months. Though not living with me, not speaking to me, not wanting to have anything to do with me, she had to make her case to me, the abominable mom, instead of to her dad, the car enthusiast, because under the terms of my divorce all the children's expenses, other than tuition and health care, were my responsibility. I had to admire her for signing it, "Sincerely." Desperate though she was for wheels, she'd be damned if she'd suck up to me and lie through her teeth and sign it, "Love."

The week after the Malibu wreck, I was at my friend Cory's for dinner and told her about Ella's latest accident and her car-request letter and my agony over what to do about my daughter's transportation crisis. To Cory it was a no-brainer. She was outraged I was even considering getting Ella another car. She called it "condoning" her. How could I jeopardize Ella's safety and that of everyone else on the road by putting her behind the wheel of yet another car? Did I want to get her killed? What more proof did I need that she was incapable of driving responsibly? Didn't I see that Ella's accidents were automotive reenactments of what she herself felt like? A wreck!

Cory was right.

But my daughter had to get to school, and no city bus, school bus, classmate, or car pool came anywhere near her father's house. And he wasn't about to chauffeur her: He was fighting cancer. Besides, disruption of his ironclad daily routine had never been tolerable to him. As far as I could see, it was essential, not optional, for Ella to have a car.

I came home from Cory's tormented about what to do, anguished with indecision, and at the end of my rope. I went straight to bed but sat bolt upright, sobbing and praying for real, praying like crazy, praying like the psalmist who says, "In the day of my distress I sought the Lord; my hands were stretched out by night and did not tire." I jackknifed over, elbows on knees, and pounded my fists against the covers and prayed out loud—*loudly* out loud—a prayer of such last-ditch, no-shit desperation that to even call it "prayer" is putting it way too politely. I cried out to God from the sum total of my whole being.

"God, oh God, oh *God*, tell me what to do. I don't know what to *do*, I don't know what to *do*! Help me, help me, *help* me. I'm so tired, I'm so tired, I'm just so fucking *tired* of having to know what to do. Tell me what to do! You have to, you *have* to. You've *got* to *tell* me, just *tell* me. Tell me what to *do*!"

And God did.

In the middle of the night, he woke me up. I don't know how. I did not hear my name called the way Samuel did in the temple. All at once

I was just totally awake. I knew I had not awakened on my own. I had been awakened, explicitly awakened. But I was not afraid.

I sat up and looked around my nighttime room—without my contact lenses, there was a fuzzy nap to it—and the room was just itself, nothing more, nothing less. I touched Quita, curled up asleep on the bed, and she raised her head for a moment. I was awake, not dreaming that I was awake. I knew I was sitting up in my bed and that my eyes were open and I was seeing my room and that my room looked as usual. I was puzzled but not afraid.

Then God spoke to me. God told me what to do. In two words God answered my prayer. A two-word sentence with an imperative verb and a direct object. I don't mean I heard a voice telling me. Nor did I think the words. God made the words present in my mind. Anyone who meditates regularly knows how pesky and intrusive thoughts can be—how you catch yourself thinking thoughts and you relinquish them only to have them rise again, and so forth and so on. It's what Buddhists call "monkey mind." But I knew this two-word commandment was not a thought *I* had had.

My prayer of sheer despair had made room for God's presence, and now God filled the space I had created. My awareness of his presence was in the words uttered—not spoken but somehow uttered—into my consciousness. I heard nothing. An auditory hallucination—"hearing voices"—shows that we hear with our brain, not merely our ears. But there was no reason for me to look around to see who had spoken: I heard nothing.

The words God spoke were like inaudible sound—no, *legible* sound, like puffs of skywriting on my forehead, as if, had I gone to a mirror, I might have seen the words vaporously on my forehead—or the *sensation* of the letters there, the way I used to write words on my kids' backs with my finger for them to guess from the sensation of the letters on their skin.

The words were like two small objects—two pebbles—that I could pick up and stick in my pocket. I did not manufacture them. They were not of my mind's making. They were instilled, implanted, introjected, blended into my mind. I don't know how—that is the divine mystery—but I heard words within my mind that did not come from my mind. I had no doubt as to their source.

Show faith, God said.

Those were God's words. Those were God's instructions. That was God's command to me. Not to *have* faith but to *show* faith. To show faith in God to keep Ella safe. And to show faith in Ella herself—a faith that, given her driving record, was like grace itself: unearned, unmerited, pure gift. To *show* faith is to demonstrate it, to *do* something about it. I understood what that meant. I knew what it required of me: another car for Ella.

Out of God's tender mercy, God's loving-kindness, God saw fit to grant me a two-syllable sliver, a linguistic glint, of his vast, transcendent, radiant powers. *Show faith* shines in my heart as a reminder of my encounter with the holy, of having received a nod from God's own being. The perceptible intensification of God's presence that I experienced—a heightening, a deepening, call it what you will—left no leeway for any doubt whatsoever. Theologian Marcus Borg compared mystical experience to orgasm: "You don't say, 'Hmm, I think maybe I just had one.' You *know* it!"

Although unquestionably outside the norm, my experience was not something I could explain away, talk myself out of, or pooh-pooh as imaginary. My experience of God was a self-authenticating experience that lifted me from the realm of faith, with its ever-shifting tides of doubt, into a realm of quiet confidence.

Even so, having a mystical experience of God is not the same thing as having a spiritual life. My experience, once over, was *over*, and as with any memory, gradually lost its immediacy and vigor. It remains the epicenter of my spirituality, a singular, treasured touchstone of my brush with the ultimate reality, but the goal of the spiritual life is not to have a one-night stand of intimacy with God but to have a long-term, ongoing relationship with God.

I did not tell Ella she had God, not me, to thank for her third Volvo, a ten-year-old with 110,705 miles on it. She drove it without incident, with nothing more serious than parking tickets, until it finally gave up the ghost. Had I gotten a vanity plate for it, it would have said: SHO F8TH.

29

END-TIMES

The time of my departure has come.
I have fought the good fight.
I have finished my course. I have kept the faith.
—II Timothy 4:6–7

D aniel's college graduation came right smack in the midst of my final exams. There was something wacky but wonderfully symmetrical about our coast-to-coast, back-to-back commencements: the middle-aged grad-school mom flying to the West Coast for her son's BA ceremony, the new grad flying to the East Coast for his mom's MA ceremony.

Daniel's graduation was one of those milestone family occasions where Alan's absence was painfully glaring. There was still enough of a lingering formality between Ella and me that, rather than share a room at our hotel, I got her a room of her own. Besides, I needed to burn the midnight oil studying for exams.

The title of the commencement speech at Daniel's graduation was "The Immediacy of Sacred Things." I took notes as if I were at a lecture at YDS with material that was bound to be on the exam.

"I left here with a mental and spiritual backpack I knew how to keep full," said the illustrious alum who delivered the speech.

The previous October, at Yale's tercentennial ceremony, Harvard president Lawrence Summers had said virtually the same thing in his congratulatory speech: "One of the things a great university does," he said, "is to increase one's capacity to flourish."

The ceremony was so late getting under way I had to dash off to catch my plane as soon as Daniel was handed his diploma, flipped the mortarboard's tassel to the "graduated" side, and marched across the stage to Ella's and my unrestrained whoops and cheering. I landed in Hartford, Connecticut, at midnight, drove to New Haven, and took my final exam in Power, Art, and Magic in the Renaissance at 9:00 a.m. I got an A.

The night before my Old Testament final I dreamed I was sitting in the lecture hall and someone called me a cow. I said, "I am not a cow." I was angry. I woke up and knew it was about that line, "Listen up, you cows of Bashan." I was absolutely convinced that it was going to be one of the IDs on the final exam, and I couldn't remember which book in the Old Testament it was from. I lay there thinking of good reasons it could be in several different ones, but I was pretty sure it was from Amos. He's all about social injustice, and Bashan was famous for its sleek cattle: "Hear this word, you cows of Bashan on Mount Samaria, you women who oppress the poor and crush the needy and who say to their husbands, 'Bring us some drinks!'"

Then it hit me that I was lying there in the middle of the night racking my brain over a biblical citation—meaning I now knew the Bible well enough to think about the likely source of one particular quotation.

Daniel did not come to my graduation after all. He called from the airport in Portland, Oregon, first to say his flight had been delayed, then to say it had been cancelled, and then to say he would now be arriving in Hartford the next morning after spending the night in *Atlanta* unless anticipated thunderstorms delayed departure from *there*.

I went in to wake Ella from a nap—she had arrived from LA the day before—and clue her in to what was happening. I floated the idea that maybe Daniel shouldn't try to come. I put them on to talk to each other, and they concluded that it made sense for him not to come but the question was: How would Mom be about that?

Fine, thank you. I really was. My graduation was something I wanted to share with both my kids, but I could well have wound up in the supremely ironic position of missing one of my graduation events in order to meet Daniel's delayed flight from Georgia.

So I did the sensible thing: I released him from having to come. The word *released* was a key word around the div. school in May. Whether or not the bishop of an Episcopalian MDiv's sponsoring diocese released a candidate to seek employment outside the diocese was the determining factor in his or her immediate future. He had done his best to come. Now that he wasn't coming, I also could stay put for the entire commencement ceremony and not have to leap up, disrobe in public, and dash out of Woolsey Hall to get him *back* to Hartford for his return flight.

Releasing Daniel also meant I could now spend time alone with Ella. In a way, though, I wished I were capable of releasing her as well—releasing her not from my graduation but from *me*. I pictured the way I open my hands to free a bird that has flown into the house and been unable to find its way out again. Standing at the open window, I launch it from my cupped hands with a little dip and a gentle upward toss, saying, "Off you go! See? You're just fine now."

My MDiv friend Dollink got it right when she said that graduation was either church or cocktails for three days straight: The Yale University baccalaureate service was the kickoff event. Then came the YDS community worship service at a local church, followed by an evening prayer service at Berkeley, followed by an elegant sit-down dinner that was a far cry from the previous week's backyard pig roast. Finally, on Monday, May 27, 2002, gowned and with devil's horns and/or aluminum halos adorning our mortarboards, we lined up at YDS and then marched down Prospect Avenue to the Yale University Commencement Exercises on Old Campus, where Steven Spielberg, among others, received an honorary degree. Finally, after the YDS lunch at the Omni Hotel—where cocktails ensued—at three o'clock came the final event: the divinity school's diploma hand-out ceremony at elegant Woolsey Hall.

The final word in the benediction that ended the whole commencement extravaganza was "Good-bye." Before saying it, the

Right Reverend Frederick Borsch, Episcopal bishop and interim dean of Berkeley Divinity School at Yale, reminded us that "good-bye" is a contraction of "God be with you." He then uttered it softly and with such poignant sweetness that it felt like what it originally was: a farewell blessing.

The YDS faculty in all their velvet-striped, silk-hooded regalia processed ahead of us out of Woolsey to form a cheering gauntlet as we graduates marched out behind them. It was a simply splendid moment, being swamped by our high-fiving, hugging, fist-pumping professors, who were beaming with parental pride at us, their theological progeny.

Voice mail congrats awaited me at home. My sister's was a biblical quotation about having run with perseverance the race that was set before me. (Hebrews 12:1, thank you very much.) My friend Chase's said, "Good omen! Twelve oaks have sprouted from the Yale acorns I collected while visiting you last October." What, I wondered, would come of *my* Yale acorns: those sixteen courses; all the elective extras; a bazillion worship services. And what about my fellow seminarians— would any mighty oaks of friendship sprout from them?

I was glad my brother's "Attagirl!" was on my voice mail, so I could listen to it over and over. An "Attagirl!" was Art's highest accolade, and he awarded them very sparingly. One time, though, when I was freaking out over a paper on Anselm's *Cur Deus Homo,* "Why God Became Man," Art bestowed an "Attagirl!" on me in advance. My brother gave me an "Attagirl!" on *credit*!

My next-to-last night in New Haven I finally had dinner at Mory's, that quintessentially Whiffenpoofy, Yale-of-yore eating club and watering hole. I went with my YDS friends Steve and Mark and their respective partners, Andrew and Pete. The menu was outdated, the food simply dreadful, and the ritualized shenanigans performed with the alcoholic concoctions served in two-handled, silver-plated Mory's Cups hopelessly sophomoric. The drink we ordered for the table was the toxic blue of Tidy Bowl.

Billy, our waiter, had been serving the tables down at Mory's for thirty-two years. I asked him if he was glad when women were admitted.

"To Yale or to Mory's, madam?" said he.

Our conversation, of course, centered on what we would be doing now that we had graduated and on our classmates' post-YDS plans. For most, seminary was a means to a known end—ordination or a religious studies PhD program or some kind of lay ministry. Since I didn't know my "end," I didn't know if YDS was a means to it or not. I'd had to check the last box on the YDS form for new alums: "My plans at this time remain uncertain."

All four of them were off to new lives in New York City. I would be resuming my former life in Los Angeles. Concerned I might be feeling left out, Pete turned to me and, in the upbeat, encouraging voice with which one makes a child's small accomplishment sound grand, said, "And, Melinda, now you're *edified*!"

After I got home, I thought about Pete's sweet effort and decided it was high time to find out just what "edification" actually meant. The word had been tainted for me ever since my interview at Harvard Divinity School when the admissions person made me feel reprimanded by suggesting that, should I be applying elsewhere, in lieu of my verbose, intense ramble of an explanation, I might want to simply summarize it as "personal edification."

I looked it up in my Webster's Tenth, the one I'd purchased to look up the seventeen vocab words from Looking on Darkness. Edify, I learned, means "to spiritually enlighten, uplift, and improve, especially in moral and religious knowledge." Poof! My hostility toward it vanished. I *had* gone to YDS just for my own edification: Yes, "just" exactly that!

What's more, now that I knew what it meant, I suddenly noticed that *edified* is an anagram of *deified*. All the while I was becoming edified, I was also being God-ified.

My movers were supposed to have come and gone by the time my YDS friend Stephen A. arrived to unload his U-Haul truck and take possession of my apartment. It was supposed to dovetail perfectly. But my moving men arrived at five o'clock instead of noon. Stephen was bringing his stuff up the back stairs while my movers carried my stuff down the front stairs. It was like a bad case of diarrhea: in one end and out the other.

By eight o'clock the apartment was emptied of my belongings and stuffed with Stephen's. There was an interlude, though, when he was through unloading his truck but the driveway was blocked by my movers' truck. He pulled out a couple of folding chairs, and we sat by the open windows in the empty living room idly chatting and gazing out over the treetops at a glimpse of Lake Whitney. We talked, fell quiet, and then talked a little more. After roaming through the empty rooms, Quita came and settled into her sheepskin bed I had placed near me and went to sleep. It was so pleasant, so peaceful.

When I commented on his patience, Stephen said it came from having lived in a village in West Africa for ten years. He said that's what so much of his life had been: waiting for something to happen. Sitting by the bedside of a dying person for four days; waiting in line for an official stamp in a government office with signs forbidding bribes.

And now there was the patient, calm, leisurely way he sat by a window in a second-floor apartment in a Silly-Putty-pink house overlooking Whitney Ave., enjoying his view for the first time while I took it in as mine for the last time.

30

HARD LANDING

When troubles come, they come not single spies,
but in battalions.

—William Shakespeare

My favorite deli guy at Vicente Foods in Brentwood thought I'd been away at massage school. Confusion seems to have been the hallmark of our acquaintance: For years I called him Marty; it turns out his name is Chuck.

"Hey, welcome back," he said. "You back for good?"

"And how!" I said. "I graduated."

"You gonna open up a place?"

"Like what?" I asked, mystified. "A church or something?"

"That's a new one! I was thinking more along the lines of a spa-type thing."

That's when we got it straightened out.

Chuck shrugged, grinning. "Oh, okay. Divinity school. What's that, massage for the soul?"

Ella came over to welcome me home. Though by then she'd been a redhead for six years, I still kept forgetting it, but as always, was floored by her loveliness. On the eve of my departure, she'd brought a rosebud to our Last Supper. Now, on my return, she brought me an ethereal blue hydrangea the color of her and her father's eyes.

Three days after I arrived home, my architect friend Nick invited me to a lecture at the Skirball Cultural Center titled, "Searching for the Sacred through Art and Architecture." Sitting in a darkened lecture hall, taking illegible notes on a slide show, I felt as if I were right back in Professor Lara's The House of the Lord, a historical survey of church design and worship spaces.

The next night I had dinner with my friend Cory at a restaurant she suggested with a laugh, saying she thought I'd really like it, a little Italian place called Divino.

The following Saturday I went to an exhibit of illuminated medieval manuscripts at the Getty Center.

Enough already, I told myself. *Get thee to a beach. Hie thee to Barnes & Noble for a best seller. Get thee to a first-run movie that won't open in New Haven for six months.*

The eighteen-wheeler moving van descended on my cul-de-sac like Godzilla on a village. Standing in the doorway of my house with a clipboard, I checked off items on the inventory sheets as Doc Harmon, the long-haul driver, and a local helper carried in a procession of boxes and furniture that had taken up just one little corner of the ginormous van.

Packing up in New Haven, I'd thought I was judicious about what I kept from my student digs. I had given away tons of stuff to YDS friends who still had another year to go: the Pier One wicker; my Goodwill prayer chair and the six mismatched dining room chairs; the Staples collapsible table; the T. J. Maxx lamps and the Salvation Army odds and ends; the makeshift tables of framed old sepia photographs atop hotel-closeout luggage racks.

I knew perfectly well that, thanks mainly to furniture inherited from my mother's place, my house in LA was furnished to the hilt. I also knew it had no attic, no basement, and not even a garage, just a carport, and that the sole storage room doubled as the laundry room and was already filled to the rafters. What's more, I knew I would not rent storage space for any overflow, because I do not believe in paid storage: it encourages gratuitous accumulation.

But there were pieces that were supposed to have been temporary that I found I could not bear to part with: the old enamel-topped kitchen table that had been my desk, with a pull-out cutting board perfect for my laptop; the 1838 backwoods Maine table with the gimpy leg; the funky trunks; the primitive wooden ironing board. And the chairs! The mismatched bentwoods and the pair of rusty Bertoias I'd spotted curbside for trash pickup and grabbed in the nick of time.

By the time the last carton, hooked rug, and Yankee antique had been unloaded, the downstairs looked like a major pileup on the freeway. The head-on collision of my two worlds created such gridlock I had to zigzag sideways to get to the kitchen. After the moving van left, restoring proportion to my neighborhood but leaving me in chaos, I sat down in one of the umpteen chairs and burst into tears. The pressing need to integrate all my New Haven stuff into my Los Angeles house was the furniture version of the problem I now faced in my life. I did not know what to do with my belongings, my divinity school degree, or myself.

I sat in my living room in my former div. student desk chair and despaired of ever getting it all sorted out and meaningfully incorporated—the furniture *or* my life. I hadn't a clue how to integrate the two worlds of furniture any more than how to integrate my shiny new MA religion degree with my regular old writing life. One life was finished and the other not yet resumed or recalculated. The richness and coherence of the YDS life was wonderful, but LA is home—and all I had to do was look at Quita lolling on the deck and chasing squirrels in the backyard to know it.

It wasn't that I wanted to be back at Yale; it was that I didn't yet know how to be home. The grace period of YDS had been extended by a ten-day, cross-country joyride with my YDS friend Liz, with stops in Kansas City and at the Trappist monastery in Snowmass, Colorado, where I'd once had a ten-day silent retreat under the aegis of Father Thomas Keating. But now Liz had flown back to the man she'd met and married at YDS, and I was home and on my own. Time was up: grace period over.

I called my friend Carol back East from my gridlocked living room. Not only did I feel terrible, but I felt guilty about feeling terrible. I was in a double bind. I was mad at myself for having shipped all this stuff to LA, but I was also upset that stuff was *missing*—namely, medium carton #165 on the inventory sheet and one extra-large, bright blue Eddie Bauer duffle bag containing approximately three-fourths of my clothes. Doc Harmon had a clear memory of having dropped off the duffle in Arizona, but he couldn't for the life of him remember whether it was at a house in Phoenix or the one in Show Low that burned to the ground the day *after* he made the drop-off. It became clear which one when, six weeks later, my clothes turned up, reeking of smoke.

Before I left for divinity school, everyone wanted to know why on earth I was going. While I was there, everyone wanted to know what I was going to do after I graduated. Once I was back in LA, everyone wanted to know how I planned to put my YDS degree to use.

Two weeks after I got back, a priest from my church took me out for lunch to sound me out on my plans. The priest, a YDS grad herself, suggested I not limit my "ministry" to writing.

"Don't exclude writing," she said. "Don't *not* write. But don't view that as exclusively what you do."

All I could think was: *I am going to be such a disappointment to so many people when "all I do" is write a book.* Besides, I had never thought of my writing *as* a ministry. Writing had begun for me as an attention-seeking enterprise, a stammering child's means of expression and of being noticed, set apart. Perhaps writing had been my vocation all along—that is, a calling from God—but typing my first story at age seven on a raucous Remington Noiseless, my sole hope was that it would make me the apple of my *earthly* father's eye.

And, too, I thought, what if I don't want to write about my YDS experience? What then? What if I don't want to do anything with this theological education of mine? What if, like Buddhist monk Thich Nhat Hanh, I'd like to start doing more manual work and less writing? What if, like Thomas Merton, I'd like to outgrow writing altogether? What if I were to start praying Merton's antiwriting prayer like a rosary?

> Please pray for me that, instead of merely writing something, I may be something and indeed that I may so fully be what I ought to be that there may be no

further necessity for me to write, since the mere fact of being what I ought to be would be more eloquent than many books.

I told my brother I was worried that if I wrote a book about going to YDS, people would think I had gone there in order to write about it—as if I had been "committing experience" by going there. Art wanted to know what people I was so worried about. He made me laugh about it.

Talking to him left me feeling much better about my plan to write about my YDS experience. I told him I wouldn't know what I thought about it until I had written about it. Art understood that, for me, putting it in writing, getting it down on paper, is what cements—even *creates*—the meaning of what I experience: "Writing is finding out what you don't yet know about what you know." But I had no idea whether pondering my muddle and poring over my theological midden pile, divining its contents like an oracle with a mound of animal innards, would be seen by others as using my YDS education to good purpose. Especially by the priest who'd taken me to lunch.

I was glad I'd talked on the phone to Art about it before he and his wife left on vacation. They were going back to Popham Beach, Maine, where I had joined them two summers before. As we were saying good-bye, Art kept saying, "I love you," with this effusive, escalating, nutty sincerity, and I kept saying, "Yes, I know you do. I love you too, Art." But he kept saying, "No, you're not hearing me: I *love* you."

He wouldn't let me hang up until I had assured, reassured, and re-re-reassured him that, yes, I really *do* know how much you really, really, really seriously love me. It took *forever* for him to finally let me hang up. It was just so Art.

When the phone rang at 2:10 a.m. on Sunday, July 28, I assumed it would be a wrong number. But it was Art's wife, and she was telling me that he'd had a stroke on the plane as they were flying home from their vacation in Maine.

My sister and I met at SeaTac and went straight to Tacoma General Hospital. Even unconscious, on a respirator, and with his head bandaged from brain surgery, Art still looked like himself: rosy-cheeked, burly, amiably white-bearded. He was fifty-two.

On Wednesday morning, July 31, we took him off the respirator, gathered around the bed, and sang him his favorite hymn, "Take Me Out to the Ball Game."

In the last picture of Art and me, taken on Yale's Old Campus when he and his wife visited a month before I graduated, I'm doubled over in laughter at the wisecrack he has just made. They say that hearing is the last sense to go. With Art, I bet it was his sense of humor.

My brother's best friend wrote me to say that if Art had known he had only a month to live, he would have spent it just the way he did. I agree except that if he had seen it coming he could have provided me with a trust fund of "Attagirls!" and maybe even bequeathed me his ability to see the funny in things.

Ten days after Art died, back from his funeral in Tacoma and having no idea what to do with myself, I took Quita for too long a walk on too hot a day. At bedtime, noticing how "off" she seemed and fearing heat stroke, I rushed her to the twenty-four-hour vet's. An X-ray showed she was so dehydrated her heart had shrunk. I told the vet I had just lost my brother and that losing my dog would just be too fucking much. He assured me she would be okay but wanted to keep her overnight for IV infusions and observation. Coming home without my dog at midnight, grief-stricken over my brother and guilt-stricken about my dog, I knew for a fact what I had told the vet was the simple truth.

Now it was not only the adjustment of being back in LA with too much actual and figurative furniture to cope with, it was the adjustment of being in a world without my brother, of having to figure out how to reconfigure my world.

In those first raw weeks after Art's death, one of the few things that could get the lead out of my heart was serving as a lay Eucharist minister at church or in a hospital room or parishioner's home. Sometimes I would see in the eyes of the one whom I fed the wafer and tipped the chalice to that an indefinable but genuine thing had just happened: real presence.

Seeing it had the power to momentarily abate the pain of Art's absence because it reminded me that he was with the one he loved "above all."

Just in time to change the inscription chiseled on his headstone, Art's wife had discovered in a tottering pile of legal pads atop his rolltop desk a page headed "Tombstone" on which Art, ever the wordsmith and communicator, had composed his own epitaph:

> Art loved his family, baseball, toy trains, and Tacoma.
> Above all, he loved our Lord and Savior, Jesus Christ.

The question of what I planned to do with myself really hit home a month later when I received my first "Dear Alumni and Friends" letter from YDS's new dean, Harold Attridge. For the first time ever, both Yale and Harvard now had nonordained deans at the helm of their divinity schools: an Islamicist Episcopalian at Harvard and a Roman Catholic New Testament scholar at Yale.

"The class of 2002 has gone forth," Dean Attridge wrote, "to turn learning into productive service. The new class, consisting of some 150 students, promises to make an equally important contribution to the life of our churches and society at large."

I'm from the class of '02, but I sure hadn't turned my learning into an important contribution to society. Here it was, four months since graduation, and while my classmates had fanned out in "productive service" all over the country—heck, all over the *globe*—I was still just trying to sign up for a Virtual Yale e-mail address before my student e-mail got cut off on October 1.

At Yale, it had been a breeze to "theologically process" the secular material in my non-YDS courses as well as a pregnant turtle and a shining meadow. Now I was having doubts whether turning my learning experiences—theological *or* spiritual—into a memoir counted as productive service worthy of a YDS grad. The one thing I knew for sure was, if I *did* write it, it would be a story about not only my study of God but God's ongoing education of me.

31

CONCLUDING REFLECTIONS
ADVANCED BEGINNER

Give the Holy One the benefit of believing
that God's hand is leading you
and accept the anxiety of feeling yourself
in suspense and incomplete.
—Teilhard de Chardin

In T. H. White's *The Once and Future King*, there is an endearing oddball named King Pellinore who has devoted his life to an eternal, gung-ho quest for a creature known only as the Questing Beast. Like Quita chasing squirrels—did she know there was more than one?—the pursuit of his beloved quarry is the whole point. Capture would utterly ruin it. Where, then, would be his *raison d'etre*? The meaning resides in the quest, in the journey, in the process, not the end result. And who knows, at the tail end of my life, maybe I'll find out that, as Buddhist Ram Dass says, "You *are* the answer—but you cannot know that you are."

I may have spent my life "questing" for the answer to a question I don't even know how to ask, but one thing I do know is that the purpose of life is not to be happy. The purpose of life is to matter. I don't want to snack myself to death on cheap choices that at the end of my life will leave me feeling empty, unfulfilled, and starved for the infinite. I hope I will not fear the end of my life so much as not having had enough of a life. I hope it measures up. I hope it feels *tall*.

Perhaps we are meant to be in a state of longing for completion. Perhaps that vacancy is like negative space in sculpture—not a void but a defining, shaping absence, like the God-shaped hole in our inmost being. It hit me with the force of an epiphany that my struggles and confusion aren't an impediment, they are the impetus for my spiritual growth.

No sooner had the notion of my inadequacies as an asset occurred to me than I ran into it all over the place, the same way that, once I'd caught a whiff of God's aroma, references to it cropped up everywhere. The uncertainty, raw bewilderment, and sense of incompleteness I have always seen as my failings are weaknesses that strengthen me. They are what keep me keepin' on.

Remaining incomplete and unfulfilled keeps me in a state of tension between who I am and who I can become: that *new self* that Jesus talks about and that St. Paul goes on and on about and that spiritual masters Merton and Keating call the true self, the one attained by becoming who you already are. The same goes for "getting to" God. I have been there all along, just as the Hindu scripture says: "Lead me to the place I never left."

When I consider just what it might take for me to feel complete, it pretty much comes down to the very things asked of God for a newly baptized infant: "an inquiring and discerning heart; the courage to will and to persevere; a spirit to know and to love you; and the gift of joy and wonder in all your works." Whenever I am feeling incomplete and lacking, it is usually due to one of those items being temporarily out of stock.

As for having "a spirit to know and to love God," that's what sent me to YDS. From horses to newborns, from coyotes to Christ, from adolescent depression to mysticism, the knowledge I have sought has been the truest indicator of what was uppermost for me at the time. I went to YDS to study theology because I wanted in-depth knowledge of this God I had come to love, this God who, when I cried out to him from the depths of my being, told me, *Show faith.*

I had to go. And I had to go to a tip-top, super-duper, all-the-trimmings Ivy League seminary, or else I would have always had the nagging thought that if I had gone there and not some convenient local seminary, I would have finally figured it all out and would have come away with the decoder ring on my pinkie, knowing everything I really, really, *really* need to know. Instead, I can now live happily in the knowledge that having gone to Yale Divinity School falls into the category of One of Those Things You Have to Do in Order to Know You Didn't Have to Do It After All.

I completed what I set out to do: I took the checkered flag. I got my degree. I got another notch on my Knowledge Seeker belt. But I found that, for me, the way to God does not lie in scholarly study. I am not a knowledge seeker after all. I am a God seeker. But I had to go to the universities of Chicago, Stanford, Oxford, and Yale before I could finally shuck off my backpack and say: Enough! Done! I have had my fill of great institutions of "higher learning."

Divinity school made me book-smart about God, but it was the testing, terrifying, shitty times in my life that made me street-smart about God. I had to come up against something in order to grow. Just as bulbs need the shock of winter to reach maturity, it is our dark, wintry, dug-up times that create the conditions for our greatest spiritual growth. In horticulture it's called "forcing." I had to be "forced" to grow.

Instead of piling up heaps and gobs of theological knowledge, I want to deepen my relationship with God through relationships with people, starting with Ella. My mother-son rapport with Daniel had never gone through the same kind of wringer.

One day, calling me out of the blue from college, he'd said, "I wanted you to be the first to know. I just cut off my dreads."

"Daniel! Wow! That is huge," I'd said. "Be sure to save them. Okay? Every last one! Put them in a Ziploc. I'm serious."

Far more than the lock of hair I'd saved from his first haircut or the jumbled smile of his baby teeth between cotton pads in a little box, Daniel's cutting off the dreadlocks he'd started growing when he left home for boarding school at fourteen marked something momentous. This was a rite of passage symbolizing *metanoia*, inner change, and I'd felt honored that he'd anointed me the first to be told.

I had kicked the can down the road long enough with Ella. After she had initiated our get-together at Pink's, I'd gratefully settled for a superficial relationship as better than none at all. But she was now twenty-one, and though the exacerbating effect of adolescence had dissipated, the same "Mom issues" that had sparked the rupture of our bond still made her wary of closeness to me. I longed for a more genuine, less hesitant and tentative connection, but my fear of driving her away had been holding me captive in a relationship that felt unsettled, timid, and provisional.

For starters, I'm just trying to be a little less me: "I must decrease, you must increase." St. Paul puts it this way: "It is no longer I who lives but Christ who lives in me." The Zulu word *ubuntu* means "I am because you are." It means that a person is a person through other persons and that a solitary human being is a contradiction in terms. What it comes down to is an increased capacity to love. My friend Chase said hers shot up by about a third when she had her first child. That's the kind of increase I'm looking for. It's a mighty tall order.

Shortly after graduating and returning to LA for good, I signed up for tennis lessons at the rec center in Santa Monica Canyon. The enrollment form provided guidelines for assessing whether your level of play was beginner, advanced beginner, intermediate, or advanced. I was torn between advanced beginner and intermediate. I wished there were an in-between category, the way that, ordering a steak, I can say, "medium/medium rare." As I was deliberating over the various guidelines, it occurred to me that, had I been signing up for spiritual lessons instead of tennis lessons, I would have known that advanced beginner was right where I belonged: "You know the basics but don't apply them with consistency."

I find it hard to welcome—much less cultivate—what Buddhists call beginner's mind. I don't like being a beginner, a rank novice who has to learn how to do something. I want to just know how. A spiritual life does not require a permit from a religion, but to have a spiritual life you do have to learn how to be spiritual—how to be wide awake, brimful, and a really good listener. You have to work at it. You have to get the hang of it. And sometimes, to make sure you're awake, you even have to have a wake-up call the way I did once at Zion National Park.

I was loafing on the hotel veranda after dinner when I heard someone mention that the Perseid meteor shower was happening that night. Most of us were thrilled by our luck in being at such a spectacular site—the catbird seat!—for viewing heaven's annual August fireworks display without any city glow watering it down. But then someone remembered a ranger having said it would peak from 4:00 to 5:00 a.m., and jokes ensued about catching it next year.

My wake-up call came at three fifty. And that's exactly what it was: a call to be awake and to be wonder-struck. Every single time I have gotten up at some ungodly hour to witness some purely elective celestial event—an Easter morning sunrise at Canyon de Chelly on the Navajo tribal lands; a lunar eclipse; a bushy-tailed comet shooting across the sky; the Milky Way flung across the sky like a starry scarf as I walked to Vigils at 2:00 a.m. at a mountain monastery—I have been rewarded with the presence of holiness in its Hebrew meaning: otherness.

As a beginner, all I can do is take my baby steps and when I fall down—lapsing in my practice, drifting away from attentiveness—do what any self-respecting toddler does: get up and start over again. Beginner's mind is a state of mind to be nurtured long after you are begun. A new member of a Benedictine monastic community put it this way:

> I came expecting to be taught a prayer technique. Instead, you are told that when you take your shoes off, you put them parallel to each other and not pigeon-toed, that you should close the door behind you quietly, that you should walk calmly and eat slowly and leave things ready for the next person to use. At first I thought this stuff is for the beginners. The real stuff will come later on. Then I came to understand that that is the real thing. It is how we do the little actions that make us mindful of God or our neighbor.

Like the Benedictine beginner, I have come to see that it's the "little actions" that are the real stuff. I want to live an ordinary life in a spiritually amplified manner, work at being a lot less me, and be available to serve God at a moment's notice.

When I was growing up, I abhorred the ordinary and was afraid that just being from Kansas City would doom me to mediocrity. All the greatness I wanted to achieve was predicated on getting the hell out of there. Now I find the extraordinary *in* the ordinary, and it is my similarity to others, not my singularity, that I want to cultivate. My ordination to ordinariness has even brought me to consider Kansas City a jim-dandy place not only to be from but to have been formed by.

Everything I studied back East, from sacred texts to New England foliage, served as preparation for my true vocation: my ordination not to the priesthood but to my secular divinity, my holy human nature, my plain old ordinary sacred self.

One summer morning when I was five or six years old, I woke up in the room I had until recently shared with my sister but that was now mine alone. It was just light enough outside to feel safe from the monster under my bed, but the dormant silence of the house meant it was too early to get up. To pass the time, I sat up against the headboard and removed the *X*'s of bobby pins from the pin curls my mother had put in my hair after washing it at bedtime. Seeing the bobby pins all helter-skelter on the sheet, I started playing pickup sticks with them without even realizing it.

Rapt in the task at hand, for once there was not one blessed thing I was worried about or trying to figure out except how to free one rubber-tipped bobby pin without disturbing any others. Suspended in a state of equipoise, maybe even of grace, my entire being was riveted, *rooted*, in each timeless, flawless moment. Playing bobby-pin pickup sticks at the dawn of dawn, engrossed in the bounty of the moment at hand, I was, quite simply, at peace. It may not have been "the peace that passes all understanding," but it was a peace that easily met folk musicians' guitar-tuning benchmark: "close enough for folk."

Had attendance been taken that morning, I could have answered, "Present." That rare moment in my childhood is paralleled by the photo of Alan as a towheaded toddler immersed in contemplative scrutiny of a wispy little flower in his grasp: a rare moment of oblivious, unmediated presence in the moment.

Fears and sorrows are what first made me take God seriously, but I discovered that pain is not required to experience him, because God is the now, whatever *now* is at the moment. When Moses asked God to reveal his name, God responded, I Am that I Am. The now and the I Am are one and the same: a fusion of the *be*-ing of God and the *is*-ness of the moment.

My uncle saw right away what my going to divinity school was all about: "Probing the mystery! Yessiree Bob."

Now that I have spent thirteen years writing about my two years at YDS and the era of holy hell that preceded it, I have come to see that this is not only a story about probing the mystery. It's also a story about showing faith.

NOTES

Grace Period: My Ordination to the Ordinary
"You need only claim ..." Florida Scott Maxwell, *The Measure of My Days*
"God comes to you ..." Paula D'Arcy, *Gift of the Red Bird*

Prologue: Looking on Darkness
"Perfect love casteth ..." John 4:18
"My God will enlighten ..." Psalm 18:28

Holy Hell
"It is life-affirming to look ..." James Carroll, *An American Requiem*

1. Unknowns
"I am that background figure ..." Sharon Olds, "Sleep Suite," *The Unswept Room*
"The ennobling difference ..." John Ruskin, *Sesame and Lilies*
"a very present help in times of trouble ..." Psalm 46:1
"Oh God, come to my assistance ..." Psalm 69:2

2. Up in Smoke
"It is easy to see ..." Joan Didion, "Goodbye to All That"
"... to whom all hearts are open ..." *Book of Common Prayer*, p. 355
"... deliverance from hardness of heart ..." *Book of Common Prayer*, p. 360

3. My Getting-to-God Machine

"Our hearts are restless …" St. Augustine, *Confessions*

"Be still and know that I am God." Psalm 46:10

"Come to me, all you who are weary …" Matthew 11:28

"functional atheist," Gerald G. May, MD, *Dark Night of the Soul*, p. 44

"my strength and my refuge …" Psalm 91:2

"the divine therapy," Thomas Keating, *Open Mind, Open Heart: The Contemplative Dimension of the Gospels*

"May the words of my mouth …" Psalm 19:14

4. The Red Phone

"one brand-new book stood out …" *A Mood Apart: Depression, Mania, and Other Afflictions of the Self*, Peter C. Whybrow, MD, Basic Books, 1997

"My grace is sufficient for you …" 2 Corinthians 12:9–10

"shield the joyous," *Book of Common Prayer*, Compline, p. 127

"If the light that is in thee …" Matthew 6:23

5. Perfect Symmetry

"Come to me all you who are heavy-burdened …" Matthew 11:28

"I invite you, therefore …" *Book of Common Prayer*, Ash Wednesday Liturgy, p. 265

"Save me, o God, for the waters …" Psalm 69:1

"We experience the inner attraction of God …" Thomas Keating, *The Daily Reader for Contemplative Living: Excerpts from the Works of Father Thomas Keating*

"You breathed your fragrance …" St. Augustine, *Confessions*

"Those who sow with tears …" Psalm 126:5–6

6. The Inciting Incident

"Come and see." John 1:38–39

The Element of Lavishness: Letters of Sylvia Townsend Warner and William Maxwell, edited by Michael Steinman

8. A Loved Person

"All shall be well, all shall be well, and all manner of thing [sic] shall be well." St. Julian of Norwich

Grace Period

"Now shall I make my soul ..." W. B. Yeats, "The Tower"

9. Journey-Proud

"After great pain, ..." Emily Dickinson, poem 372

"Go from your country ..." Genesis 12:1

10. Boola, Boola, Alleluia

"In the time of my trouble ..." Psalm 86:7

"And when you pray ..." Matthew 6:5

"But when you pray ..." Matthew 6:6

11. The Shining Meadow

"Take off your sandals ..." Exodus 3:5

"I am the light and the way ..." John 14:6

"not only for solace ..." *Book of Common Prayer,* Holy Eucharist II, p. 372

"Arise, shine, for your light ..." Isaiah 60:1–5

"His appearance was like lightning ..." Matthew 28:3

"His face shone like the sun ..." Matthew 17:2

"This is my beloved son ..." Matthew 17:5

12. Theology on the Hoof

"Restore a right spirit within ..." Psalm 51:10

13. Gotcha

"There's just no accounting ..." Jane Kenyon, "Happiness," *Poetry* (February 1995)

"while he was still far off ..." Luke 15:20

14. Thank God It's Monday

"Jesus wept." John 11:35

"Selfyeast of soul a dull dough sours." Gerard Manley Hopkins, "I wake and feel the fell of dark, not day." *Poems*

"... ferment and season you ..." Hafiz, "Don't surrender your loneliness so quickly"

15. A Dollar-Bill Madonna

"Leave her alone. The poor ..." Matthew 26:9–10

18. Holy Spirit Mojo

"Take, eat ..." Matthew 26:26

"Suffer the little children ..." Luke 18:16

"When you awake, you shall have cake ..." from the traditional American lullaby "All the Pretty Little Horses," a.k.a. "Hush-a-bye"

"... when you have to go there ..." Robert Frost, "The Hill Wife"

19. Paradise Lost

"the mountain of the Lord," Micah 4:2

"Take up your cross ..." Matthew 16:24

20. Those Beneath Me

"Remember that you are dust ..." Genesis 3:19

"The pride, hypocrisy, and ..." *Book of Common Prayer,* Litany of Penitence, p. 267

"And who is my neighbor?" Luke 10:28

"You shall love the Lord ..." Deuteronomy 6:5

"Without the inconsiderate neighbor ..." Pema Chodron, *The Places That Scare You: A Guide to Fearlessness in Difficult Times*

"Above all else, we admonish you ..." St. Benedict's *Rule,* chapter 40

"... put on the armor of light ..." Romans 13:12

"Beware of practicing your piety ..." Matthew 6:1

"The more I dislike my neighbor ..." Frederick Buechner, *Listen to Your Life,* originally published in *Wishful Thinking*

21. Zen in the Shell

"Sales were brisk …" Nathanael West, about his novel *Miss Lonelyhearts*

"… come up higher …" Luke 14:10

"We are as much as …" Thoreau, *Journals*

"… the color of the sherry …" Emily Dickinson, letter to Thomas Wentworth Higginson, July 1862

23. Unleashed

"… the one less traveled by." Robert Frost, "The Road Not Taken"

"A life is either all spiritual …" Thomas Merton, *Thoughts in Solitude,* p. 55

"… gonna wash that man …" *South Pacific*, Rodgers and Hammerstein

"There is no light without …" Carl Jung, quoted in *Urgings of the Heart: A Spirituality of Integration*, Wilkie Au & Noreen Cannon, p. 24

"I cannot understand …" Romans 15:20

"… that which we have no wish to be," Carl Jung quoted in Au & Cannon, p. 25

24. My Div-ersity

"My Lord God, I have no idea …" Thomas Merton, *Thoughts in Solitude,* p. 89

25. That Sudden Tuesday

"That sudden Tuesday" Verlyn Klinkenborg, "The Quiet Consolation of the Material World," *New York Times* editorial, September 22, 2001

"Feed my sheep …" John 21:17

26. Altarpieces And Academics

"All that I have written …" Thomas Aquinas, spoken to his *socius* Reginald of Piperno, December 6, 1273

27. Show and Tell

"self-communication of God …" Karl Rahner, a phrase coined by Karl Rahner

28. A Glint of God
"In the day of my distress …" Psalm 77:2

31. Concluding Reflections: Advanced Beginner
"Give them an inquiring and …" *Book of Common Prayer*, Baptism, p. 308
"I must decrease …" John 3:30
"It is no longer I who …" Galatians 2:20

ACKNOWLEDGMENTS

Gratitude is the most human sentiment.
—Elie Wiesel

Any book that takes thirteen years to complete becomes a roly-poly tumbleweed of accumulated thanks. Where to begin? How to stop?

To my screenwriters' group for not kicking me out while I was writing a spiritual memoir and they were writing screenplays: Ron Wilkerson, Tom Virtue, Adam Carl, Vanessa Ioppolo, Carlos Lacamara, Carol Barbee, David Cowper, and Laura Picard. To the Fe Peepers, my former students and *other* writers' group: Rachael Jordan, Elise Moore, David Gonzalez, Jessy Goodman, Kathy Pasha, Rachel Hadlock-Piltz, Chris O'Neal, Luis Marayana, and in memoriam, Julius Glover III.

To Nikki Meredith, Steve Smith, and Chase Collins Levey for their input early on. To my sister, Carole McKnight, for hawkeyed proofing and praying without ceasing. To Connie Linesch for the blessing of her wisdom. To the Rev. Dr. William Wallace for theological stunners and getting me over many a hump. To Elizabeth Nordquist, pastor and spiritual director, for her prayers and timely poems. To Jan Parkinson for always asking, "How's the book?" To Joan Peters for bold suggestions and bracing pep talks. To Betsy Amster and Sarah Sentilles for helping me wrestle with it. To Christopher Noël for a transformative eleventh-hour edit and the rustic haven of his Tall Rock Retreat. To Carol Coates Wolfe for being my editorial sidekick.

From Yale Divinity School, to the Rev. Dr. Marilyn McCord Adams; Professor Margot Fassler; Dale Petersen, dean of students;

Anna Ramirez, admissions dean; and the ever-gracious Jackie Corning, formerly at Berkeley Divinity School at Yale. To my div. school friends and cohorts: in particular, Anne Turner for her off-the-cuff insights; Deirdre Eckian for her fearless questions; Stephen Gould for hangin' out; Evalyn Wakhusama for inspirational courage; Carol Hoidra for self-aware hilarity; Mark Hummel for his trick of anytime, anywhere study; Liz Hilton for the bonanza of her company on Quita's and my cross-country trip home from YDS; Steve Smith, my dearest friend at div. school, and in memoriam, his husband, Andrew Walsh, not just for the Friday night salvation of Pepe's Pizza and a Best Video movie, but for the blessing of our ongoing friendship. To Paula and Joe Reagan in Hamden, Connecticut, for their extravagant hospitality to Quita and me.

To the Center for Spiritual Renewal, Montecito, California, where I went repeatedly to read supposedly final drafts. To St. Matthew's Episcopal Church, Pacific Palisades, California, whose community and priests, past and present—especially the Rev. David Walton Miller and fellow YDS grads Rev. Betsy Anderson, Rev. Michael Seiler, and Rev. Kristin Neily Barberia—have been integral to my spiritual formation.

Above and beyond all, my thanks go to my beloved son and daughter, who lent their input and support despite wishing their mom had been an abstract painter instead of a writer.

CPSIA information can be obtained at www.ICGtesting.com
Printed in the USA
LVOW07s2044060616

491419LV00002B/395/P